POLITICS AND POLICY IN THE
AGE OF EDUCATION

POLITICS AND POLICY
IN THE
AGE OF EDUCATION

Edited by

LAURENCE R. MARCUS

BENJAMIN D. STICKNEY

CHARLES C THOMAS • PUBLISHER
Springfield • Illinois • U.S.A.

Published and Distributed Throughout the World by

CHARLES C THOMAS • PUBLISHER
2600 South First Street
Springfield, Illinois 62794-9265

© *1990 by* CHARLES C THOMAS • PUBLISHER

ISBN 0-398-05667-6

Library of Congress Catalog Card Number: 89-48907

With THOMAS BOOKS *careful attention is given to all details of manufacturing and design. It is the Publisher's desire to present books that are satisfactory as to their physical qualities and artistic possibilities and appropriate for their particular use.* THOMAS BOOKS *will be true to those laws of quality that assure a good name and good will.*

Printed in the United States of America
SC-R-3

Library of Congress Cataloging-in-Publication Data

Politics and policy in the age of education / edited by Laurence R.
  Marcus, Benjamin D. Stickney.
      p.   cm.
    Includes bibliographical references.
    ISBN 0-398-05667-6
    1. Education and state—United States.   2. Higher education and
state—United States.   3. Education—United States—Aims and
objectives.   4. Education, Higher—United States—Aims and
objectives.   I. Marcus, Laurence R.   II. Stickney, Benjamin D.
LC89.P648   1990
378.73—dc20
                                                                89-48907
                                                                    CIP

CONTRIBUTORS

Margaret Bacon is Dean of Education at the University of Colorado at Colorado Springs.

Terrel H. Bell was Secretary of the United States Department of Education from 1981 to 1985.

David C. Berliner, a professor at Arizona State University, was president of the American Educational Research Association from 1985 to 1986.

Kenneth S. Burnley, Jr. is Superintendent of Schools in Colorado Springs.

Richard A. Caldwell is Deputy Director of the Center for Public and Contemporary Issues at the University of Denver.

Stanley M. Elam is Contributing Editor of *Phi Delta Kappan.*

Martin J. Finkelstein is Associate Professor of Higher Education and Director of the New Jersey Institute for Collegiate Teaching and Learning at Seton Hall University.

Clinita A. Ford is Founder and Director of the annual National Conference on Black Student Retention in Higher Education and is Director of Title III Programs and Professor in Academic Affairs at Florida Agricultural and Mechanical University.

John F. Jennings is Counsel to the Committee on Education and Labor of the United States House of Representatives.

Marsha V. Krotseng is Assistant Director of Planning and Institutional Research at the University of Hartford.

Richard D. Lamm, former Governor of Colorado, is Director of the Center for Public and Contemporary Issues at the University of Denver.

Marvel Lang is Director of the Center for Urban Affairs and Associate Professor of Urban Affairs at Michigan State University.

Laurence R. Marcus is Deputy Assistant Chancellor for Institutional Affairs at the New Jersey Department of Higher Education.

Edward A. Morante is Director of the Office of Learning Assessment at the New Jersey Department of Higher Education.

Kim Natale, a physics teacher at Standley Lake High School, was Colorado Teacher of the Year in 1984 and one of four finalists for National Teacher of the Year in 1984.

Benjamin D. Stickney is an associate professor at the University of Colorado at Colorado Springs and Director of Program Development at the Pikes Peak Board of Cooperative Educational Services.

Reginald Wilson is Senior Scholar at the American Council on Education.

Robert C. Wood, the Henry R. Luce Professor of Democratic Institutions and the Social Order at Wesleyan University, was Secretary of Housing and Urban Development during the Johnson Administration, served as President of the University of Massachusetts and held the post of Superintendent of the Boston Public Schools.

Manuscript preparation was coordinated by Carol Adams, Karen Fernicola and Wilma Waddle.

INTRODUCTION

An Age Of Education

An "age," in the agricultural, industrial or informational sense, incorporates a good deal more than an institution viewed as intricately associated with creating wealth and strengthening the nation. If this were the criteria, humankind would have been in a "military age" since its evolution. An age must incorporate entities which not only constitute a nation's strength but permeate the life-style and fiber of a people. In the West, this billing was filled by agriculture from antiquity to the early nineteenth century and by industrial manufacturing from at least the early 1800s to the 1950s. For the next two decades, our society was characterized by the uneasy term, "post-industrial," but with the spread of computers and other high-technology machinery, we spoke of having entered an "age of information." But "information," in the context of information dissemination, is a cumbersome term. Information dissemination may incorporate the media, the computer programmer and the stockbroker, but it has a lesser relationship to the tasks of the accountant, the manager and the bureaucrat. Although information processing tells us much about the life and fiber of our people, it does not appear to encompass the strength and consciousness of the nation as did industrial manufacturing.

Since most adults have no children in school and since education's 8 million employees constitute less than 7 percent of a national work force of 120 million (Siegal, 1989), there are those who would contend that education may not fill this bill either. But, approximately 60 million people are currently enrolled in either K–12 schools or institutions of higher learning. Accordingly, in an American population of 249 million, 68 million (more than 1 in 4) are involved in formal education (U.S. Department of Education, 1989; Siegel, 1989). Moreover, in 1986 an estimated 2.8 million children were attending preschools or nursery schools which represents 45 percent of all three- and four-year-olds (Siegal, 1989). In addition, approximately 22 million people are currently participating in some form of adult education. If expenditures on public and private schools and colleges are totaled for the 1989–90 school year, the cost of American education currently stands at $353 billion, or 6.8 percent of the gross national product (U.S. Department of Education, 1989). However, if you add to formal education's $353 billion total the estimated $5 billion spent on preschool and nursery school education, the roughly $40 billion that industry spends on educating its employees and the unaccounted billions directed toward adult education, it appears that education, at well over $400 billion, is second only to health care as America's leading monetary enterprise (Kearns, 1988; National Association for the Education of Young Children, 1989).

As a result of changes in family structure and increases in women's employment outside the home, preschool and after-school education should continue to grow substantially. The number of three- and four-year-olds enrolled in preschools and nursery schools in 1986 represents a 25 percent increase from 1980 and a 400 percent increase since 1965 (Johnson et al., 1988). In addition, it is estimated that 600 American companies provide some form of child care and many states have developed, or are developing, early childhood educational programs. Currently, more than 5 million children are identified as "latchkey" children and initiatives at the federal, state and local levels are being developed to service this population during after-school hours. Currently, both the U.S. Senate and House of Representatives are in the process of legislating policies which would expend roughly $230 million on preschool and after-school day care (Johnson et al., 1988; *Education Daily,* 1989).

Numbers both of persons directly involved or affected and dollars spent, while compelling, tell only part of the story. Education has been of consistent concern and, arguably, the principal social issue of the 1980s. While the decade began with the nation's eyes focused on runaway inflation, disproportionately high energy prices, growing unemployment, and a sense of military weakness, most of these concerns are behind us and a new set of issues has emerged. However, throughout the decade and at its end, the quest for quality education has been at center stage. Blue ribbon panels at the national, state and local levels—groups composed of various combinations of political and policy leaders, corporate officials, educators and citizens—were unmistakably clear, as they issued their reports in early and mid-decade, that America's future security was tied directly to the quality of our educational system. The sweep of the resultant reforms was so broad that few, if any, schools and colleges were left untouched. And, there is every indication, particularly given the historic education summit called at the decade's end by President George Bush, that the nation's eyes will continue to be focused on education for years to come.

It seems, then, that we have emerged from a "decade of education" and may well have entered into an "age of education."

Politics and Policy

Throughout our history, education has been seen as integral to the condition of our democracy and the growth of our nation. Colonial legislatures enacted provisions for the establishment of schools almost as soon as the legislatures were formed. Similarly among the earliest acts of the national government under the Articles of Confederation was the setting aside of land in the western territories for educational purposes. Congress consistently viewed the establishment of a publicly accessible school system as a precondition for statehood. The Morrill Land Grant Act, passed by Congress in 1862 to help to develop our nation's agricultural and industrial capacity, provided support for the creation and growth of public universities in each of the states. The belief that our schools are crucial to the condition of our democracy was never more in evidence than during the Great Depression when the federal government spent millions to keep the schools open and to keep attendance high.

The two world wars of the first half of the twentieth century gave rise to a new theme, the relationship between education and the national defense. Indeed, in the midst of the Cold War, America was sent reeling when the Soviet Union hurled its *Sputnik* into earth orbit in 1957. This technological achievement not only meant that the Russians were ahead of us in what became known as the "space race" but also gave use to a new fear that powerful intercontinental ballistic missiles with atomic or hydrogen warheads could strike American targets from launching sites within the Soviet Union. Never before—Pearl Harbor included—had we felt so directly threatened by so distant a power. In *Sputnik's* aftermath came a major focus on education—the passage of the National Defense Education Act and, several years later, the enactment of broad-based elementary-secondary, vocational education and higher education acts.

The defense-related politics of that era led to belief that the strength of our nation was directly related to increasing the amount of education received by our citizenry. The policy that flowed from that belief led to a drive to increase the number of years of schooling received by our young, to increase the amount of science and mathematics instruction provided by the schools and colleges, to increase the knowledge of foreign languages and culture among the new generation of Americans who grew up speaking only English, and so on. It has always been a part of the American ethos to try to do things better, so, too, during this period. However, the focus was to a greater extent on *more* education than it was on *better* education.

Writing in 1982, John Naisbitt discussed a series of "megatrends" that he believed were occurring in America. In pursuing the analysis of his first megatrend ("industrial age $\rightarrow$ information age"), Mr. Naisbitt pointed to an "education mismatch" as providing an inadequate knowledge base for the information age. Indeed, his indictment of the state of education (as evidenced by SAT scores declining and undemanding standards) could have come from many of the ensuing reform reports. But, in that context alone, the criticism, apt as it was, was inadequate to refocus the educational enterprise.

A year later, a report, entitled *A Nation at Risk,* provided the missing impetus. Wisely drawing upon the national defense metaphor that had served education so well a quarter century earlier, the report cited the threat to our country, not from an enemy with an arsenal of superior weapons, but from the technological advances of friendly nations resulting in our fall from the dominant position we had held in the world marketplace. Without a strengthened educational system, we would not, the report held, be able to regain our economic competitiveness. *A Nation at Risk* also drew on the historic theme that the state of our democracy (indeed, our domestic tranquility) was dependent upon education's providing the way to economic security.

This new set of politics, based on the desire for renewed economic competitiveness, led to a policy thrust on the quality of education. While the concern for *more* education remains, particularly for populations still unbenefitted by our educational system, the focus has shifted substantially toward *better* education, with most reform efforts directly intended to increase achievement levels.

Politics and Policy in the Age of Education

This volume discusses both the conditions that led to the current educational reform era and its outcomes. It focuses on the politics that have driven the reform, the subsequent policy initiatives that characterized this reform era and the challenges ahead if reform is to be sustained.

It begins with a commentary on the preeminence of education on the American agenda, written by former Secretary of Education Terrel Bell. Following his remarks, Part I, entitled "The Politics of Educational Excellence," concentrates on market-related and demographic influences on the processes of education and how reform initiatives have unfolded in the many states and myriad school districts. Addressing the market-related factors, Jack Jennings contends that competitiveness in the world market ("Economic Competitiveness: The Sputnik of the Eighties") has been the principal factor in maintenance of a federal educational role in an era of decreased expenditure, program consolidation and deregulation. In reference to demographic factors, Reginald Wilson's "Democracy and Demography" provides an analysis of the relationship between increasing pluralism and the politics of educational change. Regarding the diffusion of reform initiatives, Laurence Marcus, in the chapter "Far From the Banks of the Potomac," provides testimony to the fact that preponderance of educational reform has taken place under the leadership of the states.

Entitled "Policy in the Age of Education," Part II addresses changes in instructional strategies and faculty development, the emergence of assessment of higher education's productivity and the growth of educational collaborative endeavors. In addressing teacher training, Margaret Bacon, in "Reforming Teacher Education," discusses changes in teacher educators, students and curriculum. At the university and college level, Martin Finklestein's chapter on "Faculty Development in Higher Education" presents an overview of the efforts to improve the knowledge of faculty in such areas as student learning styles and alternative teaching strategies, a departure from their historic focus solely on their disciplines. In "Unleashing Student Creativity," Kim Natale presents a theoretical and personal accounting of the dynamics of classroom instruction in the era of educational reform. The process of recruiting and retaining historically underrepresented students at the collegiate level is provided by Clinita Ford and Marvel Lang in their chapter entitled "From Access to Retention: Minority Students in Higher Education." Zeroing in on higher education, Edward Morante, in "Assessing Collegiate Outcomes," discusses the new emphasis on holding higher education more accountable for providing quality education. Finally, in the chapter "Empowering Education Through Partnerships," Benjamin Stickney discusses collaborative activities between the universities and the schools and between education and business.

In the third part, "Sustaining the Drive Toward Excellence," the contributors discuss the relationship between public opinion and educational policy, the challenges of urban education, the impact of classroom research on educational policy and the linkage between changes in the American ethos and educational performance. Regarding public opinion, Stanley Elam and Benjamin D. Stickney provide a synthesis of the Gallup poll findings and their projected affects on policy. In "Public Support and the Quest for Dollars," Kenneth Burnley discusses the relationship between school-community relations and a school district's financial base. Robert Wood, in "Schools, Center Stage—At Last," offers an accounting of recent trends in big city schools, and Marsha Krotseng, in "Of State Capitals and Catalysts: The Power of External Prodding," provides an overview of the political climate for school reform. The relationship of "The Research on Teaching and Educational Policy" is offered by David Berliner, who cites several examples of the inconsistencies between empirical findings and administrative practice. In the concluding chapter in this section, Richard Lamm and Richard Caldwell provide a provocative analysis of changing values and the state of education.

Finally, Marcus and Stickney examine the education reform movement from the perspective of whether it has the capacity, in and of itself, to accomplish the goals of reviving America's economic competitiveness and of securing the blessings of liberty.

REFERENCES

Education Daily. Washington, D.C., September 9–11, 1989.

Johnson, James A. et al. *Introduction to the Foundations of American Education.* Boston, MA: Allyn and Bacon, pp. 470–471.

Kearns, David T. (1988). An Educational Recovery Plan for America. In Fred Schultz (Ed.), *Education 89/90.* Guilford, CT: The Duskin Publishing Group, pp. 6–10.

Naisbitt, John. (1982). *Megatrends.* New York: Communications Co.

National Association for the Education of Young Children. (1989). An estimated number based on a telephone interview with Pat Spahr, September 1989.

U.S. Department of Education. (1989). *1989 Back to School Forecast,* August 24, 1989.

Siegal, Paul. (1989). Chief of the Education and Social Stratification Branch, The Population Division, U.S. Bureau of the Census. Interview, September, 1989.

Commentary

EDUCATIONAL EXCELLENCE AND EDUCATIONAL REFORM

Terrel Bell

At this writing it has been more than six years since the release of *A Nation At Risk,* the report that provided an impetus for an educational reform movement that was already calling for the engenderment of excellence. The seeds for educational reform had been implanted within the American people. Increasing public concerns over allegedly mediocre educational standards, as evidenced by a ten-year decline in the public's grading of the public schools, provided testimony to the body politic's dissatisfaction. It was this grass roots malcontent that *A Nation At Risk* and other reports nurtured to bring educational issues to the forefront of the nation's attention.

Shortly after *A Nation At Risk,* there was a preponderance of opinion that the headlining of education by the nation's press was only a temporary phenomenon. It was contended that newspapers and television stations were faddishly hungry for a new political topic and that the public in general and political leaders in particular would soon embrace another newsworthy issue.

Within a year following *A Nation At Risk*'s release, however, nearly every state in the union had enacted one or more of the recommendations from the National Commission on Excellence in Education. More importantly, the flavor of the reform had become intensified in thousands of school districts across America. There was a widespread call for strengthening academic requirements, for increasing scholastic testing and for enhancing accountability. Accordingly, it has become increasingly clear that the preeminent posture that education was assuming in 1983 was not a passing fancy. During the last five years the visibility afforded the secretary of education has continued unabated. Moreover, the presidential candidates of 1988 targeted education as one of the nation's most important domestic endeavors. In a recent speech in Colorado Springs, President Bush told a group of business leaders that, "I can't think of any issue that is larger—or more far ranging in its impact than the education of our youth." When we think about America's status in the world, "then we'd better think about education" continued the president. "Do we want to talk about competitiveness and how we can improve? Again, we'd better think about education. About productivity and how to keep it on the increase? Again education."

The president's remarks serve to illustrate the reasons why educational reform has attained an invigorated enduring presence within the American consciousness. Firstly, according to various polls, public concern about educational quality continues to be at or near the top of the public's listing of political priority. According to the recent Gallup polls, the public increasingly views quality education as more important to America's future strength than either a strong military or strong industry. Secondly, the business community has put unprecedented pressure on political and educational leadership to improve the quality of America's work force. Well-educated workers are an indispensible ingredient to America's economic preeminence. Skilled employees are also the vital ingredient to establishing and maintaining an industry's competitive edge. Thirdly, the changing demographic nature of our society demands an educational agenda which addresses the improvement of standards of excellence for an increasingly heterogeneous population. Changes in family structure and increasing percentages of minority pupils places extraordinary challenge upon the schools to compensate for the difficulties of environmental circumstance. In accordance with a changing demographic America is the startling increase in recent years in the percentage of children (particularly those under 5 years old) living in poverty. According to Harold Hodgkinson, in 1950 60 percent of America's households consisted of a working father, a housewife mother and two or more school-age children. In 1987 this household number stood at 5 percent. He also reminds us that thirty years ago 17 people supported every 1 on social security. By the year 2,000, however, only three will support that one, and that one of the three will be minority. Clearly, it is the interest of all Americans for the schools to produce highly skilled and productive workers who come from all segments of our nation's population.

Accordingly, in concert with public opinion, the business community and demographic reality, the political leadership has committed itself to educational change in unprecedented magnitude. In 1988 almost every candidate aspired becoming an "education president." "Education" governors and senators now occupy state mansions and congressional halls. Local politicians wrestle with generating greater funding to support appropriate educational policy.

But political representatives must continue to be proactive as well as reactive. Addressing the fragmented educational malcontent in existence throughout the land, the National Commission on Excellence in Education coupled specific problems with specific recommendations. Embraced by many political leaders from Washington to the fifty states, *A Nation At Risk* became a rallying cry for action.

Given the time frame since the NCEE report's release, it appears we need another such rallying cry. For several years there was general acceptance of many of the principal tenets of the so-called "first wave" of reform. Now, however, there is a preponderance of discord and confusion over the future direction of educational policy. At least among educators, there appears to be a growing feeling that more substantive changes need to be made, but the definition of the so-called "restructuring" buzz word has remained elusive for at least the last three years. Does it mean repeal, reflection or revolution? Is the key to restructuring education empowering teachers, building schools within schools, fostering greater critical thinking strategies, attacking antiquated school financing or completing the unfinished agenda of reform's first wave? We need to develop greater agreement on the nation's educational course, and the impetus for developing consenses must come from those we elect to lead us.

Increasingly, the schools have been asked to assume a greater responsibility for readdressing the nation's social ills and for strengthening the nation. Obviously, such a herculean task has its limits. Accordingly, it is imperative that we identify both the mission of education and how to best accomplish it. As I have stated before, the president, the 50 governors, and the leading lawmakers must commit themselves—and us—to generating such a mission and fulfilling its attainment.

During the 1980s, discontent has been addressed, challenges have been disseminated and changes have been made. Although much of this initiative came from recommendations out of Washington, the unfolding of educational change occurred far from the banks of the Potomac. Given the critical linkage between educational excellence and national security and given the current fragmentation regarding education's course, it is imperative that we do not flounder in the choppy waters of a muddled sea. If we have experienced the beginnings of an educational renaissance, its evolution is contingent upon a steady purposeful sailing through the stormy winds of change.

In this volume you will read a chronicling of many of the reform movement initiatives, with their implications on politics and policy. An impressive group of scholars and practitioners have addressed the arena of teaching, learning, assessment and partnerships. It is the role of American leaders to familiarize themselves with such writings and to rally the nation for refocused attention and action.

CONTENTS

POLITICS AND POLICY IN THE
AGE OF EDUCATION

PART I

The Politics of Educational Excellence

Chapter 1

ECONOMIC COMPETITIVENESS:
THE SPUTNIK OF THE EIGHTIES*

John F. Jennings

The successful launch of an earth-orbiting satellite by the Soviet Union in 1957 shocked the United States out of its complacency. Americans had long considered the Soviets to be inferior, both economically and technologically. It was a rude surprise to find that this perception was not accurate.

Thirty years later, in 1987, the United States faces a similar crisis. For the first time in nearly four generations, America has become a debtor nation, dependent for its financial needs on investment from other countries. Nations that only a few years ago we considered to be economically and technologically inferior have now surpassed us in many areas of manufacturing and trade.

These recent events lack the suddenness of a Sputnik orbiting the earth. But, the harsh consequences of our economic misfortunes are seeping into the American consciousness. The United States is no longer the world's dominant economic power, and this change in our status will have an effect on the standard of living enjoyed by Americans.

In 1958 the United States responded to the Soviet technological challenge by mounting a crash scientific research and development program designed to launch an American satellite into space. We were forced to recognize, however, that the Soviets' success also required a longer-term solution.

A key component of this long-term strategy, the National Defense Education Act, was passed by a Democratic Congress and signed into law by a Republican president. That act encouraged the development of science, mathematics, and foreign languages in U.S. schools and colleges.

---

*This chapter was written by John F. Jennings, Counsel for Education, Committee on Education and Labor, United States House of Representatives. It is adapted from an article written by Mr. Jennings for the *Kappan*, October 1987 issue.

4

Today, a similar two-pronged approach is taking shape as a national response to the economic slippage of America and to the success of its competitors. Congress has passed a bill that seeks to correct unfair trade practices facing American companies trying to compete in the world market, and a longer-term national solution is also being molded through passage of various other bills.

After years of cutbacks, appropriations for federal education programs are beginning to rise, and several new education programs tied to economic competitiveness have been mounted. For instance, the same trade bill which is now public law proposes, as an integral component, new funding for programs of mathematics, science, and foreign language instruction, as well as programs to improve literacy and to promote technological innovations. By including these programs, the new trade law demonstrates the growing recognition of the tie between educational attainment and economic competitiveness.

The Sputnik of the 1980s is economic competition, and the United States is beginning to recognize that the educational attainment of its people is an intrinsic element of national economic well-being. Just as in 1957, a consensus is forming in favor of a federal response to this grave challenge. States and local school districts have made great strides in improving elementary and secondary education over the last decade, but a vital element will be missing if the national government does not provide leadership in the areas in which it performs best.

The task of improving American education is simply too important a job to allow the federal government to remain on the sidelines, even as a cheerleader. The federal government must back its calls for school reform with solid financial and research assistance to help in this immense undertaking.

A New Consensus

In the early 1980s, business groups and economists began to undertake studies comparing American society and American business practices with those of other countries. The reason for their concern was a feeling that other countries were surging ahead of the United States economically.

These early studies found a strong link between the educational level of a people and a country's ability to compete economically. As a result, business leaders who had not focused much attention on the schools before began to issue reports calling for the reform of American education.

Rightfully, most of the attention was directed to encouraging state and local efforts to reform the schools, since the basic responsibility for education resides with the states. Only in the last several years have business people and others outside of education called for the federal government to step up its efforts in support of education.

Typical of the reports of the early 1980s was a work commissioned by the New York Stock Exchange to examine the Japanese and American economies and to determine the reasons for Japan's growing challenge to the United States. A group of economists examined "quality circles" and other business techniques of the Japanese. However, when they issued their report, they decided to highlight as a primary reason for Japan's success the quality of its educational system. The report stated:

> One of the things the Japanese do right is in schooling their people; the extraordinary effectiveness of their schools is one relatively neglected reason for their high productivity. By comparison, our schools are failing to provide our young people with the preparation they need to reach their full productive potential.[1]

The New York Stock Exchange report emphasized that Japanese schools are developing a high *average* level of achievement. A whole population—workers as well as managers—is being educated to a level far higher than that in the United States. The report concluded that all American students, not just the academic elite, must be brought to higher levels of achievement if America is to regain its economically competitive position.

Educational attainment and economic competitiveness were perceived as being intimately interconnected in the New York Stock Exchange report, as well as in many other reports which were to follow during the early 1980s. Governors and national commissions all began to call for improvements in education, linking the degree of educational attainment of a state or region or of the nation to its ability to compete in the world economy.

None of these reports matched the eloquent intensity of *A Nation At Risk* issued by the National Commission on Excellence in Education. The first paragraphs of that report were a call to arms to improve education in order to restore our "once unchallenged preeminence in commerce, industry, science, and technological innovation. . . ."[2]

When he accepted this report at the White House, President Reagan appropriately used the occasion to urge states and local school districts to improve their schools. But he went on to call into question the usefulness of federal aid to education. In fact, the budget he had before the Congress that year proposed to cut federal spending on education by nearly one-third.

Taking a cue from the president, governors, state legislators, and local business groups turned away from Washington as a source of leadership in improving the schools. The states and local school districts mounted major school reform efforts of their own, efforts that affected nearly every school district in the U.S. State and local taxes were raised, teachers' salaries were increased, and graduation requirements were stiffened.

Between 1980 and 1986 an additional $4.2 billion in constant dollars was made available by the states and local school districts for elementary and secondary education.[3] Clearly, the nation was awakening to the need to improve its schools.

However, not everyone understands that these state and local increases in school funding were simply offsetting cuts in federal spending. During the same period — 1980 to 1986 — federal spending for education decreased by $4.2 billion in constant dollars.[4]

In other words, despite increased state and local spending, the net amount spent on education in 1986 was exactly the same amount in constant dollars as was being spent on education six years previously. The only difference was the revenue source — state and local or federal. What's more, it took a lot of effort on the part of state and local leaders to stay even in education as the national government was contracting its spending.

Improving education by shifting revenue sources was not among the recommendations of any of the numerous reform reports of the early 1980s. Only President Reagan and some of his supporters thought that a diminished federal role would mean a better educational system. Even the president's own National Commission on Excellence in Education urged a continuation of federal support for education. It stated that "the federal government has *the primary responsibility* to identify the national interest in education. It should also help fund and support efforts to protect and promote that interest."[5]

The National Commission also urged the federal government, in cooperation with states and localities, to help meet the needs of key groups of students, such as the gifted and talented, the socioeconomically disadvantaged, minority and language minority students, and the handicapped. Meeting the needs of these groups has been the special concern of the national government since 1965, when the Elementary and Secondary Education Act was signed into law. The National Commission evidently saw a need to continue that effort as essential to reviving the nation's economy.

In contradiction of the recommendations of the National Commission, the needs of students in these special categories have been slighted by the federal government over the last six years. The national program for gifted and talented children was repealed in 1982. Between 1980 and 1986, the Chapter 1 program, which provides remedial education for poor and minority children, was cut by 23 percent in constant dollars. As a result, 500,000 fewer students were being served. The Bilingual Education Act was slashed 47 percent in constant dollars over the same period, and the Education of the Handicapped Act was reduced in spending by 7 percent. Overall federal spending for all levels of education was reduced by nearly 11 percent in constant dollars between 1980 and 1986.

Moreover, the special needs of these students were usually not the object of state school reform legislation during those years. Most state and local reform was focused on increasing academic requirements for all children and on raising the professional competence of teachers. New money was most frequently made available for raising teachers' salaries. Only one state enacted a major new program aimed at the economically disadvantaged.

In sum, the mid-1980s saw the implementation of a policy which may not have been articulated by many people but was nonetheless carried out. That policy asserted that the federal government could do less while the states and local school districts could do more and that the schools would come out better in the end.

This policy not only ignored the recommendations of numerous reports that more (not less or the same amount of) financial assistance was needed by education, but it also overlooked the fact that *the different levels of government supported different activities.* States and districts paid for teachers' salaries, and the national government paid for special services for particular groups of children with special needs. States and local school districts certainly needed to increase teachers' salaries but not at the expense of doing away with innovation or eliminating remedial reading programs for academically disadvantaged students.

Not surprisingly, the mid-1980s also saw the issuance of numerous reports that noted the growth of an "underclass" in America, a class composed to a great extent of children born into poverty and locked into that status during their formative years. These same reports pointed out that the numbers of disadvantaged children who composed this "underclass" were rising while the numbers of children from more advantaged backgrounds were declining.

Harold Hodgkinson of the American Council on Education has been especially persuasive in showing these developments through an appraisal of demographic data. As he has pointed out in many reports and in countless presentations to Congress, to state legislatures, and to business groups, the future is already known because the students of tomorrow have already been born.

The key fact, which Hodgkinson and others have emphasized, is that 20 percent of the students currently in public elementary and secondary schools are economically disadvantaged. As a group, these students do least well in school. By the year 2000, fully one-third of all students will be economically disadvantaged.

In response to these facts and based on their own experiences, business leaders have become more aware that their own economic well-being depends on the availability of well-educated workers, who will have to be drawn increasingly from among the poor and minorities. In the late 1980s, the educational status of such children is a growing cause of concern to U.S. business.

As a noteworthy example of this concern, this year, for the first time, corporate leaders asked to testify before Congress in favor of expanding federal aid to education, especially for the disadvantaged. Charles Marshall of the American Telephone and Telegraph Company explained the presence of business leaders before Congress:

> We are not interested in education simply for altruistic reasons; we need knowledgeable, well-educated, highly-skilled employees if our business is to succeed. The educational system prepares the young people from whom we will enlist our future employees. If their preparation falls short, we wind up with less able employees and it is more difficult for us to reach our goals.[6]

The joint statement of these representatives of manufacturing, financial services, and telecommunications companies was delivered by William Woodside of Primerica (formerly the American Can Company). It said:

> Despite the diversity of our businesses and our regional locations, we are agreed that the quality of public schooling we provide to all our children, including disadvantaged children, will play a major role in the ability of the United States to develop a competitive economy and a strong society. Our collective appearance here today is intended to underscore the importance we attach to national efforts to provide

educational opportunities for disadvantaged and low-income children and our specific support for the renewal of the Chapter 1 program of Federal aid for disadvantaged and low-income children.[7]

Woodside urged Congress to give special attention to the costs imposed on the nation of leaving unserved half of the children who are eligible under Chapter 1 but who are not now being helped. He pointed out that "enhancing educational opportunity is an investment."

A further indication of the shift in business thinking toward a more active federal role in education comes in a report issued in September 1987 by the Committee for Economic Development (CED).[8] The CED is a prestigious group of leaders of major corporations who review the state of the economy and make recommendations for economic improvement. In the past, these business leaders have had reservations about federal efforts to fund educational and social programs.

In a significant departure from past practice, however, the CED is now calling for full funding of two major programs for the disadvantaged: Chapter 1 and Head Start. Those programs, which focus on providing remedial education for poor children, are now less than half funded. Consequently, full funding to reach all eligible children will cost the federal government many billions of dollars more.

The CED urges this increased federal spending for economic reasons. Its report asserts that for every dollar spent today to prevent educational failure, $4.75 can be saved in the future in the cost to society of remedial education, welfare, and crime.

Such statements of support for federal aid were not heard from business groups in the early 1980s when President Reagan was urging severe cutbacks in federal aid to education. An evolution of thinking has taken place. The involvement of the federal government is now seen as an essential component of a comprehensive effort to improve American education in order to meet foreign economic competition.

Congressional Action

During the early 1980s Congress reflected the prevailing belief that school reform was a job for the states and local school districts. Although the draconian spending cuts proposed by the Reagan administration were not approved, neither was federal funding increased enough to allow federal programs to maintain their levels of services. As measured in constant dollars, federal aid gradually contracted. As a result, the major federal programs lost some of their former effectiveness. Dozens of programs, such as the program for gifted and talented children and for desegregation assistance, were repealed outright.

The net effect was that by 1986 federal support for education had fallen to its lowest level in 20 years. Federal spending for elementary and secondary education constituted only 6.2 percent of all assistance provided in that year, down from 9.2 percent in 1979.

A turnaround began in 1984, but it has gained momentum only within the last three years. The first indication came when Congress enacted the Education for Economic Security Act of 1984. The sponsors of that legislation, Senators Robert Stafford (R–VT) and Claiborne Pell (D–RI), intentionally sought a title for the bill that would make the point that economic success depends on educational attainment. That legislation created the first new federal aid programs since 1980.

The cornerstone of the bill was a program to improve the teaching skills of math and science teachers. Only $100 million was appropriated for that purpose, but that amount was the first new money for education in four years. All the discussion in Congress on the need for that program centered on the declining math and science skills of American students and on what that decline meant for the economic competitiveness of the U.S. The report of the House Committee called the situation in math and science a "crisis" and suggested that "these problems threaten to compromise America's stature in the international marketplace, further weaken our industrial base, and undermine our national defense." The committee called for a renewal of the commitment to strengthen science and math education that was made in 1958 with the National Defense Education Act.

A related action taken in 1984 was the resurrection of the education directorate of the National Science Foundation (NSF), which had, in effect, been abolished in the early 1980s. During the budget cutting of 1981 and 1982, elementary and secondary education programs had been eliminated from the NSF. Once again, congressional debate about restoring these programs stressed the economic harm caused to America by a poorly trained work force.

In 1984, Congress appropriated $52 million earmarked to restore curriculum development and related NSF programs for elementary and secondary schools. In 1985, an additional $42 million was appropriated for the same purposes. Literacy in math and science was seen as essential to economic competition.

Usually when Congress passes a law or appropriates funds, the effects of these actions are not felt in the states or in local school districts until a year, or even two years, afterwards. This time lag is partly caused by the fact that most federal appropriations for education are intentionally made a year ahead of time in order to permit advance planning and partly caused by the need to develop regulations or establish programs.

Therefore, the effects of this congressional about-face were not felt locally until 1985 or even 1986. Similarly, the substantial shift by Congress toward greater funding for the major federal education programs that began in 1985 was not felt locally until 1987.

In 1986 Congress continued to fund federal education programs at higher levels than in the early 1980s. In the appropriations bill that year, the Chapter 1 program was increased nearly 12 percent over the amount appropriated for the previous year. The Education of the Handicapped Act was increased 15 percent. Both the Bilingual Education Act and the Vocational Education Act were increased 8 percent. Other programs received more modest increases.

Appropriations made by Congress in 1987 and 1988 confirmed this pattern. The major programs, in general, received adequate appropriations to maintain their current levels of services and, in some cases, to expand modestly.

This modest growth in current programs was significant, but equally as meaningful was the first-time funding of 16 new categorical aids in 1988. Since such programs are narrowly focused, limited funding can usually bring about significant changes. For instance, a new program for gifted and talented children received $8 million, which will go a long way towards spreading interest in offering special programs for such children. Similarly, new efforts to stem school dropouts began in 1988 due to a $22 million appropriation for that new program.

This expansion of federal aid should not be overstated. The contraction of aid was so severe in the early 1980s that it will take several more years to merely regain the levels of spending of 1980. To be specific, in fiscal year 1982 spending on federal programs was 12 percent less than it had been in 1980; but by fiscal year 1989, that gap has narrowed to 4.7 percent less than 1980. In other words, solid progress has been made and the prospects of further improvements are promising.

It cannot be overemphasized that these increases are a significant reflection of the belief of the Congress about what is most important to the national well-being. The national debt has more than doubled during the years of the Reagan administration, and the Congress is under enormous pressure to reduce federal spending in all areas. Yet, the members of Congress have singled out education as an area in which substantial growth in spending should occur. A grave concern about the economic well-being of the country was the motivating force for this action.

Policy changes slowly in Congress, and the movement from support for reducing federal aid to support for restoring such aid has not happened overnight. The report of the National Commission on Excellence in Education was a significant contribution to that change, as were countless other reports that followed. As each new report urged that more be done to improve education as a matter of national economic security, it gradually became more difficult for Congress to justify holding down federal spending for education—even under great pressure from the president.

The clearest sign that the Congress sees a connection between the need for better schools and our national economic survival was shown when Congress considered trade bills in 1986 and 1987. Both the House and Senate versions of these bills either called for the creation of new educational programs or proposed the expansion of current programs.[9]

The final bill which became public law established new programs in both areas of traditional federal interest: innovation and equity. Innovation is encouraged through grants for the development of educational telecommunications, exchanges of educational software, training for the better use of technology, funding of exemplary foreign language programs and expansion of science and mathematics programs. Equity is addressed through new initiatives to improve literacy training in the workplace and among those who do not speak English.

Another major new public law which would substantially expand Federal aid is H.R. 5, the Hawkins-Stafford School Improvement Amendments of 1988 (P.L. 100–297) H.R. 5 reauthorizes through 1993 all the federal elementary and secondary education and adult education programs, except for the handicapped education program which was extended last year. The largest programs which are reauthorized are the Chapter 1, the Chapter 2, the impact aid, the adult education, the magnet schools, the bilingual education, the Indian education and the science and math teacher retraining programs.

Although H.R. 5 proposes the greatest expansion of federal education programs of any bill considered by Congress in the last ten years, the House approved that legislation on May 21, 1987 by a vote of 401 to 1 and the Senate followed on December 1, 1987 by a vote of 97–1. That margin of approval was the largest ever received by a major reauthorization bill in the 20-year history of substantial federal aid to elementary and secondary education. The congressional representatives who spoke in favor of the bill returned repeatedly to the theme that the schools must be improved to make America competitive again. Increased federal aid was seen as vital to that undertaking.

Congressman Augustus Hawkins (D–CA), head of the Committee on Education and Labor, said that "education is the single most important issue facing the nation today. It is the foundation upon which our economic security, international competitiveness, and national defense are based. It is the key to a balanced budget and a growth economy."

Congressman William Goodling (R–PA), the Republican leader in the House in the area of elementary and secondary education, continued during the debate on H.R. 5 with the same theme:

> For the last three or four weeks we have heard a lot of discussion on this floor in which we were solving all the trade problems, all the trade deficit problems, all the defense problems, and all the foreign policy problems, and I am here to say that we cannot solve any of those unless we solve another serious problem we have in this country. That problem is that we have somewhere between 26 million and 60 million functional illiterates. Unless we attack that problem, all the rest of the things we do will go for naught.

No member of Congress spoke against H.R. 5, and only one member of each house voted against it. Those facts are extraordinary in a body that reflects the full range of the political spectrum from the extremely conservative to the extremely liberal. This near unanimity demonstrates that a new consensus has emerged in Congress regarding the need for school reform and for a strong federal role in that effort.

The provisions of H.R. 5 would expand current programs in order to provide services to a greater number of children. A policy was adopted urging that the funding for Chapter 1 be doubled in six years in order to reach all eligible children. The authorization for the program for math and science teachers was also doubled. In addition, the funding was increased for the adult education program, the bilingual education program, the magnet schools program, and the Chapter 2 block grant program.

Several new programs were proposed as well. A school dropout program and a program for gifted and talented children were included in the bill.

A proposed expansion for Chapter 1 would create a remedial reading program for high school students and a preschool program that would combine the education of young children with that of their illiterate parents.

In all, H.R. 5 proposes increasing federal spending by nearly $800 million next year. If fully funded, this new law would come close to returning federal support for elementary and secondary education to the levels of the late 1970s. The first appropriations bill enacted after passage of H.R. 5 did not provide full funding for these programs; but, as already noted, significant increases in funding did occur for current programs and new categorical programs were funded for fiscal 1989. The erosion of federal aid has been stopped, and the national government is moving in the direction of providing much needed assistance to improve education.

The presidential campaign of 1988 shows that this trend should continue. George Bush distanced himself from President Reagan's attempts to cut back on federal aid and he pledged to become an "education president." Only time will tell if the new president follows through on that campaign promise with a commitment of sufficient funds to earn that title.

Conclusion

National reports on education, statements from business groups, and congressional action have moved in tandem during the 1980s. In the early years of the decade, the realization that America was not keeping up economically led to a call for school reform—a task that was thought to be the exclusive responsibility of the states and local school districts.

Later in the decade it became clear that the job of improving education was so large that the national government had to do more—not less—if all parts of the population were to be served. Federal programs have a proven track record of success in assisting the economically disadvantaged and other special groups of children. Federal aid can also highlight areas of education that need improvement, such as the science and math skills of the nation's children.

The Congress, with the important support of business groups, is undertaking an expansion of federal aid in order to provide special assistance for improving educational attainment, and the prime motivating force is the need to make America economically competitive again.

Economic competitiveness is the Sputnik of the 1980s. It led to state and local school reform in the early years of the decade and now it is leading the federal government to give serious attention to the problem of improving education for all children.

ENDNOTES

1. New York Stock Exchange, Office of Economic Research, *People and Productivity: A Challenge to Corporate America* (New York: New York Stock Exchange, November 1982), p. 39.
2. National Commission on Excellence in Education, *A Nation At Risk* (Washington, D.C.: U.S. Government Printing Office, 1983), p. 5.
3. National Education Association, *Estimates of School Statistics*, 1985–86 (West Haven, CO: NEA Professional Library, 1986), p. 20.
4. Ibid.
5. *A Nation at Risk*, p. 33.
6. Hearing on H.R. 5, School Improvement Act, and S. 373, Elementary and Secondary Education Amendments of 1987, by the Subcommittee on Elementary, Secondary, and Vocational Education of the U.S. House of Representatives and the Subcommittee on Education, Arts, and Humanities of the U.S. Senate, 16 March 1987.
7. Ibid.
8. Committee for Economic Development, *Children in Need: Investment Strategies for the Educationally Disadvantaged* (Washington, D.C.: CED, September 1987).
9. H.R. 4800 passed the U.S. House of Representatives on 13 May 1986; H.R. 3 passed the House on 30 April 1987; and S. 1420 passed the U.S. Senate on 21 July 1987. This legislation was subsequently signed into law on August 23, 1988 as P.L. 100–418.

Chapter 2

DEMOCRACY AND DEMOGRAPHY: THE IMPACT OF DEMOGRAPHIC CHANGE ON EDUCATIONAL POLICY

Reginald Wilson

I

Higher education in the United States has been traditionally characterized as a privilege extended to a small elite of upper-class white males, much as it was in the English and European institutions on which it modeled itself. Indeed, education was not even mentioned in the U.S. Constitution and was presumed to be primarily the responsibility of the states or private entities. The general populace accepted this characterization for much of the early history of the nation since territorial expansion seemed to offer unlimited economic and vocational possibilities in the westward movement of the immigrant population. The social mores of the antebellum society also motivated acceptance of the restrictions of educational access as a given.

Moreover, educational theorists such as John Dewey saw the essential purpose of primary education as the socializing of the populace for work discipline and for exercising enlightened citizenship.[1] No need was perceived for mass higher education, since the majority of work available was in manual or farm labor. Eighty percent of the population lived on farms or in rural areas even after the turn of the century. Despite the Industrial Revolution in the nineteenth century, most heavy industry required little education to perform its tasks.

Nevertheless, the citizens excluded from educational institutions— racial minorities and women—yearned for educational opportunity. Women's colleges were established, mostly in the northeast, and private colleges for blacks in the South were founded by northern churches and missionaries. In 1890, an act of Congress, the Justin Morrill Land Grant Act, required Southern states to establish public colleges for blacks paralleling those inaugurated for whites by an 1862 congressional act.[2] Even so, higher educational opportunity remained considerably restricted for minorities and women until the Civil Rights movements of the 1960s. Beginning with the *Brown v. Board of Education* decision in 1954 desegregating public schools and continuing with the enactment of a number of civil rights laws and Supreme Court decisions, an explosion of educational opportunity occurred for both minorities and women. While overall higher education enrollments increased from eight million in the 1960s to over twelve million in the 1980s, black college enrollment multiplied from 150,000 in 1960 to over one million in 1980. College enrollment of Hispanics, Asians, and Native Americans also rose dramatically during that same period. Nevertheless, the progress for America's two largest minority groups—blacks and Hispanics—has begun to stagnate for the past decade or more, and for blacks has even begun an ominous decline, portending serious problems for American society for the future. American Indians and some Asian immigrants are also not doing as well as expected.[3]

II

Demographic changes in the American population since the 1960s have considerable implications for the establishment of educational policy. The dramatic increase in the proportion of racial minorities in the population, for example, is a result of both high birthrates and high immigration. While white birthrates have leveled at 1.7 children per female (below a population replacement level of 2.1), black and Hispanic birthrates are 2.4 and 3.1 children, respectively. In addition, taking 1985 as representative, immigration to the United States has been 40 percent Asian, 45 percent Hispanic, and only 15 percent white European. Indeed, the "new majority" in the 18- to 24-year-old college-going population will be women and minorities, and that proportion will increase into the twenty-first century. No longer can higher education be characterized as the exclusive preserve of white males. Minorities will be one-third of the American population shortly after the year 2000 and will be over 40 percent of the elementary and secondary school students by that time as well.[4]

As these dramatic demographic changes in the populace have been occurring, there have been equally dramatic changes in the nature of work in American society. No longer are manual and farm labor and heavy industry the norm. Now over 80 percent of the American population reside in urban areas rather than on farms or in the countryside. High technology and service industries dominate the workplace and will increasingly do so in the future. Not only will most jobs be increasingly technical but they will require a greater amount of education to perform them. It is estimated that over 80 percent of jobs will require some form of postsecondary education in the future. And while over 70 percent of the work force of the year 2000 is already employed, nearly 60 percent of the jobs of that time are in the process of being created.[5] Thus, massive retraining and upgrading of skills will be required. Therefore, the need for higher education will be even greater in the future.

Additionally, international competitiveness between sectors of the world economy will require more emphasis on the acquisition of technical skills and the maximum education of the American populace. The Pacific Rim countries already exceed the United States in many areas of high technology, and the consolidation of the European Economic Community in 1992 will present a formidable economic challenge to America's position as a leading nation.

The fact of America's higher percentage of students entering higher education institutions (approximately 50 percent of high school graduates compared to 10 to 20 percent in most countries) gives a false sense of security to Americans. Recent studies have shown that American high school students rank near the bottom among most nations in knowledge of the world, math skills, and reading and writing competencies. Indeed, most secondary school graduates of other countries exceed many American college freshmen and sophomores in general knowledge and math skills. As a consequence, substantial changes in the level and quality of American education will be required if the United States is to remain a leading industrial nation.[6]

III

The needed changes in American education will require considerable restructuring at both the primary schooling and postsecondary levels. It will be particularly necessary to improve both the academic achievement and success of minority students at these levels. Since the educational expansion of the 1960s, minority access and success in higher education has lagged considerably despite greater high school graduation rates, as Table I indicates.

Nevertheless, increased high school graduation percentages for minori-

Table I

	1976	1986
High School Graduation:		
Whites	82%	83%
Blacks	67%	76%
Hispanics	55%	60%
College Enrollment:		
Whites	33%	34%
Blacks	34%	27%
Hispanics	35%	29%

Source: American Council on Education, 1988.

ties mask real differences in the quality of the secondary educational achievement of minority and majority students. Substandard inner-city schools, predominately attended by black and Hispanic students, are often lacking in computers and scientific laboratory equipment and classes are frequently taught by uncertified or substitute teachers. Students have generally taken mathematics only through algebra, rather than calculus and trigonometry which is usual in suburban schools. Thus, even with higher graduation rates, minority students are often less competitive for admission to selective colleges and universities. These educational deficiencies are usually compounded by physical and nutritional deficiencies visited inordinately upon low-income and poverty-stricken families.

Despite these substantial handicaps, minority students have proven themselves capable of significant higher education achievement when provided with good teaching, sympathetic counseling, and effective academic support services. The historically black colleges, for example, which educate only 18 percent of the black students in college, nevertheless, produce 35 percent of the baccalaureate degrees blacks earn. Additionally, programs such as Upward Bound have a 20-year track record of considerably improving the college success potential of high-risk minority students. Yet, such programs reach only a small fraction of the students capable of benefitting from them, and funding for them has been cut during the Reagan years despite their proven success.

Often because of elementary and secondary schooling deficiencies, disproportionate numbers of minority students begin their higher education experience in open-door community colleges: 55 percent of Hispanics and 43 percent of blacks compared with 30 percent of white students. However, few of those students complete associate degrees and even fewer transfer to four-year colleges or complete baccalaureate degrees. Among 1980 high school seniors who enrolled in college, 21 percent of the white students, compared with 10 percent of black students and 7 percent of the Hispanic students, had earned a bachelor's degree or higher degree by spring 1986.[7]

Given the modest figures cited above, it is evident that even majority students have modest success rates in higher education, their figures only look better compared with the graduation rates of minority students. Thus, it seems evident that improvements in college retention will benefit all students, not just minorities. Programs to improve the effectiveness of the teaching-learning process in higher education have shown some remarkable successes. For example, a computerized program to improve the learning and study of introductory biology, developed by Professor Lewis Kleinsmith of the University of Michigan, increased black and Hispanic success rates to over 80 percent, equal to the achievement to white and Asian students. Yet, despite their success, such programs exist in isolation in various universities and have not enjoyed widespread proliferation even in the institutions where they have demonstrated their effectiveness.

Obviously, the earlier social and academic handicaps are addressed, the greater the likelihood of their success and also the more likely are they to prevent dropouts at later periods in the academic process. Forty percent dropout rates for blacks and over 50 percent for Hispanics before high school graduation in most of our inner cities depletes the pool of college-eligible minority students. However, despite their greater need, inner-city schools are habitually underfunded and are served by the least prepared teachers. Sociologist Gary Orfield's studies of big city school systems conclude decisively that these schools program their students for academic failure and limited capability of pursuing post-secondary education.[8]

In addition to the needed changes described above, more minorities need to be persuaded to pursue technical and scientific fields of study. Certainly, as has been indicated, inadequate preparation in substandard secondary schools is itself a barrier to selecting technical majors in university study. Without adequate mathematics and laboratory courses in high school, the possibility of making up these deficiencies in college is slim. Nevertheless, even minority graduates of excellent secondary

schools tend inordinately to select non-scientific majors in college, and
many of those who initially pursue technical majors change their field of
study before completing their degrees. With few minority scholars in
scientific and technical fields there are few role models and mentors to
urge and counsel minority students to pursue these disciplines and to
motivate them to success once matriculated in these fields. Although
good mentors can be of any race, Walter Allen, of the University of
Michigan, conducted research which documents that white professors
spend less time with their minority students and are less comfortable
with them.[9] James Blackwell, of the University of Massachusetts, has
published research which, on the other hand, confirms the strong correlation between the increased presence of minority professors and the
academic success of minority students.[10] Thus, increasing the number of
minority professors in the academy is a paramount need.

Currently, only 4.1 percent of professors are black and 1.8 percent are
Hispanic. Since nearly half of those black professors are in historically
black colleges, their real representation in majority institutions is closer
to 2 percent. With black and Hispanic students making up 8.8 percent,
and 5.6 percent, respectively, of higher education students, their likelihood of interacting with minority professors is exceedingly slim, and
when it does occur it is likely to be in only a few disciplines. For
example, although blacks, Hispanics and American Indians earned,
respectively, 462, 188 and 26 doctorates in education in 1986, that same
year they earned only 6, 12 and one doctorates in mathematics. Therefore,
the need to get more minority students into scholarly careers and more
of those into scientific and technical disciplines is alarmingly obvious.

Despite the evidence of the needed changes required in American
education from kindergarten through graduate school, substantial impediments to those changes occurring are present. For those impediments to
be removed, significant educational policies, institutional practices, and
legal strictures will have to be addressed.

IV

Institutional inertia is one of the major impediments to change. Institutions keep on doing things the same way even when those methods are
no longer effective. For example, financial aid policies have long been
predicated on the belief that the "typical" undergraduate student is 18 to
24 years old, attending school full time, and is dependent on parents for

support. The reality is that nearly half of students are older, attend school part time and are working. Yet only recently have financial aid policies recognized this reality that has been with us for over a decade.

Similarly, many of the assumptions that educators have about the nature of the educational process are so deeply ingrained that they are seldom raised to conscious critical awareness. For instance, the usual perception of "college-ready" means that students should be prepared to sink or swim according to their own devices. Indeed, many educators praise the Social Darwinism of the educational weeding-out process as a positive disciplining function. Many professors pride themselves on how few students pass their tough examinations rather than the greater number of students they effectively teach to pass their tests. Indeed, most educators suspect their colleagues who give many passing grades are "easy markers" rather than effective teachers. Individual study is praised while collaborative learning is seen as somehow "cheating." Yet, studies that show collaborative learning as most effective for larger numbers of students make relatively little impression on the professoriate. Thus, there is little incentive in the academic reward structure to stress improving the teaching-learning process to maximize student academic achievement.[11] Little wonder that the degree attainment indicated in Table II suggests a substantial waste of talent by students leaving college without completing their degree.

Table II
BA Degrees attained by 1980 H.S. Seniors by Spring 1986

Hispanic	6.8
American	10.8
Asian	27.3
Black	10.0
White	20.2

Source: American Council on Education, 1988.

It is well known that the overreliance on standardized tests for college admissions purposes has had a disparate impact on minorities and women. These disparities have usually been shrugged off by the test manufacturers as tests simply being the "messenger" of the bad news of inadequate early educational preparation. Nevertheless, test makers have had difficulty explaining why women, who do less well than men on tests, get consistently better grades than men in high school and college. And why, of two black students with identical Scholastic Aptitude Test scores, the one enrolled in a historically black institution is more likely to succeed academically, to graduate, and to go on to postgraduate studies. Recognizing that tests do not measure such factors as motivation, nurturing, and mentoring, institutions should understand that tests tell you more about where to begin instruction with a student than why you should keep the student out.[12]

Nevertheless, the pressures to get into selective (and more costly) institutions is becoming so fierce that a "bumping down" phenomenon is occurring. That is, students with high grades and scores who are not accepted by the most selective private institutions are raising the competitive stakes at the more prestigious public universities, thus "bumping down" students with lower test scores into the less selective institutions and community colleges. Enrollment trends confirm that minority enrollments are decreasing in selective institutions and any increases are being registered in state schools and community colleges. Therefore, quality institutions are becoming re-stratified by class, race and income levels instead of achieving the "diversity" that was the goal of many civil rights initiatives of the 1960s.[13]

Moreover, the civil rights initiatives that gave such impetus to the early advances of minorities in higher education and other areas of American life are now themselves becoming the subject of stricter scrutiny and narrower interpretation by the federal courts and the executive administration.

During the Reagan presidential years, the Civil Rights Commission, the Justice Department and the Education Department took consistent positions in opposition to the civil rights initiatives of previous administrations: school transportation for desegregation became "forced busing," affirmative action became "reverse discrimination," and higher education desegregation was achievable with only "good-faith efforts" rather than meeting goals and timetables.[14]

During the same period Reagan appointees to the Supreme Court, now constituting a conservative majority, began narrowing the interpretation and effect of previous civil rights decisions and laws. For example, the court ruled that Title IX discrimination complaints of women could only be brought against departments of an institution that directly received federal funds rather than against the whole institution. It took over two years for an act of Congress (the Civil Rights Restoration Act) to overcome that decision. More recently in the Richmond, Virginia case of minority set-asides, the court ruled that, despite the long history of discrimination in the "capital of the Confederacy," it was not justified to set aside 30 percent of city contracts for minority businesses which previously had been awarded less than 2 percent of city business in a city over 50 percent black in population. Most recently, in June 1989, the Supreme Court ruled that minority workers in Alaska must not only provide statistical evidence of alleged discrimination but must as well identify the specific employment practice which led to the discriminatory effect. The Court has since ruled in *Martin v. Wilks*, that court-approved affirmative action plans can be challenged by white workers, and in *Patterson*, that only discrimination in *making* a contract can be the basis for a suit, not discrimination that occurs in carrying out the contract. The conservation consistency of the new Supreme Court majority now seems set and clear.[15]

Certainly in light of the Reagan administration's eight-year opposition to various civil rights initiatives and the Supreme Court's narrowing of effective means to redress historic discrimination, it is not surprising that institutions of higher education, as well as other American institutions, have become lax in vigorously enforcing civil rights or affirmative action measures. Franklin A. Thomas, president of the Ford Foundation, was certainly right in characterizing the history of affirmative action as "an almost inescapable phase of our long journey toward social equality. Without affirmative action as a transitional and hence transitory remedy, and without the other civil rights laws that are sometimes characterized as intrusive, I doubt that the pace of progress toward the inclusion of all our citizens would have been as brisk." That significant progress was made by minorities and women during the period of strong enforcement of affirmative action there can be no question. That stagnation, indeed retrogression, for minorities has occurred during the decade-long opposition of the administration and the courts, there can equally be no question, as attested to by numerically measurable evidence. Despite the complaints of many higher education administrators about the intrusive nature of affirmative action laws, none has been able to demonstrate their vigorous actions to achieve equal opportunity before these laws were enacted or offered better alternatives to achieve the same desirable result.

V

As the United States prepares for the world of the twenty-first century it must increasingly recognize that its future success as a competitive society is intimately tied to the viability and enpowerment of its racial minorities. Blacks, Hispanics, Native Americans and many Asians are seriously underrepresented in American institutional life, particularly in its higher education institutions. The increasing technological and scientific work force required for jobs in the next century mandate that all of the citizens of society receive the maximum education they are capable of if that society is to prosper both domestically and internationally.

Shortly after the year 2000 minorities will constitute one-third of the American population. If substantial numbers of those minorities are mired in inner-city school systems that are ungovernable, and locked out of access to upwardly mobile training and jobs, the entire nation suffers as a consequence. It is axiomatic that the cost of prisons exceeds the cost of schools and that uneducated masses drain societal resources for the provision of welfare, courts, and rehabilitation services. Moreover, there is no return from these expenditures in meaningful contributions to society. Yet, despite the inexorable logic of these assertions, making the necessary changes in educational policies and institutional practices to address them faces formidable obstacles.[16]

Among the most intractable obstacles to change and the most difficult to discuss dispassionately is the deep current of racism in American societal history. Contradicting all of the egalitarian beliefs upon which this republic was founded have been the insidious practices of, first, slavery, then legal discrimination, and, now, systemic institutional policies and practices which operate to deny equal access and opportunity to racial minorities. Some of the most well-trained minds in our society go to extraordinary lengths to rationalize inequality and discriminatory institutional practices, and have done so throughout Western and American history. Most of the intellectual justification of status inequalities was produced by scholars in academic institutions. Thus, one of the issues least confronted in discussing needed changes in educational policies to increase opportunities for minorities is that the academy is being asked to repudiate itself as well as practices and belief systems which it has created.

Nevertheless, despite the formidable barriers to substantive changes in educational policy and institutional practices, significant changes have occurred in the past in American history with remarkable effect in achieving far-reaching and long-lasting changes in societal behavior. For example, the Flexner Commission at the turn of the century examined the widely varying quality of medical education and practice in the country and recommended sweeping changes in upgrading the level of medical training and the delivery of health services that had momentous and permanent consequences. Following the devastation of Europe in World War II, the American government created the Marshall Plan, a rapidly developed massive program to send billions of dollars in goods and services to rebuild European economies and infrastructures. When the Russians launched the first satellite, Sputnik, the Congress quickly developed the National Defense Education Act which provided millions for the education of scientists and engineers that ultimately resulted in America landing a man on the moon.

When the challenges have been dramatic and compelling, this nation has responded to crises with alacrity and good effect. Part of the present difficulty is that two of our most important challenges—international economic competitiveness and maximum technical education of the populace, particularly minorities—do not appear sufficiently dramatic or compelling enough to mobilize the kind of resources of the magnitude necessary to adequately address these challenges.

This is not to suggest that there are no educational programs of excellence in operation. Indeed, a number of outstanding initiatives are achieving dramatic successes in various parts of the country. A few examples are worth briefly describing:

1. The state of New Jersey probably has in operation the most comprehensive and long-standing effort to improve minority educational achievement. Under the governor and state chancellor's initiatives, challenge grants have been awarded to both public and private collegiate institutions for innovative minority college recruitment and retention strategies; outreach to elementary and secondary schools for earlier preparation and motivation for college has been supported; and loan-forgiveness grants have been made to support the doctoral study of minority scholars who plan academic careers. Other states such as California and Wisconsin have now emulated many of the New Jersey initiative's, but their programs are in too early stages of development to measure their success.

2. Phillip Uri Treismann of the University of California, Berkeley,

received the Charles A. Dana Award for Exemplary Service to Education for the development of significant improvements in the teaching-learning process in mathematics and science that achieved, among other things, the astonishing diminution of black and Hispanic failure rates in calculus from 60 percent to 4 percent! Other programs have been established in various colleges that either focus on improving the teaching process—such as Kleinman's work in biology at Michigan—or improving student's skills in learning—such as courses in critical thinking as offered at LaGuardia Community College.

3. A number of corporations and foundations have invested considerable funds in study for minorities at the doctoral level, particularly for those in scientific and engineering fields. Dupont, IBM, AT&T, and Hewlett-Packard are among corporations that have made such awards. And the Ford, Mellon, Dana, and National Science Foundations have been among those supporting various minority educational programs.[17]

However, the conclusion that can be drawn from all these pockets of excellence in various places is that they are insufficient to address problems that are nationally pervasive and that will require substantive federal policy initiatives and congressional action as well as state, corporate, and institutional initiatives. For example, in 1975 American universities awarded black Americans a total of 1213 doctorates. In 1987 the total was 765. Despite the pockets of excellence described above, these initiatives were insufficient to stem the disastrous decline in universities meeting their responsibilities for the production of minority scholars and scientists.

VI

Two areas of national self-interest which are raising issues of concern to both the educational and corporate worlds may provide part of the compelling motivation for both these sectors to urge the development and expansion of policies and programs to increase minority participation in American institutional life. One area is demographic. Population projections well into the twenty-first century suggest that an increasing proportion of the 18- to 24-year-old college-age cohort will consist of racial minorities. The other area is the corporate and industrial need for a highly trained work force. If colleges and universities are to maintain student bodies and class sizes, they will increasingly depend on minorities in the educational pipeline to fill them, and they will have a vested interest in retaining them successfully throughout the educational process. Corporations now spend over $5 billion a year in training and retraining workers. The need for highly skilled and trained workers is increasingly a bottom-line issue of corporate profit and competitiveness.[18]

In the 1960s, it was the leadership of the U.S. presidents and the courts, which, declaring the need for a "new frontier" and a "war on poverty," pushed other societal institutions, often reluctantly, into initiating long-overdue programs and to partially tearing down long-standing barriers to bring minorities into the mainstream of American life. That effort has now stagnated and, in some areas, has alarmingly retrogressed. In the 1980s, it is the presidents and the courts which have now become major obstacles to overcoming those last systemic, thus most intractable, barriers to minority access and empowerment. As a consequence, it is the academic, the legislative and the corporate sectors which, in their self-interest, may be the leaders in the 1990s in insisting on national policy and program initiatives to achieve that which in the past had been motivated on basically moral and legal grounds. If that be the case, then the broad outlines of some of the most needed considerations of policy change can be clearly identified:

- Increased federal and state funding to improve both the quality and efficiency of American public elementary and secondary schooling is urgently needed, particularly for major urban areas where most minorities reside. Efforts by states in recent years to "raise standards" by requiring more high school academic courses and higher standardized test scores, without providing both the resources and skills to underachieving schools and students to meet those standards, simply condemns a larger number of students to academic failure.

- Entrance to higher education institutions should be based on variable admission criteria—grades, leadership, community service, etc.—without overreliance on test scores, in recognition of the latter's limitations in predicting both what institutions and students can do to improve their academic achievement success.

- Colleges and universities *must* provide more incentives and resources to motivate faculty to improve the efficiency of the undergraduate teaching-learning process. Less than 50 percent graduation rates for all students after 5 years of collegiate experience is a grievous waste of talent, both of students and for the nation. Improvements in student academic achievement by better faculty teaching need not detract from the production of research and scholarship. Challenge grants to institutions that increase their undergraduate graduation rates (*not* by raising entrance criteria) might be an incentive, particularly if increased retention efforts are aimed at chronically underachieving students.

- With 45 percent of black, 55 percent of Hispanic, 43 percent of Asian, and 65 percent of American Indian students (compared with 30 percent of whites) beginning their higher education in a community college, emphasis on improving the transfer rate and baccalaureate success must be a high priority for state and institutional policy. Currently, an average of only about 15 percent of community college students transfer (fewer of minorities). Early identification and motivation of students with potential as well as easing the transfer process should be supported by state policies and institutional plans.[19]

- Increasing the number of minority students pursuing doctorates, particularly in technical fields, and urging interest by them in academic careers is paramount for the continued viability of American leadership in science and technology. With 59 percent of engineering doctorates and 51 percent of physics doctorates from American universities being awarded to foreign nationals, America is in serious danger of undereducating its domestic population (and especially minorities) for technological leadership. A recent bill introduced in the Congress to ease immigration requirements for foreigners with "certain skills" only avoids addressing the critical issue of American universities declining production of *American* scientists and scholars. Congressional and state policies should motivate initiatives to redress this decline.

The demographic and competitive realities of the twenty-first century will provide the impetus for a much-needed critical reevaluation of educational policy and practice that will be crucial for the future well-being of American society. That the increased educational viability and societal participation of racial minorities is a key ingredient of that well-being is becoming compellingly clear to thoughtful educational leaders and corporate executives. What has been conspicuously absent has been the comprehensive planning at national and state levels, the significant reordering of financial and material resources, and the concerted leadership to initiate programs of sufficient magnitude to effect measurable and urgently immediate changes to achieve the results required.

REFERENCES

1. R.D. Archambault (Ed.), *John Dewey on Education* (Chicago: University of Chicago Press), 1974.
2. Allen B. Ballard, *The Education of Black Folk* (New York: Harper and Row), 1973.
3. American Council on Education, *Minorities in Higher Education: Seventh Annual Report, 1988* (Washington, D.C.: American Council on Education).
4. *One-Third of A Nation,* A Report of the Commission on Minority Participation in Education and American Life (American Council on Education — Education Commission of the States), 1988.
5. *Opportunity 2000,* U.S. Department of Labor (U.S. Government Printing Office), 1988.
6. *Barriers to Excellence: Our Children at Risk,* National Coalition of Advocates for Children (Boston: NCAC), 1985.
7. *Minorities in Higher Education.*
8. Gary Orfield et al., *The Chicago Study of Access and Choice in Higher Education* (Chicago: University of Chicago Committee on Public Policy Studies), 1984.
9. Walter Allen, "The Education of Black Students on White Campuses: What Quality the Experience?," in Michael Nettles (ed.), *Toward Black Undergraduate Student Equality in Higher Education* (New York: Greenwood Press), 1988.
10. James Blackwell, *Mainstreaming Outsiders: The Production of Black Professionals* (New York: General Hall), 1981.
11. Madeleine F. Green (Ed.), *Minorities on Campus* (Washington, D.C.: American Council on Education), 1989.
12. Wanda E. Ward and Mary M. Cross, *Key Issues in Minority Education* (The University of Oklahoma: Center for Research on Minority Education), 1989.
13. Robert Atwell, *Competition and the Commonweal* (Washington, D.C.: American Council on Education), 1986.
14. Reginald Wilson, "Affirmative Action: The Current Status," *AGB Reports* (Washington, D.C.: The Association of Governing Boards), May/June, 1985.
15. "Strike Four," *The Washington Post,* June 16, 1989, A26.
16. *One-Third of A Nation.*
17. *Minorities on Campus.*
18. *Opportunity 2000.*
19. Richard Donovan et al., *Transfer: Making it Work* (Washington, D.C.: American Association of Community and Junior Colleges), 1987.

Chapter 3

FAR FROM THE BANKS OF THE POTOMAC: EDUCATIONAL POLITICS AND POLICY IN THE REAGAN YEARS

Laurence R. Marcus

Throughout most of our history and in many quarters today, an Alexis de Tocqueville would hear that the strength of the educational system that underpins our democracy lies in the local control of the schools. Yet, while municipal and regional school boards have traditionally maintained a preeminent role in the establishment of educational policy, they have not been the only players. In response to social concerns, states established mandatory school attendance policies and mandated minimum curricular requirements. In times of concern regarding national defense and economic security, there have been federal interventions. The Great Society education bills dramatically increased the federal role in education and led to the 1979 establishment of a cabinet level Department of Education (ED) (see Stickney and Marcus, 1984, for a discussion of federal educational involvement in the schools). If de Tocqueville had spoken with Americans in the late 1970s, he would have heard a growing anguish about the performance of our schools: some would have blamed local politics; others would have focused on the teachers; and some would have pointed to misguided policies that came from Washington.

Ronald Reagan's landslide election in 1980 was based in part on a perception that the reach of the federal government had extended too far and that Washington was involved in too many ventures that were best handled at other governmental levels or by the private sector. Reagan's education platform called for the replacement of "the crazy quilt of wasteful [education] programs with a system of block grants that will restore decision making to local officials responsible to voters and parents" rather than Washington bureaucrats. Complaining that the attention of teachers had been diverted from teaching and a concern for maintaining standards of excellence (since their time was consumed by "the task of complying with federal reporting requirements"), he campaigned for the "deregulation by the Federal Government of public education and elimination of the Federal Department of Education" (1980 Political Platforms, 1981:101–103). And while he achieved substantial success in much of his educational agenda, the president's desire to strengthen the position of local school officials fell short of his target.

Reagan's Education Goals

As Susan Fuhrman (1987:135) has noted, Reagan had five initial goals in the area of education: disestablishment of the Education Department; deregulation; decentralization; deemphasis of education as a federal priority; and diminution of federal education spending. In his first term, he accomplished much of what he had set out to do.

Deregulation was a hallmark of the early 1980s. In addition to revoking at least 30 sets of education-related regulations, the administration retreated from its responsibilities as enforcer of civil rights statutes. Not only was ED's Office for Civil Rights precluded from aggressively pursuing the bilingual education requirements (Astuto and Clark, 1988:362–3), but the government actually changed its position in celebrated cases that had the effect of supporting the racially discriminatory practices of Bob Jones University and the Goldsboro Christian Schools and of disregarding the failure of Grove City College to comply with anti-sex discrimination regulations. In fact in those cases, the administration sought to narrow the reach of civil rights provisions, both as it argued before the Supreme Court and in its subsequent interpretation of the decisions, particularly that in *Grove City* (see Marcus, 1988, for a discussion of these cases).

Decentralization was accomplished through the replacement of categorical programs with block grants. Originally, the president proposed a massive reorganization of 85 social service and educational categorical programs into seven block grants. Congress would not go that far and chose to consolidate 57 programs into nine block grants. The Education Consolidation and Improvement Act of 1981 merged 40 programs into a block grant. Included were most programs authorized by the Elementary and Secondary Education Act of 1965, part of the Higher Education Act of 1965, a section of the National Science Foundation Act of 1950, the Alcohol and Drug Abuse Education Act, the Career Education Incentive Act, and, on a phased basis, the Follow Through Act. These programs were refashioned into three broad subchapters, "Basic Skills Development,"

"Educational Improvement and Support Services" and "Special Projects," and much greater latitude was accorded to the states in spending the funds that flowed to them through this new approach. (It should be noted that political pressure and congressional interest kept some categorical programs including compensatory education, Head Start, bilingual education, education of the handicapped, vocational education and the Women's Educational Equity Act from consolidation into block grants [Stickney and Marcus, 1984:110–112].)

While the previous categorical programs had been targeted toward equity issues, disadvantaged students and school improvement, block grants gave the states increased opportunity to direct federal education dollars toward more locally perceived needs. As a result, spending shifted to the acquisition of instructional materials, library resources, computers and software and other educational equipment, on curriculum development and on district-initiated activities (Astuto and Clark, 1988:365).

President Reagan's own words best exemplify his desire to deemphasize education as a federal priority.

> American schools don't need vast sums of money as much as they need a few fundamental reforms. We must restore parents and state and local government to their rightful place in the educational process. Education begins at home, where it is a parental right and responsibility. Decisions about discipline, curriculum and academic standards—the factors that make a school good or bad—shouldn't be made by people in Washington. They should be made at the local level by parents, teachers, and administrators in their own communities. (Astuto and Clark, 1988:361.)

Washington's disengagement was also felt in higher education. University of Vermont president Lattie F. Coor (1988:34) lamented that he found "very little evidence that higher education has a place of any significance on the Federal political agenda."

As might be expected, the deemphasis in priority was accompanied by a diminution of federal dollars directed toward education. Between 1980 and 1986, federal education expenditures increased slightly in absolute terms but declined by $1.3 billion in real terms. A comparison of fiscal years 1980 and 1985 reveals that the consolidation of programs into block grants resulted in a current dollar reduction of 34 percent (which translates into a 53.5 percent reduction in real terms) for those programs (Astuto and Clark, 1988:363). The proportion of the federal share of public elementary and secondary school funding fell from more than 9 percent to 6.4 percent during the same period (Fuhrman, 1987:135–6).

Efforts were also made in the first six years of the Reagan administration to reduce sharply the amount of federal financial aid provided to college students (Coor, 1988:36). While the student aid agenda was not fully implemented, eligibility requirements were tightened so extensively as to gut assistance to students from middle-income families and to remove from guaranteed student loan eligibility a significant proportion of the population previously served by that program.* Between FY80 and FY87, the federal share of total education spending dropped from 21 percent to 14 percent and the proportion of the federal budget spent on education declined from 5.8 percent to 4 percent, although in the following year it rose very slightly (Finn, 1988:347).

The one goal where the president ran into a brick wall was his attempt to disestablish the Department of Education. Ironically, it was a Reagan administration initiative that provided the death knell to the effort. In April 1983, ED Secretary Terrel Bell published the report of the National Commission on Excellence in Education, *A Nation at Risk: The Imperative for Educational Reform*, which decried "a rising tide of mediocrity" in American education that was threatening our future (1983:5). The report drove home the point that something was amiss with our schools, so wrong that "[i]f an unfriendly foreign power had attempted to impose on America the mediocre educational performance that exists today, we might have viewed it as an act of war" (p. 5). The report captured the country's attention in its message that "[o]ur Nation's people and its schools and colleges must be committed to achieving excellence . . ." (p. 13).

Over 700 newspaper articles were written about *A Nation at Risk*, and 70,000 copies of the report were sold in its first year (Fuhrman, 1987:36). Its recommendations received America's rapid and overwhelming support according to a June 1983 poll conducted by *Newsweek* (June 27, 1983:61). According to one analyst who tracks education reform for the Education Commission of the States, *A Nation at Risk* "transformed 1983 into a watershed year for American education" (Pipho, 1986:K1). The report ushered in a new focus on educational excellence and defined a new role for the federal government as the patron of excellence.**

---

*Student loans were dealt another blow when the 1986 Tax Reform Act phased out the deductibility of interest for all educational loans except those based on home equity.

**While he was forced to live with ED, Reagan was able to rein it in significantly by reducing its complement of staff by some 35 percent (Finn, 1988:348).

Excellence and Politics

Chester E. Finn, Jr., the Vanderbilt educator who served as ED's Assistant Secretary under Terrel Bell's successor, William Bennett, believes that the call for excellence was "the most visible and . . . most consequential of the Reagan Administration's endeavors in the field of education" (1988:349). Prior to *A Nation at Risk*, the administration, despite its successes in Congress, had little to brag about in education. Deregulation, particularly with regard to the handicapped, gender and race, was extremely controversial. Few at the state and local levels found anything positive in the federal funding cuts. The president's efforts to put prayer back in the public schools and to provide tuition tax credits for parents sending their children to private schools had support from some quarters, but fell flat with both the educational establishment and the Congress. As the 1984 election campaign approached, Reagan needed an educational strategy with broad popular appeal, and *A Nation at Risk* gave him that opportunity. He seized the opportunity to use his office as a "bully pulpit" to catalyze a nationwide educational reform movement. The timing was right, as business leaders and governors were beginning to express their concerns about the quality of the schools. Despite defensiveness in some quarters, leading educators jumped at the chance to begin to build coalitions that would direct more dollars to their programs. It was, as Finn (1988:350) said, "good politics."

William Bennett assumed the top spot at ED after the 1984 election and took the bully pulpit role seriously. And while some of his utterances were pure opinion (sometimes very inaccurate, like his generalization about college students complaining about federal financial aid reductions at the same time that they were spending their own money on stereos and trips to Florida), he kept education in the news. Central to his strategy was the unleashing of a flood of unequivocal and often controversial reports and policy papers that received wide publicity. Educators were often the target of his criticisms; the public, governors and legislators were his audience. His message was almost always grounded on the excellence theme.

With Washington content to proselytize, it fell not to the local districts (which had come to be viewed as having lax standards and thus as being a part, if not the source, of the problem) but to the states to identify their concerns and to develop reforms that would be seen to resolve local problems—and to find a way to pay for them. Complementing the more than 40 national reports that were issued, at least 275 state-level blue ribbon committees and task forces were established in the early and mid-1980s to discuss issues of educational reform (Reilly, 1988–9:92–3), most of them using *A Nation at Risk* as their springboard. Contrary to the oft-held view that such reports have their greatest utility as dust collectors, most served as the basis for tangible, sometimes widespread, reforms.

The States Empowered

In earlier times a Washington withdrawal from educational policy preeminence would have resulted in a concomitant rise of power among local school authorities, but not this time. Conditions were correct for an ascendancy of the states. First, the rise of collective bargaining, teacher militancy and single-interest advocacy groups in the decade that preceded Ronald Reagan's arrival in Washington caused educational problems to spill out of the non-partisan arena of local boards and into the partisan political arena. At the same time, local property taxes were strained in many places, and court-ordered, cross-district funding equalization requirements caused an increased flow of state tax dollars to the schools. These phenomena increased the interest of governors and legislators in education.

In addition, the capacity of the states to deliver the political goods had developed over time to the point where a heightened state role in education was possible. Demonstrating that the flow of federal dollars to the states between 1945 and 1984 contributed to increases in the size and reach of state government in two-thirds of the 50 states, James Garand (1988:837, 847) has argued that, as the federal government shared its revenues, state governments became dominated by "self-interested actors who utilize at least some of the tools at their disposal to increase the size of the state public sector." Gubernatorial and legislature staffs are visible evidence of his thesis. While the average governor's office had only four staff members in 1956, it had 35 in 1979; nearly all included a planning and development staff. Similarly, state legislatures across the nation had an estimated 16,000 full-time employees in 1980, many serving in research, evaluation and audit positions (Fuhrman, 1977:137), often to keep an eye on the governor's staff and the executive branch (Kritek et al., 1988:2–3). As the new "age of education" was about to be born, governor's offices and legislatures both had full-time staff members whose responsibilities were focused on education, these in addition to (and sometimes more

influential than) the personnel in the state's education and higher education agencies.

A study conducted by Kritek et al. (1988:10, 14) of legislative actions
concerning public elementary and secondary schools in 18 states reveals
the increase of state educational activity in the wake of *A Nation at Risk.*
The number of education bills passed in each year of the 1970s was
relatively stable, increasing from 393 in 1971–72 to 407 in 1979–80. In
1983–84, the number of legislative actions jumped by more than 60
percent over 1979–80 to a level of 661. In many instances, legislatures
were responding to the leadership of a reform-minded governor committed to educational improvement. Among the "education governors"
during this era were both liberals and conservatives, Republicans and
Democrats, including LaMar Alexander (TN), William Clinton (AR),
Pierre Dupont (DE), Robert Graham (FL), James Hunt (NC), Thomas
Kean (NJ), Charles Robb (VA) and William Winter (MS) (Krotseng,
1987:8–9, 30).

Characteristic of earlier educational reform efforts was a focus on
specific programs for discrete concerns, each moving through the legislature or the state board of education independently of any program for
any other concern. States would, for example, enact a program for the
handicapped on one occasion, a set of programs for the educationally
and economically disadvantaged on another, a program for the gifted on
another. During this wave of reform, however, the belief became widespread that educational change requires comprehensive and systematic
approaches. Fuhrman (1987:133) has pointed out that Arkansas, Florida,
South Carolina and Texas each packaged in the vicinity of a hundred
different programs into omnibus legislation. In addition, California's
Hughes-Hart Education Reform Act of 1983 included 83 different provisions (Likens, 1985:146). While other states may not have bundled together
so many items, the omnibus approach was frequently used. Further, to a
larger extent than before, the new set of reforms restructured state
education agencies, initiated new programs, raised statewide standards
for educational practice, provided financial incentives to schools that
made progress toward state goals, and provided for legislative oversight
of school performance (Kritek et al., 1988:22).

More important than either the approach to reform or the form of
policy mechanism that was used, the states consistently echoed the message from Washington—that the schools should be aimed for excellence.
No player in the educational game was exempt from the imperatives

established by the state solons; more was to be expected of students, teachers and parents as well as local administrators and policymakers.

Expectations of Students

In the spirit of *A Nation at Risk,* efforts to increase both the quantity and quality of education in order to improve student achievement have been at the heart of much of the education reform in this era. On the quantity side, six states between 1980 and 1986 raised the age that they permit students to drop out of school; three of these states joined three others in lowering the age for the start of compulsory schooling (Pipho, 1986:K5). The number of states that require local districts to offer kindergartens increased to 28 after seven states joined the group in the mid-1980s. Illinois increased state funding so that local districts could extend kindergartens from half-day to full-day sessions (Education Commission of the States, 1985a:1). Further, some states moved to lengthen the school day. In addition, the school year was lengthened in six states and the District of Columbia but, counter to the trend, was decreased in seven states (Pipho, 1986:K5).

There have been instances where the zeal to increase the quantity of education has resulted in more form than substance. California provides a costly example. School districts that set the academic year five days beyond the minimum 175 received $35 per student. Incentive funding for districts that lengthened the school day provided $20 for each child in elementary school and $40 for each high school student. Ninety-seven percent of the districts serving 99.7 percent of the state's students decided to participate in this program. The price tag was substantial, originally estimated to be $460 million for the first three years but actually closer to $250 million per year during the three-year phase-in period and $450 million annually thereafter. According to the state education department, most districts needed to add not five but four days to the school year to meet the new standard. While most elementary schools already met the new criteria for the length of the school day, the average high school needed to added only six minutes per day. Some districts accomplished this by lengthening the homeroom period, while others increased the amount of time available for passing between classes. Thus, the amount of additional instructional time turned out to be minimal (Likens, 1985:147; Timar and Kirp, 1988:81–83).

Other measures to increase the quantity of education, both in California and elsewhere, hold greater promise. For example, high school graduation requirements have been changed in 45 states and the District of Columbia: eleven states set requirements for the first time; four states changed distribution requirements without increasing the number of credits; the other states and the District of Columbia increased theirs.* Acting on the belief that the dismal achievement levels in math and science have been largely responsible for America's having lost its position as the world's technological leader, most states moved to increase the number of required years of mathematics and science instruction. Of the 42 states that raised the math requirement, nearly three-fifths increased from one year to two, another fifth increased the requirement to three years and a fifth instituted a graduation requirement in this area for the first time. Of the 34 states that raised the science requirement, 22 went from one year to two, three increased to three years and nine instituted requirements for the first time. Eighteen states changed the number of mandated years of English study; one decreased from six units to three, most of the rest raised their standard to four years. Social studies graduation requirements were decreased in two states but were raised in 24 others, generally to two or three years.

Despite all of this activity, the graduation requirements in most states still fall short of what was recommended in *A Nation at Risk:* four years of English, three each of mathematics, science and social studies, two of foreign language study and a half year of computer literacy. By the end of 1986, only 15 states met the English and social studies standards, ten met the mathematics standard (with one other moving in that direction); four (with the likely possibility of a fifth) met the suggested science level; none required two years of foreign language instruction; and only six required the study of computer science (Pipho, 1986:K5).

Beyond the strengthening of graduation requirements, many states also sought to encourage additional study in crucial areas and to provide enriched curricula. For example, Iowa provides its school districts with grants of $25 for each high school student who enrolls in an advanced mathematics or science course and $50 grants for each student who takes the first year of a foreign language (Astuto and Clark, 1988:368). Alabama, Missouri, New Mexico, Oklahoma, Rhode Island, Texas and Virginia have all initiated statewide requirements for students enrolled in college

---

*Colorado, Hawaii, Idaho, Nebraska and Wyoming made no changes in their high school graduation requirements; Colorado is constitutionally prohibited from establishing curriculum requirements. Only Vermont lowered its requirement (Pipho, 1986:K5).

preparation tracks (Pipho, 1986:K5). Some states enacted sex education, drug and alcohol education and AIDS awareness programs.

Strengthening Educational Quality

Programs to improve the quality of education have been varied. For example, California provides grants of up to $2000 to teachers to develop more effective instructional approaches. Kentucky, Michigan, Tennessee and West Virginia each offer special summer programs for gifted students (Astuto and Clark, 1988:367–8) as does New Jersey. Some states have required that students attain a specified minimum grade point average in order to participate in extracurricular activities, including sports (Fuhrman, 1987:132); Texas, under the prodding of millionaire H. Ross Perot, was a leader with its no-pass, no-play rule for athletes (Timar and Kirp, 1988:77). Colorado, Hawaii, Idaho and South Carolina enacted statewide discipline codes in order to provide the structure for conditions for improved learning (Astuto and Clark, 1988:369).

Testing has been in the spotlight of state quality enhancement measures during this era of educational reform. For decades, schools have utilized standardized achievement tests for diagnostic and placement purposes. While some states have traditionally mandated minimum competency tests for certain grade levels, most local districts have overseen their own testing programs. Prior to 1979, New York (whose regents' exams must be passed in order for students to earn a state-endorsed high school diploma) and only three other states used statewide tests for the "high stakes" purposes of grade advancement or high school graduation (Kritek et al., 1988:4; Airasian, 1988:311). Between 1980 and 1985, 25 states adopted or updated minimum competency tests. Within a year they were joined by 21 more states. Some use them as a condition for promotion at certain grade levels; 20 have mandated their use as a prerequisite of high school graduation (Education Commission of the States, 1986b:1; Kritek et al., 1988:4).

Included among those states that strengthened their testing requirements was New Jersey, which replaced its Minimum Basic Skills Test (MBS) with the High School Proficiency Test (HSPT) in 1983. The new test was adopted as a result of concern over a continuing skid in SAT scores that routinely saw New Jersey high school seniors performing well below the national averages. Pressure also came from the State Board of Higher Education that had been administering the New Jersey College Basic Skills Placement Test since 1979 to all entrants into the state's

two-year and four-year public colleges and universities; performance on
that test had been so poor as to result in the placement of huge proportions of college freshman into remedial courses. The students, whose
lack of basic skills proficiency was revealed by the college test, came from
all parts of the state (from the inner-city schools and the best suburban
districts alike) and had reasonably good high school records.

The HSPT was designed to measure a higher proficiency level in
mathematics, reading and writing (the latter being tested for the first
time) than its predecessor did. After two years of pilot testing, it was
administered in the spring of 1986 to the high school freshman class.
Beginning with that group of ninth graders, students were required to
pass the test in order to graduate. Those who failed any of its three parts
were required to receive remedial instruction in the deficient area(s) in
the tenth grade as preparation for retesting in the deficient area(s). For
those still unable to achieve a passing grade, remediation and retesting
would continue in the eleventh grade and, again, in the senior year, if
necessary. Students unable to pass the test by that time would be denied a
state diploma.

The responses of the school districts to the test's implementation have
been noteworthy—and promising. In 1986, 79 percent of the districts that
responded to the state education department's survey reported that they
were revising their curricula in all grades in order to reflect the new skill
levels being tested and were developing long-range plans to improve
student achievement. Over four-fifths of the districts implemented staff
development programs as part of their efforts. To assist the districts, the
state increased its compensatory education funding that year by nearly
50 percent to $158 million (Koffler, 1987:330–1).

The effect of the HSPT in improving basic skill proficiencies has yet
to be determined, since the initial class is (at this writing) just about to be
graduated from high school. 31,000 (38.5%) of the ninth graders who took
the HSPT in 1986 failed at least one section of the test (Koffler, 1987:332–3).
By the end of the eleventh grade, 660 students who had previously failed
the reading portion of the HSPT still were unable to attain the minimum passing score; 1726 students were still unable to pass the math
portion; and 907 students again failed the writing portion. Given what
we know about the condition of the big city schools, it is not surprising
that the passage rate for all three tests was lower in the 56 urban districts
than it was in the other districts (NJ Department of Education, 1988:2–4).
In future years, New Jersey students will be expected to attain even

higher achievement levels, since the State Board of Education has initiated the process of developing a new test, raising the proficiency standard required for graduation from the current ninth grade level to the eleventh grade level.

Focus on the Teaching Profession

During the 1970s teachers saw their paychecks being eroded as salary increases failed to keep pace with inflation; they saw their status losing ground in comparison to other professions; and they saw their control over the classroom falling away as a result both of the evaporation of traditional discipline and of the replacement of their own curricula with one supplied by the district. The accompanying rise of teacher militancy, their willingness to strike, and the practice of many to work only to the letter of their collective-bargaining agreement left a bad taste with much of the public. Teacher "burnout" became a frequent topic in the media, and teachers often bore the brunt of the criticism for the lackluster performance of the schools.

The centrality of teachers to the improvement of education came to be appreciated once again in the aftermath of *A Nation at Risk.* Distinguished bodies including the Carnegie Task Force on Teaching as a Profession and the Holmes Group began to call for the empowerment of teachers—to free teachers to do their best to unleash student creativity—as an important precondition for educational improvement. In addition, it became evident that it was necessary to upgrade the teaching profession itself. In response, states focused attention both on attracting the best students into teaching, on teacher preparation programs and on teacher salaries.

At least 34 states have developed incentives to encourage the entrance of top-flight students into teaching. In most instances they follow the ROTC model of providing scholarships in return for an agreement to teach for a certain period of time. Some states, including Illinois, target their programs to areas of teacher shortage. Loan-forgiveness programs for prospective math and science teachers have been the most prominent, occurring in at least 28 states. The District of Columbia provides bilingual and elementary education majors with free tuition in return for two years of teaching. Missouri offers non-renewable $2000 scholarships to high-achieving students; the state pays half of the scholarship and the student's college pays the other half. Alaska and New Jersey offer academically talented students loans of up to $7500 per year to support their undergraduate study. The New Jersey loans are forgivable after four years of teaching in the state. In Alabama prospective teachers can receive loans for two years and are required to teach for three years to redeem each year of the loan. In return for a three-year teaching commitment, Indiana provides prospective teachers with $1000 (Leatherman, 1988:A30; Education Commission of the States, 1985d:2, 1987b:1, 1987c:1).

Many states have made it possible for prospective teachers to achieve certification despite not having completed an approved collegiate teacher education program. Some demand passage of the same core set of education courses required of students in approved programs, while others merely require the completion of an intensive course on pedagogy (Leatherman, 1988:A30). New Jersey's "alternate route" allows college graduates to become teachers if they had good grades in college, are able to pass the National Teacher Examination in the subject(s) for which they seek certification, and have been hired as a provisional teacher by a school district. In order to qualify for certification, they must undergo an intensive three-week preservice orientation course, serve for a year under the watchful eye of an experienced teacher and complete a year-long in-service seminar program approved by the state's education department.

Certification standards for students enrolled in collegiate teacher training programs have also been altered. By 1988, 21 states had set more rigorous admissions standards for students interested in enrolling in teacher education programs, and six had set a higher exit standard by increasing the minimum grade point average necessary for certification. Degree requirements were changed in 32 states. In many instances, the number of general education courses was increased (Massachusetts and Tennessee are examples), while the number of professional education courses was significantly decreased. Some, including New Jersey, went even further by mandating that undergraduate students complete a major in an academic subject rather than in education in order to qualify for certification. Only two states, Iowa and Kentucky, bucked the trend by increasing the pedagogy requirements (Leatherman, 1988:A30). Forty-three states now insist that prospective teachers pass an examination in order to qualify for initial certification; 35 enacted this requirement between 1980 and 1987. Seventeen states require passage of a basic skills test (Leatherman, 1988:A30). Many of them also require passage of a subject area test and/or an exam on teaching principles and educational foundations. The National Teacher Examination, the most prevalent of the tests, is used by at least 19 states; 12 use a test developed specifically for their state (Education Commission of the States, 1987a:1).

Only a few states permit initial certification to last an entire career. While some issue probationary certificates for new teachers for their first several years of teaching prior to the conferral of a permanent license, others, including Pennsylvania and Idaho, require additional course work. In the first half of the 1980s, at least 14 states raised their recertification standards. In California, for example, teachers must complete 150 hours of professional development in order to be recertified, while in Washington 150 hours of continuing education is required every five years. Some states, including Illinois, now test teachers for basic skills and subject area competence prior to reissuing a teaching license (Education Commission of the States, 1985c:1).

The modification of teacher preparation programs shows little sign of slowing down. Between 1986 and mid-1988, six states made changes in at least four areas, while 12 enacted reforms in three areas. Only Georgia, Hawaii, Louisiana and New York had no reforms during this period (Leatherman, 1988:A31–33).

As important as these measures might be to attracting a more talented pool of students to teaching careers, the efforts to improve teachers' salaries is more likely to have been responsible for the recent upsurge in teacher education enrollments. In New Jersey, for example, the median salary for first-time teachers in 1984–85 was $14,963; only 10 percent of the districts started new teachers above $16,453 (Richards, 1988:314). College graduates with degrees in other fields were commanding significantly higher salaries. As a result, the number of education majors dropped by more than half between 1977 and 1985 (more than twice the decline among liberal arts majors), while those majoring in the better-paying areas of business, computer science and engineering/architecture increased by 28.2 percent, over 900 percent and 44.5 percent, respectively (Richards, 1988:317). As one means of bringing a larger number of higher-achieving students into teaching, Governor Thomas Kean fought to establish a statewide minimum salary of $18,500 for public school teachers. The statute, which became effective in September 1985, requires the state to pay the full amount of the cost to raise teachers to that level during the first three years of the program. In the initial year, approximately 17,750 teachers were affected at a cost of $34.5 million to the state (Richards, 1988:307). The new minimum also resulted in pay increases to other teachers who were at different steps and ranges on the salary scale.

In the program's first year alone, 14 percent of the school districts reopened their contracts so that their teachers could receive the benefit of increased wages (Richards, 1988:312).

Other states have taken different approaches. Two, for example, index minimum teacher salaries. In Georgia, new teachers now receive ten-twelfths of the average starting salaries of other college graduates exclusive of engineers. South Carolina starts its teachers at the average starting teacher salary in the Southeast (Richards, 1988:320).

Many states have also sought to increase salaries for experienced teachers beyond the normal annual increments by adopting incentive models that encourage and reward excellent service. At least fourteen provide merit pay (or bonuses) to their best teachers (Astuto and Clark, 1988:367). Others, including the District of Columbia, Florida and Tennessee, have implemented career structures along the lines found in colleges where assistant professors may earn promotions to associate and full professorships. Incentives have been implemented, are being piloted or are under active consideration in all but a dozen states (Pipho, 1986:K6).

Supporting Parents

Rather than relying solely on the teachers to improve the quality of instruction, many states have called upon parents to take a greater role in their children's education. Colorado, for example, includes among its accreditation requirements the stipulation that local school boards establish citizen advisory committees to provide them with ongoing advice. Florida provides matching grants to districts that offer parent effectiveness training programs. Similarly, Illinois provides education, support, information and advocacy services to parents. New York offers parents of elementary school children a 15-hour series on how to work with teachers. Michigan and Washington focus their efforts on Hispanic parents in order to reduce dropout rates. The District of Columbia provides parents with "home learning recipes" to help families interact and to improve school achievement; for example, recipes offer advice on selecting television programs for the family and on how to utilize the programs as the basis for the development of intellectual and communications skills (Education Commission of the States, 1988a:6–7).

Accountability Measures

By strengthening curricula, bolstering graduation requirements and mandating competency testing, the states have established a structure for improved schools. By implementing incentives for districts, students and teachers (including better pay), they have provided an important carrot. Attention has also been turned to accountability for results. In 1983, Secretary of Education Terrel Bell issued a "wall chart" that, for the first time, displayed the performance of each of the states in a variety of educational categories (Smith, 1988:488). Seeing it to their benefit to oversee the collection and release of such comparative data, the Council of Chief State School Officers (the association of state education commissioners) took on the responsibility of developing a system that will result in a "national report card." Three years in the making, their first report was issued in 1987, with additional data elements scheduled to be phased in each year until 1990. When fully developed the report will include contextual factors such as size and complexity of the state's schools, demographic data, resources (fiscal and other) available to the schools, and number of special needs students; input data such as time devoted to instruction, content of the instructional program, characteristics of the instructional work force including teacher preparation and certification, and policies on ages of mandatory attendance; and outcome indicators such as attendance, achievement levels as determined by the National Assessment of Educational Progress (NAEP), school completion rates and the status of elementary and secondary school completers. By 1991 or 1992 it will be possible to determine how the states are doing, both in absolute terms and in comparison with states facing similar challenges (Selden, 1988:493–4). The national report card will be a useful measure for school officials and parents in their efforts to promote school quality.

Many states have begun to tackle the issue of school district accountability, with the achievement and graduation tests that were discussed earlier playing a central role. The ultimate threat of poor performance by a school district is that of a state takeover, something akin to the placement of a failing business into receivership by a bankruptcy court. At least a half dozen states have implemented takeover provisions, while others, including New York (New York State Education Department, 1988:2), are considering such measures.

In every instance, state takeover is considered a last resort, and the process is generally a lengthy one with ample opportunity for remedial action on the part of the local district once a deficiency is identified. In South Carolina, for example, the process requires the appointment of a review committee by the State Board of Education, the concurrence of a joint meeting of the Senate and House Education Committees and the approval of the governor in order for the full measure of state sanctions to be implemented (Education Commission of the States, 1985e:2–3). If a Texas school district fails to meet the 12 standards required for state accreditation, the state provides technical assistance for a defined period. If the district still fails to meet the standards, a five-step process is initiated. First, a confidential notice is sent to the district. A public notice follows. A state monitor may then be appointed to participate in local board activities. If the district remains deficient, a state master may be appointed to oversee the district's operations. Finally, accreditation may be revoked and state funds withheld (Education Commission of the States, 1985e:3). Arkansas, Georgia and Kentucky have takeover processes which are equally as cumbersome as those in South Carolina and Texas.

New Jersey is one state that has had the sad occasion to use its stick. Its school certification provisions require a review every five years of a school district's educational programs, governance, management and fiscal operations. If the implementation of a "corrective action plan," compliance investigations, hearings and a final opportunity for correction all fail to resolve the problems, a district may be declared "educationally bankrupt" and placed into receivership, with the state taking control for a minimum of five years. Under receivership, the powers of the local school board are relinquished and the superintendent and other important central office administrators are fired; a state-appointed local advisory board and superintendent replace them (New Jersey State Department of Education, 1986:i–ii).

In May 1988, New Jersey Commissioner of Education Saul Cooperman initiated legal action to take control over the schools in the state's second largest city, Jersey City. A 2000-page complaint delineated charges of continual political intrusion in the operation of the schools, a pattern of cronyism in hiring, chronic fiscal irregularities and an educational program that received failing grades. Absenteeism exceeded the state's maximum daily rate of 10 percent. Students were forced to share textbooks and desks. The buildings were in disrepair. Only 40 percent of the ninth graders passed the state High School Proficiency Test (Buckley, 1988:21A); the minimum acceptable pass rate is 75 percent.

By August 9, 1988, the takeover process had advanced to the point where the state asserted the ability to veto all personnel actions and any contracts worth more than $5000 (Glading, 1988:1B). At this writing, the complete seizure of power by the state awaits a final judicial determination. It has been estimated that the legal bills amassed by the Jersey City school board in its effort to resist the state takeover will exceed a million dollars (Braun, 1988:65); some legislative analysts believe the figure will be five times that amount—money which might have been better spent on strengthening the city's schools.

Higher Education

While the degree of independence from state government has always been greater for colleges and universities than it has for the elementary and secondary education sector, higher education has not been immune from the increasing state role in this period of new federalism. Generally speaking, the reforms of the current era can be classified according to those that promote access to higher education and those that are focused on the quality of higher education services. On the access side, numerous states have initiated efforts to recruit and to retain minority students; many of these efforts include the encouragement and funding of school-college partnerships to provide pre-collegiate enrichment programs for elementary and secondary school students. (Since these two areas of state activity are discussed in depth in other chapters, they are only referenced here.)

Access to higher education for many minority students and other low-income students has been seriously challenged by the decline in federal student assistance. Additionally, many moderate-income students along with students from families with more than one child in college have had to forego enrollment at the college of their choice in favor of lower-cost institutions. In response, some states have moved to develop or to strengthen their own tuition aid programs as well as their financial support programs for disadvantaged students. To make up for the loss of loans for middle-class students, two new approaches to financing a college education have been launched by the states.

Michigan was the first of nine states to enact a prepaid, guaranteed tuition plan (*Chronicle of Higher Education,* 1988:30) through which parents may enter into contracts to make either lump sum or installment payments into a trust fund in return for a guarantee that their child's undergraduate tuition at a public institution will be fully paid at the time of the contract's redemption; an amount equal to the cost of a public higher education will be disbursed to those who choose to attend an independent institution. The contracts vary in length from four to 20 years; the longer the contract, the lower the amount of the parental investment (Education Commission of the States, 1988b:12). While Michigan officials had expected fewer than 10,000 persons to be interested in this program, they received more than 80,000 inquiries in the first two years (Anderson, 1988:32).

The other new collegiate finance approach initiated by at least 14 states is the establishment of tax-exempt savings plans (*Chronicle of Higher Education*, 1988:12). In Connecticut, for example, parents may buy "zero-coupon" bonds in denominations beginning at $1000 with maturity dates of five to 20 years. Rhode Island will sell 15-year tax free bonds with a face value of $1000 at a cost of $344 (Anderson, 1988:30).

Higher education was not exempted from the scathing criticisms of former Education Secretary William Bennett. His description of an "educational malaise" that he believed resulted in narrowly educated and incompetent graduates prompted many states to focus on the quality of the college experience (Grossman, 1988:6). Remedial programs were among the first to come under scrutiny. California spent $82 million per year for basic skills courses and support programs for college freshmen in the early 1980s; at mid-decade Texas was spending $18 million. The Southern Regional Education Board has estimated that 40 percent of the students entering college in most of its member states require remedial course work (Reilly and Cashen, 1988:22). In response to this problem (and usually a step ahead of the strengthening of high school graduation requirements by state boards of education), at least 19 states during the first half of the 1980s revised the admissions requirements for all or some of their public colleges and universities (usually the four-year schools); six others adopted a set of "recommended" requirements. Several of these states began to mail information on their college admissions requirements to junior high school students and their parents (Education Commission of the States, 1985f:1–2).

Worried that participation of so many students in remedial courses would result in a reduction of the number of college-level courses required for graduation, 17 states banned the awarding of graduation credit for remedial courses offered by their public institutions; one other, Nevada, has forbidden its four-year public institutions from awarding credit for remedial courses but permits the practice for the community colleges (*Chronicle of Higher Education*, 1988:56).

The quality of the college-level courses has also come under state scrutiny. Since faculty play such a crucial role in the success of their students and since increasing numbers of undergraduate courses (particularly in mathematics, science and computer science) are being taught by foreign-born teaching assistants, 12 states have required the passage of English competency tests by teaching assistants whose native language is other than English (Chronicle of Higher Education, 1988:18). In addition, 21 states have mandated that their public colleges and universities implement programs to assess what students learn (*Chronicle of Higher Education*, 1988:85); at least three-quarters of the states will have such requirements before long (National Governors' Association, 1987:32). (Assessment is discussed in detail in a subsequent chapter.)

Many state initiatives to improve the quality of the collegiate experience have taken the form of incentive funding. Tennessee, for example, provides funding above the base budget to institutions that meet a variety of quality indicators. Other states, including New Jersey, utilize a competitive grant approach. Eight of New Jersey's nine state colleges, for example, received three-year grants totalling $34.5 million through the Governor's Challenge to Excellence (see Yavorsky and Marcus, 1987). The challenge approach has also been used in the other higher education sectors in the state. Competition is within sector; that is, the independent colleges and universities compete against each other, while the community colleges are in a separate competition. New Jersey also offers an array of competitive grant programs open to all institutions regardless of sector in order to upgrade curricula in the humanities, mathematics, science and computer science, and to infuse the collegiate curriculum with computers. Grants are also available to support bilingual and foreign language projects and to improve undergraduate retention toward graduation. The state's competitive grant programs provide more funds to New Jersey colleges and universities than are made available to the whole country by the federal Fund for the Improvement of Postsecondary Education.

The Road Ahead

Whether the increased state role in education was caused by or merely coincided with the federal retreat led by President Reagan, it was real. As former Assistant Secretary Finn (1988:343) has noted, "nearly all the truly significant activity occurred far from the banks of the Potomac." If funding is a barometer of commitment, the rise of the states to center stage of the education reform movement is dramatically evidenced by their having increased their educational expenditures by more than $9 billion between 1982 and 1986 (Fuhrman, 1987:132).

There are no indications that the states are looking for a return to a secondary or tertiary role. In fact, the analysis of 1988 gubernatorial budget messages and state of the state addresses undertaken by Verstegen and McGuire (1988:3–7) indicates that education is still on the minds of governors: six cited the centrality of education both to the smooth functioning of our democracy and to our ability to compete in the world economic arena; ten mentioned the need to develop stronger programs for at-risk youth; five spoke of the need to improve the accountability of the schools; six addressed the challenge of improving the attractiveness of the teaching career; and many referenced the need to keep the educational reform movement going.

Not surprisingly, many of these issues were also on the minds of state education leaders. The major elementary/secondary challenges according to those who attended the 1988 annual meeting of the Education Commission of the States were programs for at-risk youth, school finance, educational restructuring and reform, early childhood education and testing (Education Commission of the States, 1988c:1). Forty-six of the 50 State Higher Education Executive Officers (SHEEOs) indicated in a survey that the major issues facing the collegiate sector (in order of magnitude) were "ensuring the quality of academic programs, assuring students of diverse socioeconomic status access to educational programs, increasing state appropriations, attracting and retaining qualified faculty, and recruiting and retaining minority faculty and students." They also cited the need to assure adequate student financial aid (Mangieri and Adams, 1988:40–41). One can assume, then, that these will be the issues around which further state reform initiatives will focus in the coming years.

REFERENCES

Airasian, Peter W. "Symbolic Validation: The Case of State-Mandated High Stakes Testing." *Educational Evaluation and Policy Analysis*, 10(4): 301–313. 1988.

Anderson, Ellin. "State-Based College-Payment Plans." *Connection*, 3(3): 30–32. 1988.

Astuto, Terry A. and David L. Clark. "State Responses to the New Federalism in Education." *Educational Policy*, 2(4):361–375, 1988.

Braun, Robert J. "School Board Affirms State Right for Partial Takeover in Jersey City." Newark *Star Ledger*, December 2, 1988, p. 65.

Buckley, William F. "Jersey City and Choice of Schools." *Philadelphia Inquirer*, June 2, 1988, p. 21A.

"*Chronicle of Higher Education* Almanac." insert in *Chronicle of Higher Education*, September 1, 1988.

Coor, Lattie F. "Higher Education's Place on the American Agenda." *College Law Digest*, 19(2):33–45. 1988.

Education Commission of the States. "Clearinghouse Notes—Academic Bankruptcy." Denver, CO: Education Commission of the States. November, 1985e.

——. "Clearinghouse Notes—College Admissions Requirements." Denver, CO: Education Commission of the States. September, 1985f.

——. "Clearinghouse Notes—Examples of State Incentive Programs for Educational Improvement." Denver, CO: Education Commission of the States. 1987b.

——. "Clearinghouse Notes—State Characteristics: Kindergartens." Denver, CO: Education Commission of the States. November, 1985a.

——. "Clearinghouse Notes—State Activity: Minimum Competency Testing as of November 1985." Denver, CO: Education Commission of the States. November, 1985b.

——. "Clearinghouse Notes—States Implementing Changes to Teacher Certification or Recertification as of November 1985." Denver, CO: Education Commission of the States. November, 1985c.

——. "Clearinghouse Notes—States Requiring Testing for Initial Certification of Teachers." Denver, CO: Education Commission of the States. April, 1987a.

——. "Clearinghouse Notes—States with Loan Forgiveness Programs to Attract New Teachers." Denver, CO: Education Commission of the States. 1987c.

——. "Forum, Tracking the Reforms Part 4: Loan Forgiveness Programs: Will They Work?" Denver, CO: Education Commission of the States. April, 1985d.

——. "One in Five States Has College Savings or Prepayment Plan." *State Education Leader*, Fall, 1988b:12.

——. "States Have Role in Improving Home/School Relationship." *State Education Leader* Fall, 1988a:6–7.

——. "Top State Issues Run the Gamut." *State Education Leader* Fall, 1988c:1–2.

Finn, Chester E., Jr. "Education Policy and the Reagan Administration." *Educational Policy*, 2(4):343–360, 1988.

Fuhrman, Susan H. "Education Policy: A New Context for Governance." *Publius: The Journal of Federalism*, 17(Summer):131–143, 1987.

Garand, James C. "Explaining Government Growth in the United States." *American Political Science Review*, 82(3):837–849, 1988.

Glading, Jo Astrid. "State Given Veto Power Over School." *Philadelphia Inquirer*, August 10, 1988, pp. 1B–2B.

Koffler, Stephen L. "Assessing the Impact of a State's Decision to Move from Minimum Competency Testing Toward Higher Level Testing for Graduation." *Educational Evaluation and Policy Analysis*, 9(4): 325–336, 1987.

Kritek, William J. and Associates. "Dimensions of State Education Legislation: 1971–1984." Paper presented at the 1988 Annual Meeting of the American Educational Research Association, New Orleans, LA, April, 1988.

Krotseng, Marsha V. "The 'Education Governor': Political Packaging or Public Policy?" Paper presented at the Annual Meeting of the Association for the Study of Higher Education, Baltimore, MD, November, 1987.

Leatherman, Courtney. "Reforms in Education of Schoolteachers Face Tough Challenges." *Chronicle of Higher Education,* April 20, 1988, pp. A1, A30–33.

Likens, James D. "A Preliminary Diagnosis: The California Experience." in William J. Johnson (Ed.): *Education on Trial, Strategies for the Future.* San Francisco: ICS Press, 1985, pp. 141–173.

Mangieri, John N. and Larry D. Adams. "State Commissioners and the Crucial Issues." *Educational Record,* 69(3 and 4):40–42, 1988.

Marcus, Laurence R. "Federal Civil Rights Enforcement in Higher Education: Shadow or Substance." *Educational Policy,* 2(2):189–208, 1988.

Mullen, J. Michael. "College Costs and the State Role in Higher Education Funding." *Educational Record,* 69(3 and 4):9–14, 1988.

National Commission on Excellence in Education. *A Nation at Risk: The Imperative for Educational Reform.* Washington, D.C.: U.S. Government Printing Office, 1983.

National Governors Association. *The Governors' 1991 Report on Education, Results in Education: 1987.* Washington, D.C.: National Governors Association, 1987.

New Jersey Department of Education. *New Jersey's Plan to Intervene in Deficient School Districts.* Trenton, NJ: New Jersey State Department of Education, 1986.

———. *1987–88 High School Proficiency Test, State Summary – Grade 11.* Trenton, NJ: New Jersey State Department of Education, 1988.

New York State Education Department. "State Seeks More Power Over NYC Schools." *Learning in New York,* June, 1988, p. 2.

"1980 Political Platforms: The Republican Education Platform." in R. Miller, ed: *Federal Role in Education: New Directions for the Eighties.* Washington, D.C.: Institute for Educational Leadership, 1981, pp. 101–103.

Pipho, Chris. "States Move Reform Closer to Reality." *Phi Delta Kappan: Kappan Special Report* (reprint). December, 1986.

Popkewitz, Thomas S. and Marie Brennan. "Certification to Credentialing: Reconstituting Control Mechanisms in Teacher Education." Paper presented at the 1988 Annual Meeting of the American Educational Research Association, New Orleans, LA. April, 1988.

Porter, Andrew. "Indicators: Objective Data or Political Tool?" *Phi Delta Kappan,* 69(March):503–508, 1988.

Reilly, David H. "State Control of Education: An Emerging and Troublesome Issue for Administrators." *National Forum of Educational Administration and Supervision Journal,* 5(2):92–107, 1988-9.

Reilly, Kevin P. and Gail L. K. Cashen. "Remediation Revisited, States Struggle to Respond." *Educational Record,* 69(3 and 4):20–25, 1988.

Richards, Craig E. "State Regulation of Entry Level Teacher Salaries: Policy Issues and Options." *Educational Policy,* 2(3):307–322, 1988.

Selden, Ramsay W. "Missing Data: A Progress Report from the States." *Phi Delta Kappan,* 69(March):492–494, 1988.

Smith, Marshall A. "Educational Indicators." *Phi Delta Kappan,* 69(March): 487–491, 1988.

Stickney, Benjamin D. and Laurence R. Marcus. *The Great Education Debate: Washington and the Schools.* Springfield, IL: Charles C Thomas, Publisher, 1984.

"The Politics of Education: What the Public Thinks." *Newsweek*, June 27, 1983. p. 61.

Timar, Thomas B. and David L. Kirp. "State Efforts to Reform Schools: Treading Between a Regulatory Swamp and an English Garden." *Educational Evaluation and Policy Analysis*, 10(2):75–88, 1988.

Verstegen, Deborah A. and Kent McGuire. "The State of State Education Finance — Emerging Themes and Collapsing Constraints." Paper presented at the 1988 Annual Meeting of the American Educational Research Association, New Orleans, LA, April, 1988.

Yavorsky, Diane K. and Laurence R. Marcus. "Converting Crises to Challenges: New Jersey's Effort to Promote State College Quality." *Educational Policy*, 1(4): 445–459, 1987.

PART II

Policy in the Age of Education

Chapter 4

REFORMING TEACHER EDUCATION

Margaret A. Bacon

It is called the academic ghetto. Virtually anyone who wants to venture inside can do so. But most do not want to go near it. According to campus lore, it is where some of the least-qualified students study some of the least-demanding subjects at the hands of some of the least-talented professors.

These opening salvos on teacher education programs from a 1988 *Los Angeles Times* series on "Making Better Teachers" provide a fitting context for a chapter on the effects of the reform movement on teacher education. The reform movement began with the 1983 publication of *A Nation at Risk*, which criticized American schools for not producing the kind of achievement which would allow us to economically compete with other countries. The criticism then shifted to teachers (if students were not achieving, then blame must rest with their teachers), administrators (if teachers were not teaching effectively, then it must be the fault of the administrators who hire and evaluate them), and teacher educators (at least some of the blame must rest with the colleges and schools of education which train the nation's teachers). The list of ills which teacher education perpetrated and perpetuated became ever longer: they attracted and selected the least academically qualified students in the university setting, allowed them to bypass an academically rigorous curriculum by permitting them to major in the non-discipline of education, thus relegating them to a vacuous curriculum taught by professors far removed from practice in the schools.

Suggested reforms for teacher education, many of which are already in effect, consisted of raising entrance and exit requirements, allowing alternate paths toward teacher certification, eliminating the education major, and incorporating more practitioners into education programs. While these initial responses to the reform movement dealt primarily with surface features of teacher education programs, more substantial

Social Behavior in animals

Social Hierarchy in animals

WRIGHT STATE UNIVERSITY BOOKSTORE

614 CASH-1   7579 0001 002

0723832050
Pilot EZ 3pk   MDS 1   3.18
0440000679
CHIPS AHOY MINI CH   MDS 1N   .99
0121310
MOUNTAIN DEW   MDS 1   1.29
            SUBTOTAL   5.46
    6.5% Sales Tax   .30
            TOTAL   5.76

ACCOUNT NUMBER   XXXXXXXXXXXXXX1741
  Visa/Mastercard   5.76
Expiration Date   XX/XX
  Authorization   800265

REFUND POLICY EXPLAINED _____

                          2/17/09 12:19 PM

efforts were soon to follow. Chief among these were the Carnegie and Holmes reports, which addressed comprehensive changes needed in the education of teachers if teaching is to become a true profession. Currently, Goodlad's extensive Study of the Education of Educators should, when completed, contribute an excellent data base to the restructuring of teacher education.

I shall review in more detail both the background and the effects of the reform movement on teacher education by using a heuristic originally proposed by Schwab and used by Lanier and Little (1986) to examine teacher education. That is, the "commonplace of teaching" consists of someone (a teacher) who must be teaching someone (a student) about something (the curriculum) at someplace and point in time (the milieu or context). In teacher education, the teachers are the teacher educators, or "teachers of teachers," and consist of a diversity of roles and backgrounds, including college professors and public school practitioners. The students are adults who are either potential or practicing teachers. The curriculum consists of general education, subject-matter specialities, and pedagogy. The milieu or context consists of the general society, with its goals and expectations for its schools and the personnel who staff them; the university; the school district; and the professional and state agencies who govern certification and standards. In examining the relationship between the reform movement and teacher education, I shall look at each of these entities separately and then draw some conclusions about the continuing effect of the reform movement upon teacher education.

Teacher Educators

The public criticism of teacher educators in the 1980s reflected the low status of such professionals in both the university community and the practitioner community. Teacher educators were a likely target for those who felt they had designed a curriculum with no intellectual content, had limited academic backgrounds themselves, and were far removed from the realities of teaching in schools. Several of the reform reports called for the complete removal of teacher training from the "educationists" and placing it back in the colleges of liberal arts and sciences and in the schools with practitioners. To add insult to injury, several states allowed for the bypassing of schools of education altogether by providing alternate routes to teacher certification whereby those who had strong academic and subject-matter backgrounds could enter the teaching profession without going through a teacher preparation program.

Lanier and Little (1986) contend that teacher educators have never fit the norm of university professors: they are far more likely to come from lower middle and lower social class origins and have formed and maintained "intellectual propensities and working norms that conflict with the traditional values of higher education." Ducharme and Agne's study (1982) of 340 education professors in diverse institutions corroborated the tension felt by such professors, caught between campus colleagues who see them as pragmatic, unscholarly, and service-oriented, "anti-intellectuals in the house of intellect," while teachers in the public schools may see them as aloof and academic. Contrary to conventional wisdom, however, Ducharme and Agne found that education faculty's publication rate was comparable to that of higher education faculty in general and their commitment to teaching and advising students was above the norm (65% of them considered teaching to be their first priority).

But to consider teacher educators to be only the faculty in schools and colleges of education is to miss a substantial portion of those who educate teachers. Certainly, the faculty in colleges of liberal arts and sciences, who are responsible for an ever-increasing proportion of potential teachers' education, must be considered to have at least some stake in teacher education. And, indeed, one outgrowth of the reform movement has been to involve such faculty in the restructuring and reconceptualization of teacher education programs. For example, a major effort is now underway to involve the liberal arts and sciences faculty and schools of education in 30 colleges and universities nationwide in just such a project. The aim of this three-year, Carnegie-funded project, entitled "Learning for Teaching: Nourishing the Roots of the Teacher's Art," is to "redesign the way that prospective teachers are educated" (AACTE, 1988, p. 5). College presidents are increasingly being urged to join the movement to reform teacher education, and many have become advocates and leaders of their institution's efforts to revitalize teacher education. Indeed, when the Association of Colleges of Teacher Education, the primary professional organization for deans of colleges of education, formed a committee to study and make recommendations on teacher education (the National Commission for Excellence in Teacher Education), it chose a college president to chair it (C. Peter Magrath from the University of Missouri).

A third critical party in the education of teachers is the field-based practitioner who provides supervision for students' field experiences.

Because they are often perceived by prospective teachers as the most credible and practical "teachers" in their teacher education program, it makes sense that schools and colleges of education should involve them more substantially in their programs. And, indeed, one of the outgrowths of the reform movement is the involvement of practicing teachers in both the advisement and governance of teacher education (Cruickshank and Cruz, 1989). Several reformers have suggested that teachers be the primary educators of themselves; that is, that students need only serve an apprenticeship with a master teacher after completing a degree in the arts or sciences to learn the skills of pedagogy. But since reformers had previously criticized educational practice in the schools, that practice will hardly be changed by teachers who receive their sole training at the hands of practitioners. As Goodlad (1988) asks: "Is it not reasonable to believe, then, that the mentoring of a neophyte by an experienced teacher, without any accompanying sustained reflection guided by a third party with authorized opinions on pedagogy and other matters, might merely perpetuate the status quo?" (p. 107). Nonetheless, the collaborative effort between teacher educators in higher education and practicing teachers in the field is in need of enhancement and development; such efforts may well prove to be the hallmark of the eighties reform movement in teacher education. Suggestions range from the creation of laboratory schools to the use of practitioners to help design teacher education curriculum.

Teacher Education Students

In many ways, students of teaching reflect their sheer numbers in the work force; in 1982, teachers still accounted for 7.5 percent of all college-educated workers (Feistritzer, 1983). As Lortie has pointed out, "teaching is unique . . . no other occupation can claim a membership of over two million graduates and tens of thousands with advanced degrees" (1975, pp. 243–244). Yet, the character and quality of those in the profession is one of the prime planks in the reform platform; improvement of the teaching force is a major theme in nearly all of the commission reports. In the early 1980s, a Rand Corporation report stated that "recent evidence suggests that new recruits to teaching are less academically qualified than those who are leaving, and the number of new entrants is insufficient to meet the coming demand for teachers" (Darling-Hammond, 1984).

Is there, in fact, a shortage of new entrants into the teaching profession?

There seems to be no clear-cut answer on this issue. The number of students entering teaching has always been a supply-and-demand function. While the number of new teacher graduates dropped by half between 1973 and 1983, the drop paralleled the lack of teaching positions during that period. Since 1983, student enrollments in teacher education have continued to rise, despite higher admissions standards. But whether the supply will meet the growing demand for teachers has been the focus of a continuing debate, one that affects a number of corollary issues in teacher education such as alternative certification, admissions standards, and minority recruitment. Reports from the early part of the decade (Feistritzer, 1984; Darling-Hammond, 1984) estimated a growing and severe teacher shortage by the end of the decade. "Given current trends in school-age population, entrants to the teaching profession, and attrition, the supply of new teacher graduates may satisfy only about 80 percent of the demand for additional teachers by 1988" (Darling-Hammond, 1984, p. 6). However, such a shortage did not occur, except in some geographic areas and some subject fields. In a 1986 survey conducted by the National Center of Education Information, Feistritzer reported that contrary to widespread reports of a growing teacher shortage, virtually all states were able to hire enough qualified teachers over the previous two years. Feistritzer did acknowledge that some urban and outlying rural districts may have experienced shortages, and some districts have had difficulty finding teachers for mathematics, science, and foreign languages. It would appear that the recent national focus on education has begun to attract more students into teaching, more previously certified individuals back into the field, and more older adults to consider teaching as a career change.

Teacher shortages in particular disciplines, particularly mathematics and science, have led to a variety of innovative programs to attract students into teaching in these areas. The federal government, states, and professional associations have established loan and grant programs for potential teachers of mathematics and science, and a variety of incentives have been established to recruit and train persons who have not attended professional education colleges (Cruickshank and Cruz, 1989).

A recent AACTE survey of institutions that prepare teachers showed a startling enrollment upswing between 1985 and 1986, with an overall increase of 13.5 percent (Zimpher, 1988). This has occurred despite the fact that nearly all programs have raised their admissions standards during that period.

What does this group of potential teachers look like? Will they be able to carry out the reform effort in the schools? One of the disappointing factors emerging from the AACTE survey was the profile of students within teacher education programs. They remain a "culturally insular group": 91% of them are white, 4.3% are black, 1.5% are Hispanic, 2.5% are Asian, and .3% are Native-American. Only 15.5% of the students grew up in an urban area; 80% of them grew up in a rural or suburban community and want to return to such areas to teach. When one compares these demographic data to the predicted profile of students in the year 2000 (most of whom will be located in urban areas and the majority of whom will be ethnic minorities), the need for a vastly improved system of recruiting minority students into education as well as expanding the multicultural curriculum in teacher education becomes clear.

The demographic profile of those entering the profession has led to a growing concern over the lack of minority teacher candidates. A report of the American Council of Education on Minorities in Higher Education (quoted in Cruickshank and Cruz, 1989) concluded that "the use of competency testing is screening minorities out of teaching at an alarmingly high rate at every level." Other reasons, such as the recruitment of minorities by other professions and the low status of teaching, have been suggested for the lack of minorities in teacher education programs.

The American Association of Colleges for Teacher Education, in a report entitled "Minority Teacher Recruitment and Retention: A Call for Action," delineated a ten-point effort to increase the number of minorities entering the profession, including scholarships, early incentive programs, career reentry, and teacher induction programs (Cruickshank and Cruz, 1989). Both the Carnegie and Holmes groups addressed the need to recruit an ever-growing number of minority students into teaching if the teaching force is to come anywhere near the percentage of minority children in the school population. As the Carnegie Task Force points out, it is essentially a pipeline problem: "Because teaching will need a very high proportion of college graduates in the years ahead, the problem of minority teachers cannot possibly be solved without addressing the fundamental problems of minority educational preparation throughout the pipeline" (p. 83). It remains to be seen whether any of the proposed solutions will prove to be effective in attracting more minorities into higher education in general and teacher education in particular. Clearly, minority recruitment is one area which will continue to need innovative reform efforts.

One of the critical factors that emerged from the reform movement was the oft-repeated assertion that those pursuing careers in teaching are academically weak. In Feistritzer's 1983 report on teacher education and certification, she noted that "few of the institutions preparing teachers had well-defined, much less rigorous, standards for admission into their teacher education programs" (pp. 9–10). Few seemed to use high school rank or grade point average and 82 percent reported that they do not use a SAT or ACT cutoff score as an entrance requirement. The lack of use of high school data for admission, however, may be due in part to the fact that few colleges of education admit students as freshman. Seventy-five percent of the institutions did report the use of college grade point average.

Darling-Hammond (1984) documented a decline in the academic ability of students planning on becoming teachers: "the scores of students planning to major in education have traditionally been lower than those of other students; in addition, over the past decade, the scores of potential education majors have declined more steeply than those of other students." Certainly there is evidence for this if one examines the SAT scores of college-bound seniors who plan to major in education: "in 1973 they scored an average of 27 points below the national average verbal score and 32 points below the national average math score; by 1981 that difference had widened to 33 points on the verbal score and 48 points on the math score" (reported in Kluender, 1984, p. 34). Perhaps even more discouraging is the evidence that the most capable students academically are the most likely to leave the profession. Vance and Schlechty (1982) reported data from the National Longitudinal Study showing that only 20 percent of teachers in the upper 20 percent of measured verbal ability planned to teach at age 30, while 56.6 percent of those with lowest verbal ability planned to teach at that age. It should be pointed out, however, that the quality of those entering teacher education programs has improved over the past five years.

In an effort to deal with the quality issue, many institutions have raised their admissions requirements; 75 percent of them reported changes in their requirements in the 1987 AACTE survey. The key admissions requirement is still college grade point average, although the minimum average required has changed from 2.0 to 2.5. Two thirds of the institutions report using some form of testing for admission, the most common tests being the Pre-Professional Skills Test (PPST), the California Achievement Test (CAT), and SAT or ACT scores. Much of the admissions testing has come about through state requirements; twenty-five states require such testing, either through legislative or state board of education mandates (Sandefur, 1986). In addition to admissions testing, Sandefur reports that forty-one states require some form of testing prior to certification, generally the National Teacher Examination.

While we have no evidence that the new emphasis on testing is producing better teachers, it does appear to add to the status of the profession in the eyes of those considering teaching as a possible career. Since one of the hallmarks of a profession is the use of rigorous entry requirements, more academically capable students may be attracted to the profession. The current surge of applicants to teacher education programs with their newly instituted entry requirements would support this assertion, although it may also be simply a market factor. It should be noted, too, that the teacher competency testing movement has had an unfortunate side effect — that of disproportionately eliminating minority candidates from the pool of potential teachers.

As teacher education reformers have attempted to recruit more academically capable students into teaching, they have been taking a new look at the research on reasons for entering the profession reported by practitioners. Lortie's (1975) sample of teachers reported the following reasons for entering the profession; enjoyment in working with young people; pride in performing important public service; ease of entry, exit, and re-entry; time compatibility; modest material benefits; and psychic rewards emanating from student achievement. Sykes (1983) found, though, that several changes in teacher motivation had occurred in the past decade: decreased enjoyment from work with less responsive and appreciative young people; a deteriorating public image of teaching as an important service; the erosion of material benefits; and reduced psychic benefits from less regular student achievement. Goodlad's survey of 1350 teachers in *A Place Called School,* however, found that "the largest majority of our sample, on all levels, tended to be idealistic and altruistic in their views of why they chose to teach" (p. 173). Some would argue that increasing teacher salaries is the single most important factor in recruiting high-quality individuals into teaching. Others (Joseph and Green, 1986) argue that recruitment should involve emphasis on the intrinsic rewards of the profession, appealing to the altruistic motives of those who consider the profession. Whatever the approach taken, there does appear to be a gradual rise in the status of the profession during the 1980s, which has been accompanied by both a rise in teacher salaries and an increased interest in the service aspects of the profession (witness, for example, the 1988 movie *Stand and Deliver*). The 1988 Gallup poll of the public's attitude toward schools reported that 58 percent of those surveyed indicated they would like a child of theirs to pursue a career in teaching, a 10 percent increase over 1980 (Gallup and Elam, 1988).

A look at the students of teaching would not be complete without considering the substantial body of practitioners, those teachers who are not preparing for the profession but already in it. The 1980s reform efforts have included a growing interest in this group, which, as a result of limited turnover in the late seventies, is now more stable than at any time in America's past. The current trend is to look at teacher education as a developmental continuum, thus not separating out preservice from in-service education. Berliner's work (1988) on expert and novice teachers belies the notion that the development of competency and expertise can be acquired in a teacher preparation program.

A series of efforts to restructure the profession in the 1980s to continue to make it attractive to those within it have included career ladders and merit pay. The Holmes Group (1986), calling for the recognition of differences in knowledge, skill, and commitment among teachers, proposed a hierarchical structure which included career professional teachers, professional teachers, and instructors. The Carnegie Forum on Education and the Economy (1986) suggested the restructuring of teaching into four levels: licensed teachers, certified teachers, advanced certificate holders, and lead teachers. While there has been considerable resistance on the part of the teachers' organizations to any of these solutions, it seems likely that some type of restructuring of the profession to decrease its "flatness" will be an outcome of the reform movement.

Teacher Education Curriculum

The curriculum in teacher education programs has been the focus of considerable concern in the reform movement. Oft-repeated jibes about the "Mickey Mouse" nature of education courses are uttered by those who may have taken such courses many years past or who "know" someone who did. But the curriculum for teacher education is a more complex issue, partially because of varied centers of responsibility for it. Teacher educators generally refer to three strands in the curriculum: general education in the liberal arts and sciences (whatever vestiges of a core curriculum may remain), subject-matter concentration, and professional pedagogical study. It becomes readily apparent that two-thirds of a teacher's education takes place *outside* a school or college of education. One irony of the reform movement is that much criticism has been leveled at the one-third of teachers' education which takes place in colleges of education while the recommendations have unilaterally endorsed *more* of the education they receive in colleges of liberal arts and sciences. It is clear to the critics, if not the educators, that if teachers are ill-prepared, it must be the fault of their teacher education programs rather than their more general college education. Teacher educators have responded that if teachers appear to be unprepared to teach science or math or language arts or social sciences, perhaps we should examine the content and teaching methods in their college biology or algebra or American literature or history courses.

Both the Carnegie Task Force (1986) and the Holmes Group (1986) recognized the problem and call for a restructuring of undergraduate education for potential teachers. The Carnegie report states that "arts and sciences faculties must join their education colleagues, and, together with the leaders of professional disciplinary societies, begin by undertaking a thorough review of the undergraduate curriculum for the education of prospective teachers" (p. 75). This is echoed by a strong plea from the Holmes Group for institutions of higher education to address the weaknesses in their undergraduate programs: "a lack of curricular coherence and an avoidance of a core of enduring and fundamental ideas" (p. 47). These two groups thus join a growing list of higher education critics calling for universities to critically examine and revise their undergraduate curriculum (Boyer, 1987; Bloom, 1987; Sykes, 1988).

But the majority of the reform efforts have primarily addressed the professional education curriculum in schools of education. There has been an almost universal cry to abandon the undergraduate major in education, a recommendation that has been adopted by many teacher education institutions and in several states. The argument has been that both elementary and secondary prospective teachers need a stronger grounding in the disciplines if they are to teach them effectively. The elimination of the undergraduate major in education has led to the conceptualization and implementation of a variety of post-baccalaureate programs. Both the Carnegie and Holmes groups recommend graduate-level training in education, with the Carnegie Task Force suggesting a master's in teaching degree and the Holmes group proposing training based on its differentiated career model.

In terms of the sequence of professional education course work, there has been a sharp differentiation between the earlier reform reports (such as *A Nation at Risk*) and later reports from education-based groups (such as Holmes and Carnegie). The former recommended a variety of ways to avoid education courses altogether and ease the entry into the profession of qualified experts, while the latter recommended a more coherent, research-based sequence of professional education. The Holmes group states well the case for defining the knowledge base for professional education and ensuring that it becomes incorporated into the teacher education program curriculum: "Reforming the education of teachers depends upon engaging in the complex work of identifying the knowledge base for competent teaching, and developing the content and strategies whereby it is imparted" (1986, p. 49). Current research in effective teaching, which is now classroom rather than laboratory-based, deserves a more central place in the teacher education curriculum. The identification and documentation of the knowledge base for teaching will be a major effort of teacher educators in the next decade.

Another critical piece of the teacher education curriculum that has received attention from the reform movement is the field experience component. In the past, student teaching was the sole field experience requirement in teacher education, and it was universally perceived by students to be the most important part of the training (in some cases, the *only* useful part). Thus, most reform recommendations call for a dramatic increase in field experiences, and, indeed, this seems to have occurred in most teacher education programs in the last decade. The requirement for student teaching, for example, has gone from a total of approximately 280 hours in 1975 to almost 420 hours ten years later (Kluender, 1984). The research on field experiences, however, provides a less-convincing case for its efficacy: most student teachers quickly conform to the norms of the classroom and school in which they are placed and rarely attempt innovative teaching strategies from their methods courses. The problem, as Lanier and Little point out, "is not that field experience cannot be valuable, but that its value is dependent on prospective teachers being properly prepared to learn from it" (1986, p. 551).

Thus, there has been a call for renewed collaboration between colleges of education and the schools in which they place their prospective teachers. The Holmes group goes so far as to recommend the establishment of Professional Development Schools, which they see as analogous to teaching hospitals in the medical profession, bringing together practicing teachers and administrators with university faculty in partnerships designed to increase the flow of information and communication between the groups and to provide settings for the testing of alternative instructional strategies (1986, p. 67). There is a corollary interest in the idea of "clinical faculty" in schools of education; basically, school-based practitioners who supervise and/or teach in teacher education programs.

A part of the new link between universities and schools is the growing recognition of the problems of novice teachers and the need to develop collaborative approaches to the solution of those problems. Entry into the profession, commonly referred to as induction, has been seen as a likely avenue for partnerships. Some 40 states currently indicate some activity related to providing support or evaluation of entry-level teachers (Cruickshank and Cruz, 1989). And in a flurry of cooperative spirit in the mid-eighties, several universities instituted "guaranteed graduate" programs in which they assumed some level of responsibility for the performance of their graduates who were hired by local schools. "Should the graduates of a teacher education program fail to perform satisfactorily as beginning teachers, the institution that trained them promises to provide direct assistance and support to both the employing schools and the new teachers" (Barr, 1984, p. 128).

As teacher education becomes recognized as more of a developmental process, in-service education has come under increasing scrutiny and criticism. Gall (1983) has characterized staff development as "frequent, but fragmented and without depth." School districts have increased their efforts in recent years to make staff development more than a "one-shot" experience; programs in effective teaching, cooperative learning, peer coaching, etc. are now designed to be longer-term, developmental projects. With the exception of induction projects, however, universities have been noticeably absent from these efforts.

Teacher Education: Context

An examination of the reform movement and how it has affected the students, teachers, and curriculum in teacher education would be incomplete without a discussion of the context or environment in which it takes place. That environment includes social, political, and economic factors in the university community, in society at large, and in the state and professional organizations and agencies which certify teachers and accredit programs.

An historical overview of teacher education programs in university settings confirms the obvious: power and prestige are clearly lacking

(Lanier and Little, 1986). In fact, as schools and colleges of education attempted to adapt to the norms of research-based institutions, they increasingly abandoned their original commitment to undergraduate teacher education and focused on specialized graduate study (Clifford and Guthrie, 1988). Universities tended to invest little in teacher education. Peseau (1982) points out that in 1980 "the average direct cost of instruction per year on undergraduate teacher education students was only 65 percent as much as for a public education student, and only 50 percent as much as the average cost per undergraduate students in all university disciplines" (p. 14). There is some evidence of a shift in at least the attention to, if not the dollars for, teacher education. University presidents have been invited by several of the foundations funding the reform reports to become actively involved in the effort, and many have done so.

Teacher education has also been the beneficiary of the considerable national attention that has been focused on education ever since the publication of *A Nation at Risk.* Education issues have been at the forefront of the last presidential and congressional contests, and George Bush based a good part of his platform on being the "Education President." However, it is a measure of the low esteem in which teacher educators are held by the society as well as the university that they have been noticeably absent from the committees and task forces which shaped the reform movement.

A Nation at Risk also prompted state action, both from governors and legislatures, on education. While their first mandates dealt with perceived problems in K–12 education, they turned their attention to teacher education, particularly the quality of the work force, early on. A major thrust was the testing of teacher competency. In 1980, only 10 states had mandates to test teachers; by 1986, 46 states had regulations requiring some form of competency assessment of teachers (Sandefur, 1986). In a review of six years of state actions in teacher education, Sandefur drew several conclusions:

(1) the teacher testing movement grew with the educational reform movement and reflects the public's lack of confidence in teachers and teaching;
(2) the movement had its origins in the South and spread from there to the West and Northeast;
(3) early entries into teacher testing were usually the results of legislative mandates, whereas later entries were typically mandated by state boards of education;

(4) states are becoming more aware of the impact of testing on cultural and ethnic minorities. (P. 14.)

Another area of state intervention has been alternative certification. Eleven states have developed special procedures to provide certification to people who have not completed teacher education programs. Some states require those people to complete the same professional education courses and pass the same tests as those who receive education degrees, while others require only an intensive course on pedagogy (*The Chronicle of Higher Education*, 1988). The move to abandon teacher preparation entirely has come under severe criticism from teacher educators. Berliner (1984) suggests that the move toward alternative certification comes at the worst possible time because teacher education has only recently developed a scientific research base. "But now that we are capable of monumental reform in teacher education—reform guided by research—we hear only calls for the reduction or total elimination of teacher preparation programs" (p. 94).

Governors, too, have been active all along in the school reform movement, and their 1986 report, *Time for Results: The Governors' 1991 Report on Education*, invited educators to join with them in resolving the nation's educational dilemma. One of the report's major recommendations was to improve preparation and in-service training programs for teachers and administrators. Most of the governors list education as their top priority and have included educational initiatives in their legislative proposals in the past several years (Nathan, 1986). It should be kept in mind that governors' agendas are automatically passed on to chief state school officials and thus to state certification officials (Cruickshank and Cruz, 1989). Educators have been critical of policymakers' entry into teacher education, but their resistance is often seen as defensive and legislators primarily view them as protecting their "turf."

Teacher organizations have shifted gears as the reform movement progressed. The first response of both the NEA and the AFT was to oppose virtually all of the reformers' recommendations, zealously protecting the right of their constituency to determine its own future. The AFT, under Al Shanker, first stepped down from this defensive posture, and the NEA, under Mary Hatwood Futrell, followed. Both organizations now maintain a high level of activity related to teacher preparation. NEA "is making slow but solid progress toward its goals of gaining control of teacher certification and teacher education program approval through the establishment of state-mandated autonomous and advisory professional standards boards" (Cruickshank and Cruz, 1988). Teachers increased representation on NCATE committees and their majority on the Carnegie board reflect the growing role that practitioners are playing in teacher education.

Another key factor in the context of teacher education reform is the role of the new National Board for Professional Teaching Standards, an outgrowth of the Carnegie report. The 63-member board, chaired by former North Carolina Governor James Hunt, was formed in 1987 with funding from the Carnegie Forum on Education and the Economy. The board, which hopes to begin voluntary certification of teachers by 1993, using a system similar to those used by doctors, accountants, and other professionals, will assess teachers' subject-matter knowledge, teaching techniques, and knowledge of child development. The assessment is designed to go far beyond the type of multiple-choice testing currently used by the National Teacher Examination. A large research project at Stanford University under Shulman is currently developing sample protocols for the new assessment. The National Board for Professional Teaching Standards has the potential of having a revolutionary impact on not only the credentialing of teachers but on teacher education itself. It is noteworthy that the majority of board members are working teachers rather than teacher educators.

The Carnegie National Board is only one aspect of the growing movement to re-establish teaching as a true profession. Part of Goodlad's current study of teacher education involves an inquiry into the status of teaching as a profession. As a part of that study, Soder (1988) examined education along with other professions and derived 15 features that training programs in the established programs share with the professional education of educators. Along with other professional training programs, for example, teacher education programs are generally affiliated with universities, are usually accredited, recruit and select trainees, weed out unqualified trainees, and provide for continuing education. Soder wonders why so much attention has been paid in recent years to the various efforts to "professionalize" what is presumably already a profession. The answer lies in the profession's search for increased status and rewards: "If we compare the historic economic performance of some of the professions with that of most ordinary occupations, it seems reasonable for members of an occupational group seeking greater remuneration and reward to pursue professionalization" (p. 301).

Conclusions

"Nothing short of a simultaneous reconstruction of preservice teacher education, in-service teacher education, and schooling itself will suffice for significant educational change and school improvement."

Although these words were penned by John Goodlad in 1970, they might equally reflect the current realization of the reform movement in teacher education. Teacher education has come under criticism before, most noticeably in the early sixties when James Conant's study of teacher education also unearthed a movement to remove teacher education from the hands of the educationists (1963). The convergence of all the forces discussed above, however, leads one to the conclusion that the current effort is more than a flash in the pan and that real change is likely to occur. There is a growing recognition on the part of all the players that the game is far more complex than they realized, and that "quick-fix" solutions will act only as band-aids to deep wounds. After reviewing almost a decade of the reform movement as it affects teacher education, I draw the following conclusions, which merge into future directions that the reform movement will take as we prepare teachers for the twenty-first century.

(1) *Teacher education will begin to focus on individual programs as the logical sites for reform, rather than individuals or state or professional agencies* (Goodlad, 1988). This reinforces what we discovered in the reform of K–12 schooling: that individual teachers, working together under leadership with vision at a school site, are able to effect change (Sirotnik, 1987). Howey and Zimpher's (1989) study of several exemplary teacher education programs in the Midwest confirmed the notion that individual institutions were able to construct coherent programs of teacher preparation. They noted several attributes of these programs, many of which were very similar to the findings regarding effective schools. The programs had clear conceptions of schooling/teaching which they articulated clearly to their constituencies, were rigorous and academically challenging, showed evidence of faculty collegiality, and were carefully evaluated. Howey and Zimpher's research underscores another point: allowance for a variety of approaches to teacher education should accompany reform efforts.

(2) *The growing recognition of the role of practitioners in the reform of teacher education will continue.* This recognition accompanies the teacher empowerment movement in the public schools and reinforces an obvi-

ous point: change in schools is not possible without the involvement of the primary agents of schooling, teachers. University teacher educators will have to develop far more collegial stances toward their public school counterparts if they are not to be shut out of teacher education altogether. "What is practical must often control what is pure theory," Jefferson said with regards to the Louisiana Purchase, and it is equally applicable to teacher education. There is some evidence that collaboration between university teacher educators and practitioners is becoming more the norm, and that the professoriate is becoming more cognizant of what Lee Shulman calls "the wisdom of practice."

(3) *The efforts to professionalize teaching will continue and will include such reform recommendations as entry and exit requirements, certification and licensing, salary increases (although not to the degree proposed by reformers), and some version of career ladders.* Within teacher education itself, the movement to develop a knowledge base for the profession will continue, and the incorporation of that knowledge base into teacher assessment is one of the more exciting items on the reform agenda.

(4) *The movement to make teacher education more accountable will continue,* and teacher educators will need to become even more involved in putting their programs to the ultimate test: does their training of teachers increase student learning? If they are not willing to assume responsibility for their program outcomes, state legislatures and education agencies will be only too willing to do so.

(5) *The trend toward greater academic preparation in the liberal arts and sciences will continue and will spur a reform movement in undergraduate education.* This will provide a crucible for the content vs. process argument and may ultimately result in both a high school and college curriculum which will look quite different from today's.

Teacher education is at a critical point; forces have converged at this point in time so that real change is now possible. The mission is clear; the will appears to be present. The next decade in teacher education should truly be an exciting one.

REFERENCES

AACTE Briefs. (Jan.–Feb., 1988). AACTE joins cooperative to link teacher education and liberal arts. 9(1), 5. Washington, D.C. American Association of Colleges for Teacher Education.

Barr, R.D. (1984). New ideas for teacher education. *Phi Delta Kappan,* 66(2), 127–129.

Berliner, D.C. (1988, February). Teacher education: what we know and what we need to know. Charles W. Hunt Lecture at the Annual Meeting of the AACTE, New Orleans.

Berliner, D.C. (1984). Making the right changes in preservice teacher education. *Phi Delta Kappan*, 66 (2), 94–96.

Bloom, A. (1987). *The closing of the American mind.* NY: Simon & Schuster.

Boyer, E.L. (1987). *College: The undergraduate experience in America.* NY: Harper & Row.

Carnegie Forum on Education and the Economy. (1986). *A nation prepared: Teachers for the 21st century.* Washington, D.C.: Carnegie Forum.

Chronicle of Higher Education. (April 20, 1988). A survey of two years of action by 50 states and D.C. to reform the education of teachers.

Clifford, G.J. & Guthrie, J.W. (1988). *ED School: A Brief for Professional Education.* Chicago, IL: University of Chicago Press.

Conant, J.B. (1963). *The education of American teachers.* NY: McGraw-Hill.

Cruickshank, D.R. & Cruz, J. Jr. (1989). Trends in teacher preparation. *Journal of Teacher Education*, 40 (3), 49–56.

Darling-Hammond, L. (1984). *Beyond the commission reports: The coming crisis in teaching.* Santa Monica, CA: The Rand Corporation.

Ducharme, E. & Agne, R. (1982). The education professoriate: A research-based perspective. *Journal of Teacher Education*, 33 (6), 30–36.

Feistritzer, C.E. (1984). *The making of a teacher: A report on teacher education and certification.* Washington, D.C.: National Center for Education Information.

Feistritzer, C.E. (1983). *The condition of teaching: A state-by-state analysis.* Princeton, NJ: The Carnegie Foundation for the Advancement of Teaching.

Gall, M.D. (1983, winter). Using staff development to improve schools. *R&D Perspectives,* 1–6.

Gallup, A.M. & Elam, S.M. (1988). The 20th annual Gallup poll of the public's attitudes toward the public schools. *Phi Delta Kappan,* 70(1), 33–46.

Goodlad, J.I. (1988). Studying the education of educators: Values-driven inquiry. *Phi Delta Kappan,* 70 (2), 104–11.

Goodlad, J.I. (1984). *A place called school.* NY: McGraw-Hill.

Goodlad, J.I. (1970). The reconstruction of teacher education. *Teachers College Record,* 72, 61–72.

Holmes Group. (1986). *Tomorrow's teachers: A report of the Holmes group.* East Lansing, MI: Holmes Group.

Howey, K.R. & Zimpher, N.L. (1989). *Profiles of preservice teacher education.* Albany, NY: State University of New York.

Joseph, P.B. & Green, N. (1986). Perspectives on reasons for becoming teachers. *Journal of Teacher Education,* 37 (6), 28–33.

Kluender, M.M. (1984). Teacher education programs in the 1980s: Some selected characteristics. *Journal of Teacher Education,* 35 (4), 33–35.

Lanier, J.E. & Little, J.W. (1986). Research on teacher education. In Wittrock (Ed.). *Handbook of research on teaching* (3rd ed., pp. 527–69). New York, NY: Macmillan.

Lortie, D.C. (1975). *Schoolteacher.* Chicago: University of Chicago Press.

Nathan, J. (1986). Implications for educators of *Time for Results. Phi Delta Kappan,* 68(3), 197–201.

Peseau, B.A. (1982). Developing an adequate resource base for teacher education. *Journal of Teacher Education,* 33 (4), 13–15.

Sandefur, J. T. (1986). State assessment trends. *AACTE Briefs,* August, 12–14.

Sirotnik, K.A. (1987). *The school as the center of change.* Occasional Paper No. 5, Center for Educational Renewal. Seattle, WA: University of Washington.

Soder, R. (1988). Studying the education of educators: What we can learn from other professions. *Phi Delta Kappan,* 70 (4), 299–305.

Sykes, C.J. (1988). *ProfScam: Professors and the demise of higher education.* Washington, D.C.: Regnery Gateway.

Sykes, G. (1983). Contradictions, ironies, and promises unfulfilled: A contemporary account of the status of teaching. *Phi Delta Kappan,* 65 (2), 87–93.

Vance, V.S. & Schlechty, P.C. (1982). The distribution of academic ability in the teaching force: Policy implications. *Phi Delta Kappan,* 64 (1), 22–27.

Zimpher, N.L. (1988, February). 1987 national survey of students in teacher education programs: Preliminary findings. Paper presented at the Annual Meeting of the AACTE, New Orleans.

Chapter 5

FACULTY DEVELOPMENT IN HIGHER EDUCATION

Martin J. Finkelstein

The Faculty Role and Faculty Development in Historical Perspective

When we look at the college faculty member's role in American higher education over the past three hundred or so years, it is possible to identify certain watershed periods, periods during which the role was transformed from one prototypical incarnation to another. The first such watershed is located in the first quarter of the nineteenth century. That was the period when "professoring," per se, first emerged from the shadow of the tutorship, when collegiate staffing moved from the temporary pattern of tutors shepherding a student cohort through the four-year baccalaureate course to the appointment of "permanent" professors with some subject-matter specialization in which they taught (e.g. natural philosophy, divinity, moral philosophy). Although faculty continued to preach and to watch over their student charges *in loco parentis*, organizational careers were beginning to take shape during this period.

The second watershed began in earnest in the last quarter of the nineteenth century and culminated just before the First World War. Most generally, it was marked by the transition from the faculty career as primarily an *organizational* one to the faculty career as primarily a *professional* one. Faculty became preeminently members of a discipline and profession and only secondarily members of an organization. This was the period when the modern academic disciplines took form and established a foothold on American campuses in the form of academic departments. This was a time of the rise of research as a legitimate and respected role activity and the Ph.D. as the union card for entry to the academic ranks (v. Veysey, 1965; Finkelstein, 1983; Metzger, 1987). This was a period, too, of the development of the disciplinary and scholarly associations as vehicles for the expression of purely professional concerns, and the beginning of the struggle of external disciplinary concerns with

77

the organizational needs of colleges and universities. In terms of the faculty role, it meant a new and increased emphasis on basic and applied research; a decrease, especially in the universities, in the amount of time faculty devoted to teaching and a progressive tendency to focus their teaching more and more on their area of specialization; it meant a decline in faculty's custodial role vis-a-vis students (and the concomitant emergence of the student personnel movement) and the refocusing of the faculty service role from religious and/or communal activities to public activity in one's field of specialization.

The immediate post-World War II era may constitute a third such watershed involving an intensive second-order academic specialization. This is the period of Jencks's and Riesman's *academic revolution* (1968): the rise of federal research funding, the ascendence of the research university, and the advent of the faculty roles of "grants person" and advisor to presidents. It is a period of a decline in the influence of college faculties in the governance of their institutions as a function largely of increased professional and organizational fragmentation (v. Clark, 1987).

The last ten or fifteen years, I believe, constitute a fourth such watershed. This one may be as revolutionary as the first, promoting as much discontinuity. The impetus for this watershed has been the extraordinary growth and diversification of the academic professions. Increasingly, as the ranks of the full-time professoriate are being filled with full-time colleagues in the career and vocational fields (health sciences, businesses, criminal justice, etc.) and by part-time faculty in these fields and in the traditional arts and sciences, college teaching is no longer the *exclusive* career for many faculty (or it is the exclusive focus for only a brief period in the individual's entire professional career). This "new majority" who come to college teaching without the socialization experience typical of graduate education in the arts and sciences may be ushering-in an era where American higher education is staffed by a small core of permanent, full-time faculty together with a majority of temporary professors who are a "teaching" faculty and for whom college teaching is a non-exclusive career.

This restructuring of the faculty ranks has been associated, as well, with a restructuring of several aspects of the academic role. The teaching role has been both complicated and transformed by new kinds of students who are increasingly populating our campuses (the other new majority), students who are increasingly part-time adults, increasingly underprepared, and increasingly minority. The research role continues to evolve along at least two dimensions. As the academic disciplines continue to fragment and to realign themselves in new configurations (e.g. cognitive sciences, biophysics), the social arrangements for research are changing—more *multi*-disciplinary teams of faculty are crossing traditional departmental lines and new research units are forming. Second, as professors and institutions seek to find expressions of the research role that are appropriate to the diverse institutional structure of American higher education, new kinds of research roles in the area of knowledge synthesis and application (quite beyond traditional research seeking to advance knowledge) are emerging (Boyer and Rice, 1988). In addition, new kinds of faculty roles, especially entrepreneurial and dissemination roles in the areas of off-campus program development and technology transfer are on the horizon (see Lynton and Elman, 1987).

The changes currently being wrought, as those of the three previous watersheds, correspond to a variety of forces impinging on American higher education and the purposes it serves. During the 1980s, those forces have included: (1) scientific/technological development—a veritable knowledge explosion, involving the opening up of entirely new frontiers (e.g. genetic engineering, artificial intelligence), as well as the realignment of traditional academic disciplines into the formation of new ones (e.g. the cognitive sciences); (2) concern about the United States's global economic competitiveness and the role of colleges and universities in economic and technological development; (3) political concerns about social equity and expanding access to American higher education as a positive social good (and the concomitant changes in the composition of the student body of the higher education system); and (4) the fiscal constraints imposed by slower economic growth and mounting foreign debt.

Many of these same forces shaped the transformations we have chronicled in the nineteenth century. Indeed, it may be that these academic role transformations merely follow economic transformations of the larger society (agrarian/religious > industrial/secular > post-industrial) and the social and political transformations in the purposes of higher education, leavened by internal social and political factors (v. Martin Trow's 1973 "Transition from Elite to Universal Access").

At all events, these watershed periods of academic role transformation thrust issues of faculty preservice preparation and the development of faculty already in service into bold relief. The more drastic the transformation, the more urgent the need and frenetic the pace of activity. The peculiar nature of the transformation is reflected in the substantive nature of the need and the substance of programmatic response. Thus, in the early nineteenth century, there was a need to *prepare* "Godly" individuals (i.e. those who would provide sound religious influence on students) for teaching a subject-matter specialty; and the practice evolved, at many institutions, of hiring individuals, sending them off to European training centers for one or two years to prepare for their position (in effect, melding development and preparation together). By the late nineteenth century, faculty needed help in securing and maintaining expertise in their fields of study, thus giving birth to sabbaticals for study and research and funds for travel to the meetings of learned societies and professional associations. In the first half of the twentieth century, as the faculty role became more highly differentiated, faculty development opportunities emerged that were sub-role specific. To sabbaticals and travel funds were added research grants and fellowships (both internal and external), grants, seminars and services, and instructional development grants and opportunities. As faculty shortages developed in the 1950s and early 1960s, prospective faculty were being recruited in the midst of their doctoral programs, and faculty development came to include the granting of leaves, reduced loads, or funding to complete work on the terminal degree. (In effect, the support of preparation for faculty positions.)

Current Needs for Faculty Development

The past generation has seen a tremendous expansion and differentiation in the scope of faculty development needs corresponding to changes in the profession, its role and condition, and in higher education, generally. *Profession Development* opportunities to enhance the expertise of faculty in their primary disciplines have continued to expand in response to the general knowledge explosion, but also in response to the progressive vertical expansion of American colleges and universities into graduate education. More faculty than ever are teaching graduate students and more faculty than ever hold a terminal degree in their discipline. *Instructional Development* since the late 1960s has become a nearly equal partner with professional development. Early on, instructional development focused on the use of what were then new technologies (including media of all kinds and computer-assisted instruction) to handle the tremendous influx of students into American higher education in the

1960s while still managing some individualization of instruction. As the growth of higher education leveled off in the 1970s and 1980s, a second wave of instructional development turned its focus much more on the new *kinds* of students populating colleges and universities, including the returning adult students as well as the increasingly underprepared students (much like the first wave, the second wave of instructional improvement sought to achieve its goal through the use of teaching improvement grants and various kinds of faculty workshops).

As the profession and the faculty role have changed, a third wave of instructional development is discernible—on at least two fronts. First, there has been a general reaction to the increasing ascendance of research over teaching, even in the teaching-oriented institutional sectors of American higher education. Thus, instructional development has emerged as a *remedy* to the neglect of teaching. Second, instructional development has emerged as a reaction to the increased use of part-time and other non-regular full-time faculty. Many institutions, including a majority of two-year community colleges, have most of their courses taught by part-timers, who may sometimes have minimal teaching experience and motivation or opportunity to improve. Instructional development thus is a matter of *extending* faculty development to non-traditional faculty groups (i.e. non-full-time and non-tenure-track).

Both the second and the third waves of instructional development we have described have been associated with *curriculum development* along at least two dimensions. First, curriculum development has emerged in terms of a need for faculty to meaningfully deal with the increasing underpreparedness and cultural diversity of their students. This is reflected in the recent movement away from relegating all remedial/basic skills programs to one department or organizational unit toward promoting reading/writing/speaking *across the curriculum*. Second, curriculum development has emerged as a reaction to the curricular fragmentation of the past twenty years, taking on the search for integration and coherence in undergraduate education reflected in the recent work of Ernest Boyer (1987), Allen Bloom (1986), and recent reports from the National Endowment for the Humanities ("To Reclaim a Legacy," 1986) and the Association of American Colleges ("... the College Curriculum," 1985). We are dealing here not merely with disintegration in the face of the student upheavals of the 1960s but with the fact that these upheavals coincided with the increased fragmentation of faculty who were all too frequently more than willing to abandon required general education courses for their more strictly disciplinary concerns.

Finally, there are the personal and career needs of faculty associated with the conditions of decline that higher education has been experiencing over the past decade. The abrupt end to growth in the early 1970s, and faculty personnel policies that "tenured in" a large majority of that very large cohort of young faculty hired to staff the growth of the late 1960s and early 1970s, have left us with a *greying* and increasingly *stuck* faculty, a faculty that is older and that has nowhere to go in the depressed academic job market. Beyond the organizationally stuck, are the professionally stuck, those anachronistic professors trained in academic fields in which an increasingly career-oriented student body is no longer enrolling (e.g. classics, languages, history) or those trained in professional fields with declining enrollments (e.g. education, nursing). These conditions have spawned a variety of efforts in the personal, career and organizational development of faculty. In terms of personal development, institutions are concerning themselves with promoting and maintaining the health of an older and more permanent core of faculty. Institutions are also helping faculty either change careers (i.e. move out of academe entirely or move into fundamentally different kinds of organizational responsibilities like administration) or move into new subjects within academe for which there appears to be stronger or growing demand (faculty retraining). Finally, insofar as mobility has declined and insofar, too, as faculty sense of community is declining, institutions have begun to recognize the need for organizational development to enable a fragmented and more diverse faculty to function effectively as a coherent force within the institution.

Current Faculty Development Activity

Having identified the emergent needs for faculty development over the past decade, the question arises as to what colleges and universities are currently doing about those needs. How much faculty development activity is taking place? In what areas of need? Where? Who is responsible?

Beyond traditional sabbaticals and research grants/travel, one can discern two waves of activity over the past twenty years. The late 1960s and early 1970s represent the first sprouting of the faculty development movement, characterized as we have suggested above by a heavy emphasis on instructional development. Following a period of retrenchment in the late 1970s, the faculty development movement arose anew in the early and mid-1980s with a more holistic focus on faculty vitality (personal, professional and organizational) and on the second and third waves of instructional and curriculum development we have described above.

According to John Centra's landmark study (1976), approximately three in five colleges and universities surveyed had faculty development or instructional improvement programs in 1975 (and, to a lesser extent, programs for personal and professional development of faculty). Typically, institutions did not build organized programs that systematically addressed a clearly identified array of needs, but rather put together a smorgasbord of choices, including one-shot workshops and seminars (both on-campus and off), small instructional improvement grants programs, teaching awards, retreats and conferences, etc. Each item on the smorgasbord tended to focus on a fairly narrow aspect of faculty activity, typically relating to classroom teaching (and including the retraining of faculty in low-demand fields for teaching in allied fields of considerable growth). Statewide activity was sparse. The State University of New York (SUNY) and the University of Wisconsin systems were two notable exceptions. At SUNY, teaching improvement grants were awarded to faculty statewide to provide released time or to defray costs associated with classroom improvement projects. A statewide program of teaching awards was created as well as a new system-wide academic rank: Distinguished Teaching Professor (Francis, Finkelstein, and Stratton, 1978). These grants and award programs were supplemented in the mid-1970s by a grant program to fund the retraining of faculty statewide to teach in higher-demand fields (v. Neff, 1978). Such statewide programmatic efforts at faculty retraining were also underway in Wisconsin (the Faculty Development and Renewal Program). Similarly, as well, the University of Wisconsin system initiated and sustained an undergraduate teaching improvement grants program for faculty.

While there were, then, a few isolated instances of statewide funding (and a few, as well, of institutional funding), the lion's share of the cost of the early faculty development movement was borne by the private philanthropic foundations. A number of the more notable foundation funding efforts remain as part of the higher education landscape even today: the Center for the Teaching Professions, funded by the Kellogg Foundation at Northwestern University; and the Centers for Learning and Teaching at both Harvard and Stanford funded by the Danforth Foundation. The programs at liberal arts colleges were supported by the Lilly Endowment, the Bush and Mellon Foundations (Eble and McKeachie, 1985). But such "soft money" funding ultimately requires a movement to an institutional base of support. That transition came at precisely the time that "retrenchment" was becoming the watchword of American higher education. Faculty development programs, thus, found themselves "under the gun" in the late 1970s: to prove themselves in the face of tight budgets before there was adequate time to determine their effectiveness. In an effort to assess the movement, the Fund for the Improvement of Post-Secondary Education (FIPSE) funded a national project at the University of Michigan in 1978. The results of that national survey raised some serious questions about the early programs. The primary problem appeared to be that faculty did not see programs as meeting their needs as they saw them, but rather their needs as administrators and state policymakers defined them (Blackburn et al., 1979). That is, the programs tended to be administratively driven and to be activity or sub-role specific, focusing on what was to the mind of the faculty the wrong sub-role, teaching rather than research, and they did not help faculty achieve integration between those two major sub-roles. Moreover, the prototypical form that faculty development programs tended to take was the one-shot workshop or seminar, frequently off-campus. Thus, the programs did not provide for *sustained* learning nor for *in situ* learning readily transferable to the individual professor's day-to-day context. It was, thus, that during the late 1970s many of the year faculty development programs found themselves either discontinued or suspended (v. Centra, 1985).

During the decade of the 1980s but especially since 1985, we are seeing a *resurrection* and what may be the bare outline of a *transformation* in the faculty development movement. I use the qualification *appears*, since there is not to my knowledge any reliable, comprehensive empirical charting of the faculty development terrain since Centra's 1976 survey and the Blackburn et al.'s 1978–79 survey with three exceptions: a 1985 survey of faculty development practices at 33 colleges and universities nationwide by the California Post-Secondary Education Commission (CPEC, 1986); a 1985 update of the earlier Centra survey by the Professional and Organizational Development Network in Higher Education (Erickson, 1986); and NCRIPTAL's 1987 survey of Academic Management Practices in the teaching-oriented sectors of American higher education (Peterson, forthcoming). These efforts are, however, too limited in their sample, scope or depth of coverage to permit us to chart national trends—although NCRIPTAL's results are clearly the most comprehensive.

The resurrection is clear simply from the pace of activity: the numbers of institutions and, for that matter, the number of states involved with formal faculty development programs. The California Post-Secondary Education Commission (1986) reported that three out of four colleges and universities provided organized instructional development services and *23* states were subsidizing statewide faculty development programs. The Professional and Organizational Development Network (POD) reported a doubling of membership during the last two years, reflecting at least in part an increase in the number of individuals, both professional staff and faculty, concerned with faculty development on campuses. Moreover, the POD survey found that of the extant faculty development programs at nearly 900 colleges and universities nationwide, fully half were new (i.e. had begun after 1981). These findings are lent further credence by NCRIPTAL's 1987 Survey of Academic Management Practices at 1053 two-year, four-year and comprehensive institutions with undergraduate arts and sciences units (Peterson, forthcoming). The average such teaching-oriented institution reported employing 62 percent of the instructional development practices surveyed, fully half of which were initiated since 1984. Beyond the ubiquitous sabbatical and conference travel funds, about one half offered peer teaching consultation programs and nearly two fifths had established faculty development or instructional improvement offices—and in one-third cases within the past three years.

The purported transformation of the faculty development movement is reflected in what is fast becoming the watchword in faculty development circles—faculty *vitality,* a term legitimized by Shirley Clark and Darrell Lewis (1985) in the University of Minnesota faculty studies. Vitality is a very robust and somewhat amorphous concept that focuses attention on the *whole* faculty member as s/he functions in his/her professional life (directing faculty development beyond the development of isolated sub-roles or skills or activities to a functional *gestalt*). And as an emerging literature clearly shows, "vital" professors can be distinguished on a whole array of variables from a representative sample of their colleagues: vital professors have more defined and more concrete goals; they spend more time on non-teaching activities, especially scholarship; they have more complex, diversified and multi-dimensional careers that are more fluid and peppered with risk-taking and role change; they are also more enterprising and they exploit external resources and professional growth opportunities (Clark and Lewis, 1985). And vitality is the polar opposite of *stuckness.* Rosabeth Kanter (1981) is, of course, the individual who has raised the currency of the concept of being "stuck" in a job. What Kanter as a sociologist has done and colleges and universities have begun to do is relate individual vitality/strictness to organizational vitality/stuckness or "opportunity structure." An opportunity structure is provided most obviously by the employing organization (the college or university) in terms of faculty opportunities to do different kinds of things as well as to emphasize different aspects of the academic role differentially (v. AAHE Task Force on Professional Growth, 1984). It is also provided by the profession (the professoriate and/or the discipline) in terms of opportunities for developing multiple variants on the traditional academic career—one career in one field for a lifetime (v. Baldwin, 1981). What has happened, then, at least at the conceptual level in the group psyche of American higher education, is that a holistic focus on individual functioning across roles has met with a complementary rethinking of organizational and career opportunity structures and examining major reconfigurations of faculty roles and careers. This is reflected in a new emphasis on *sustained* learning for faculty, on *organizational development* (examining organizational opportunity structures and organizational arrangements for faculty development, especially faculty "ownership" of programs), on *career development* (re-examining the traditional career trajectory and certainly doing so within a developmental perspective that indeed assumes that what is appropriate for one stage may not be appropriate for another), and broadening the conception of the prototypical faculty to include college teachers in the "newer" professional/career fields who may teach only part time or full time for short periods in a more diverse professional career.

Emergent New Models of Faculty Development

This emergent (nascent) new emphasis on faculty development—more holistic, more faculty driven—is cropping up in a number of ways. Organizationally, colleges and universities that may in the past have allowed faculty development to "happen" in academic departments/divisions/colleges are now organizationally focusing (centralizing) their efforts in newly established organizational units, variously called Centers for College Teaching, Offices of Teaching Effectiveness, Teaching Resource Centers, etc. And while these units may be headed by a professional staff person (a faculty development specialist), they are now more than ever faculty influenced and faculty centered. At the large institutions, a professional staff person typically works with a faculty advisory body;

at the middle-size institutions, the units are frequently headed by faculty members themselves; at smaller institutions the work of such centers is typically performed by faculty development committees of full-time faculty and appear to be springing up with increasing frequency (Svinicki, 1988). Beyond organization, the transformation is manifesting itself programmatically. While sabbaticals and research grants remain the mainstays of faculty development at many campuses and while instructional development still frequently takes the form of one-shot workshops or technical consulting, new programmatic models of instructional development and more broadly of professional/career development for faculty are emerging that promise more substantial individual and organizational impact. The first of these that is clearly emerging is the "train the trainers" model wherein individual faculty or teams of faculty are provided with *sustained training* for working with their colleagues and then move into such *in situ* roles with their colleagues—a classic organizational development strategy. An example here would be the Integrative Skills Reinforcement program (ISR) developed at La Guardia Community College that has been exported to campuses nationwide via train-the-trainers seminars (J. Anderson et al., 1983). Another example would be the New Jersey Master Faculty Program wherein faculty coordinators from some two dozen campuses statewide are being trained to train their colleagues in working collaboratively with each other on enhancing student learning in their classrooms. This variant not only trains "trainers" on a campus but builds support for a collegial culture based on the classroom teaching role. Both of these are examples of faculty-driven, group-oriented, and *in situ* interventions.

A second model is provided by the Program in College Teaching and Academic Leadership (CTAL) at Teachers College, Columbia University, established in 1984. CTAL is an intensive, sustained three-year experience for faculty already in service who do not possess a doctorate— typically community college faculty or four-year college faculty in career programs. The doctoral program specifically encourages students to work on institutional problems and to assume faculty leadership roles at their own campuses. Beyond the doctoral program, Teachers College is now attempting to expand the scope of CTAL to serve a broader array of faculty development functions for institutions in the tri-state (New York, New Jersey, Connecticut) area. A third emergent model is the effort currently underway in New Jersey (beyond the Master Faculty Program alluded to above) to establish a statewide Institute for Collegiate Teaching and Learning. The institute will serve as a statewide focus for programmatic efforts in enhancing faculty understanding of student development, learning styles, alternative teaching strategies, and in promoting faculty research on teaching and learning. It, along with its proposed companion, the Center for Higher Education Leadership, will also seek to develop a cadre of faculty leaders to work with campus administrators in vitalizing higher education in New Jersey. It will no doubt give rise to a wide variety of new kinds of arrangements for facilitating faculty and organizational development. Among the critical populations to be served are part-time adjunct faculty and graduate assistants. Ambitious as it is, the institute is embedded as one initiative (albeit a centerpiece) in a multi-faceted statewide plan to strengthen and to vitalize college faculties throughout the state of New Jersey, including fellowship programs, the development of disciplinary networks, research grants for study, and reformulating organizational awards systems, etc. (v. NJDHE, 1987).

Future Priorities for Faculty Development

Undergirding the New Jersey plan as well as the stepped-up and *transformed* activity in faculty development that appears to be emerging is a conviction that developing human resources in higher education to their fullest potential is one of the surest steps to enhancing the quality of higher education as it is *experienced* by our students and faculty in their daily lives and as it is *reflected* in the capabilities of our students after they graduate (student outcomes) and in the scholarship of our faculty. While it is discomforting to learn how late we have arrived at that conviction in higher education (in comparison to American business and industry), it is profoundly disturbing to see how little we actually know yet of the precise contours, let alone the impact of the second incarnation of the faculty development movement (in reality, we do not even yet have substantial empirical verification of its existence—which we only believe we see). The very next task we need to attend to, then, is to systematically explore what kinds of faculty development efforts are underway, where, and with what, if any, effect in our states and on our campuses across the nation as a whole—to what extent is the nation's principal developer of human resources optimally developing its own human resources. That question must find itself at the very top of the political/policy agenda if public policy truly aspires to make higher education better as the cornerstone of our national economic resurgence (Newman, 1985).

In the meantime, the foregoing analysis has highlighted some clear substantive challenges to be taken up by leaders in higher education and public policy. A primary challenge will be to continue the development and testing of models or approaches to faculty development that—

(1) Focus on real faculty needs as these relate to achieving institutional mission.

(2) Provide opportunities for sustained learning for faculty that is readily transferable to their daily work context.

(3) Develop the capacity of institutions to organize and to plan systematically for faculty development that will be self-sustaining (i.e. that will allow faculty to work with their colleagues).

(4) Maintain professional development, but extend their purview to the development of the whole faculty member as teacher, scholar, etc.

Moreover, as we contemplate the development of the academic professions over the coming decade, certain substantive priorities will clearly need to be addressed by higher education leaders and public policymakers. First, we must continue to address the needs of that large cohort of faculty within ten to twenty years of retirement who are largely immobile and many of whom are currently feeling and acting "stuck." Second, we will need to think about the development of "newly hired" and "to-be-hired" faculty members. Over the next ten to fifteen years a large cohort of newcomers will be entering the academic professions (v. Bowen and Schuster, 1986). While some inroads in graduate education, particularly in the training of graduate assistants, may be made in the next five to seven years to prepare these entrants, most of the needs we have identified will nonetheless fall to faculty development. Third, we will need to think now about the developmental needs of the "new" professoriate, i.e. those part-time faculty and faculty in career fields who are increasingly coming to constitute the majority at most two-year and some of the four-year institutions. As we contemplate the depth and array of needs represented by these groups, it appears that we may be contemplating a human resource need in the staffs of our colleges and universities that may be so large over the next decade to require substantial outside assistance—from the private sector, but also from government. How we respond to faculty development over the coming few years will go a long way to shaping the quality of American higher education well into the twenty-first century.

REFERENCES

AAHE Task force on Professional Growth. "Vitality Without Mobility: The Faculty Opportunities Audit." In *Current Issues in Higher Education,* no. 4. Washington, DC: American Association for Higher Education, 1984.

Anderson, JoAnn, Nora Eisenberg, John Holland, and Harvey Wiener. *Integrated Skills Reinforcement.* New York: Longman, 1983.

Baldwin, Roger (Ed.). *Expanding Faculty Options.* Washington, D.C.: American Association for Higher Education, 1981.

Blackburn, Robert et al. "Are Instructional Improvement Programs Off Target?" In *Current Issues in Higher Education,* 1980. Washington, D.C.: American Association for Higher Education, 1980.

Bloom, Allan. *The Closing of the American Mind.* New York: Simon and Schuster. 1987.

Bowen, Howard, and Jack Schuster. *American Professors.* New York: Oxford University Press, 1986.

Boyer, Ernest L. *College: The Undergraduate Experience in America.* New York: Harper and Row, 1987.

Boyer, Ernest L. and L. Eugene Rice. "Broadening Conceptions of Faculty Scholarship," manuscript in process, November 1988.

California Postsecondary Education Commission. "Faculty Development from a State Perspective." Sacramento: CPEC, 1986.

Centra, John A. *Faculty Development Practices in U.S. Colleges and Universities.* Princeton, NJ: Educational Testing Service, 1976.

———. "Maintaining Faculty Vitality Through Faculty Development," In Shirley Clark and Darrell Lewis (Eds.), *Faculty Vitality and Institutional Productivity.* New York: Teachers College Press, 1985.

Clark, Burton. *Academic Life.* Princeton, NJ: Princeton University Press, 1987.

Clark, Shirley and Darrell Lewis (Eds.). *Faculty Vitality and Institutional Productivity.* New York: Teachers College Press, 1985.

Eble, Kenneth, and Wilbert McKeachie. *Improving Undergraduate Education Through Faculty Development.* San Francisco: Jossey-Bass, 1985.

Erickson, Glenn. "A Survey of Faculty Development Practices," In *To Improve the Academy,* edited by Marilla Svinicki. Stillwater, Oklahoma: New Forums Press, 1986, pp. 182–196.

Finkelstein, Martin. "From Tutor to Specialized Scholar: Academic Professionalization in Nineteenth Century America." *History of Higher Education Annual* (1983): 99–121.

Francis, J. Bruce, Martin Finkelstein, and Lisa Stratton. *The Recognition and Reward of Teaching Excellence.* Albany, NY: State University of New York, 1975.

"Integrity in the College Curriculum." Washington, D.C.: Association of American Colleges, 1985.

Jencks, Christopher and David Riesman. *The American Revolution.* Garden City, NY: Doubleday, 1968.

Kanter, Rosabeth M. "Career Growth and Organization Power: Issues for Educational Management in the 1980s." *Teachers College Record* (Summer 1981): 553–566.

Lynton, Ernest and Sandra Elman. *New Priorities for the University.* San Francisco: Jossey-Bass, 1987.

Metzger, Walter P. "The Academic Profession in the United States." In Burton Clark (ed.), *The Academic Profession: National, Disciplinary and Institutional Settings.* Berkeley, California: University of California Press, 1987.

Neff, Charles. "Faculty Retraining in Four States," *AAHE Bulletin,* 31 (October 1978): 1.

New Jersey Department of Higher Education. *Supporting and Strengthening the College Faculty.* Trenton, NJ: Office of Policy Studies and Faculty Development, 1987.

Newman, Frank. *Higher Education and the American Resurgence.* Princeton, NJ: Carnegie Foundation for the Advancement of Teaching, 1985.

Peterson, Marvin W. et al. *Academic Management Practices Technical Report.* NCRIPTAL: Ann Arbor, Michigan (forthcoming).

Svinicki, Marilla. personal communication, November, 1988.

"To Reclaim a Legacy." Washington, D.C.: National Endowment for the Humanities, 1985.

Trow, Martin. "The Transition from Elite to Mass to Universal Access in Higher Education." Paper presented at OECD, Paris, 1973.

Veysey, Laurence. *The Emergence of the American University.* Chicago: University of Chicago Press, 1965.

Chapter 6

UNLEASHING STUDENT CREATIVITY

Kim Natale

Learning and Society

A rare experience: a high school teacher who is given the chance to teach in the elementary school for a day. "Just bring whatever you have that the children will be interested in" was the only instruction given to me by my son's second grade teacher. What would interest a second grader? Can they understand anything? Sure, my son is one of them, but I have no idea what he does all day in school.

The dreaded day came that I had volunteered for in some weak moment. I had to go teach these children. What a surprise was in store for me! They were interested in absolutely everything that I brought. In fact, I am convinced they would have been interested in almost anything. Their enthusiasm and their curiosity about how things worked amazed me. Their questions went on and on. Then I realized that their teacher was not grading them for their class participation. They were not being required to take notes. Their only motivation for listening was the sheer joy of learning something new! What a contrast this presented to me, a high school teacher. So many students in high school seem to have no internal motivation and all types of external motivators need to be used. High school teachers often require students to hand in their notes, or outline the chapter for a grade. If homework is not collected for a grade, most students will not do the assignment. Extra credit points are needed before students will research a topic or watch a program related to their interests.

Learning is not an exciting journey into the unknown in many of our schools today. Instead, it is more like forcing a child to eat everything on his plate. Our children do not dislike school. They just dislike going to class. They enjoy the times when they can visit with their friends and not be bothered by people trying to teach them something. In the *1985 Survey of the American Teacher,* pollster Lou Harris found, "A substantial 66-34 percent majority feel lack of student interest in their classes is a serious

92

problem." He also found that only 42 percent of all teachers polled would rate their schools as excellent.

What is it that happens between second grade and twelfth grade to remove the zest for learning from most students? What happens to diminish their creativity? Watch students entering a high school classroom. They will do only the work that is required of them and graded (and sometimes not even that). A common question is, "Does this count on my grade?" with the implication that if it doesn't, then why should it be done. Reading is a lost art in high school. The textbooks provided, at great expense, in our public schools are only read by a few. When questions are assigned to test the reading, students will talk to their friends to find out the answers or ask the teacher to tell them what it says; however, they rarely read the material for themselves. Students have become masters at extracting the answers from teachers so that they do not have to do the work on their own.

The loss of an excitement for learning is even more apparent in teaching adult classes that teachers are required to take to become recertified. The teachers in these classes not only show a lack of interest but in many cases they show signs of outright rebellion. Perhaps this is due to some dissatisfaction with the teaching profession. The Harris poll found that only 40 of every 100 teachers would say they were "very satisfied" with teaching. The refusal of many teachers to learn is reflected in our society as a whole, a society that does not hold reading or learning in high regard but stresses pursuit of pleasure as the highest goal. Ways to get rich by expending the least effort is an attitude which predominates this materialistic society. It is within this society that our education system must raise the children with a different spirit, a spirit of learning and creativity.

Hopefully, this picture is too bleak. In a few high school classrooms there are students who display an ember of creativity remaining from the fire that engulfed them in their youth. Educators must find a way to fan the fires of creativity to ignite that skill once again. What are some ways that teachers can foster creativity? How can administrators help teachers develop this skill, one that is disappearing? What can people who establish public policy in education do to stimulate creativity in our students?

False Assumptions About Education

Before any discussion about creativity in our schools may begin, there are two common assumptions about education that must be recognized as false. First, there is the common belief in behavior modification that assumes that a dog may be taught to salivate everytime a bell rings. Therefore, a student's behavior may be changed by a skilled teacher using the correct reward and punishment routines. The second assumption made is that great teachers can be made. People who believe this are constantly training teachers to teach in some new way, a way that is currently in fashion. Both of these assumptions are wrong. It is important that both assumptions are dismissed.

Behavior modification is a product of our society. In the United States the past century has been one of great trust in science and technology. Our society is one that searches for a logical explanation of everything. It is commonly believed that there are causes for every action. Teachers have been taught to modify behavior by precise methods. Some theorists believe that students can be made to do anything and learn anything if the teacher is creative enough to dangle the correct carrot in front of the student. Just as a rat may be taught to run through a maze by using a series of rewards, it is also believed that students can be directed if the correct rewards can be found.

Education policymakers must realize that not all students will respond to behavior modification in a reasonable amount of time with reasonable stimulation. In fact, it may be impossible for the average student to be reasonably stimulated in the traditional classroom setting by a teacher using behavior modification. This is a result of the restrictions placed on the teacher by our society and the relative lack of influence of the public school in the life of the typical student.

The cultural emphasis on science has been reflected in the training of future teachers. Many education departments in major universities teach that there are schemes and methods that anyone can follow to be a good teacher. These methods can be taught to anyone with the desire to teach. The human mind is viewed much like a computer. If the right set of inputs is placed in the mind of the prospective teacher, then the right set of outputs will be achieved. Depending on the style of teaching that is in vogue at the time, the prospective teachers are taught to emulate that particular method. This may be asking the correct questions, or observing and scoring the number of students that are participating in a class, or teaching for mastery learning, or the list goes on and on.

The scientific culture has forced an erroneous view of teaching. For too long we have tried to reduce teaching to a science. A positive step in helping our students become creative would be to recognize that teaching is not a science. Teaching is an art. Consider this analogy for a moment. A real artist is very different from a paint-by-number painter. The scientific approach to painting would be a paint-by-number painter. It is more efficient and the product is more uniform. There is hardly any chance of painting a poor painting, so the risk to the employer of the painter is very low. The employer allows a technician to place the correct color in the correct numbered area. If the technician is doing the job correctly or incorrectly, it is easy to evaluate the performance. A chart can be kept of the number of colors placed in the correct area. The pay of the technician could be linked to the percent correct each month. The efficiency of the company could be determined by the number of paintings produced each month. The production model of painting would produce more paintings of more uniform quality than our present painting-by-artist approach. In spite of all these apparent advantages, most people do not have paint-by-number paintings hanging in their living room. Instead, they have, or would like to have, paintings done by an artist and not a technician.

In the same way, superior teachers are artists, and most people find it boring to sit in a technician's class instead of an artist's class. In viewing a variety of great teachers, a person will see a variety of techniques. What is really amazing is the way the great teacher can take the subject and make it come alive. They generate excitement and exude a love for learning. They are doing far more than can be quantified. Most of their reactions are intuitive. They seem to be able to take the correct action without even pausing to think about what they are doing. These teachers are viewed highly by former students. These are the teachers former students remember with statements like, "She taught me more about life than anyone, and at the same time we learned Shakespeare."

Writing in the *Wall Street Journal*, September 8, 1986, Irving Kristol stated, "Teaching is a talent, and very good teachers, like very good actors, are bound to be in a minority. There are 2,182,000 public elementary and high school teachers in the U.S. From such a large population, the most one can reasonably expect is an average level of minimum competence. And on the whole, that is what we get." One reason for the average level being one of minimum competence is that the right people are not being attracted to education. More effort needs to be given to helping people try teaching for a short period of time to see where their gift really lies. Then those in the population with a gift of teaching would become teachers. Just as there are many potentially great actors who never have an opportunity to act, so there are many potentially great teachers who never have a chance to teach. Once the people with the basic ability to teach have been identified, they should be helped to develop and perfect their skills. Much as an artist needs certain basic skills such as mixing colors, using perspective, and using effective brush strokes, so a teacher must have a solid base in his or her subject matter and in pedagogy. Training and experience will allow a person with the basic genetic gifts to become a superior teacher.

Education policymakers must find a way to encourage the type of teaching that is an art form. However, in most schools the art of teaching is being stressed less, not more. There are several trends that show a movement away from quality teaching. For example, when a school is viewed as a company and the product is the students, then the administration of the school will begin to measure the productivity of the teachers. They will develop specific criteria that define "good teaching" and observe classrooms looking for these criteria. The teachers will then be scored on the number of the points they have made. Notice how similar this is to rating an artist by how many times he or she has painted the correct color in the numbered area. There are many schemes where the salary of the teacher is linked to these observations. These measures of productivity must be avoided by schools.

Ways to Stimulate Classroom Creativity

Once these false assumptions are dismissed, it is possible to discuss ways to stimulate creativity in the classroom. These methods include the removal of standardization, the empowerment of teachers, the development of quality curriculum, the recognition of quality teaching, the improvement of school organization, and the development of clear expectations of student outcomes.

Destroying Creativity Through Standardization

The first way to stifle the creative spirit is to demand a measure of the quality of the education through some "objective" means and the use of that means to form a judgment of the quality of instruction. The measure is usually some form of standardized test. For many years SAT and ACT scores have been used to judge the quality of high schools. Admittedly, this has not been official policy, but it has been used by the community and the higher scoring schools for this purpose. Other methods being used are the number of National Merit scholars, scores on achievement tests, advanced placement scores, and many other standardized test results. Policymakers must not rely on final product measurement to judge the quality of instruction. Other means should be developed to gauge quality instruction that do not treat a school as a factory with a product being produced.

The correct and necessary use of standardized tests is to gauge the progress of individual students. Each individual's scores will show if a particular skill has been mastered or if some attention is still needed. Many schools housing students with marginal skills effectively encourage students as they demonstrate progress in each area. Unfortunately, the teachers in these schools are often looked down upon because the students do not compare favorably to others who started with much higher skills.

The danger of improper use of standardized tests is the pressure that may be created for standardization of courses. In his book, *Free to Teach*, Joseph Nathan tells of his experience and a far too typical reaction.

> Our Superintendent of Schools issued a new directive about junior high course credits. He was responding to strong pressure from the Board, which was concerned about test scores and the complaints of some parents about proliferating elective courses in which youngsters apparently acquired few skills. The superintendent also was concerned about reports from high schools that many youngsters entered tenth grade without basic writing, computing, and reading skills. Some experts suggested that the way to handle these problems was to have a standard curriculum for everyone. The Council for Basic Education's *The Paideia Proposal* recommended that "All sidetracks, specialized courses or elective choices must be eliminated. The course of study to be followed in the twelve years of basic schooling should, therefore, be completely required, with only one exception. That exception is the choice of a second language."
>
> The Superintendent directed junior high schools to offer one basic course in English and one in social studies, with no electives in these areas without his approval. The effect was chilling.

A standardized curriculum is a surefire way to destroy the creative spirit of the most artful teacher. There is a correct way to use a curriculum.

Certainly a teacher should know what the course requirements are as set by the administrators. However, they should never be told to teach that material in only one way. The parallel is again drawn to the artist. It is perfectly acceptable for a buyer to commission an artist to paint a certain subject. But the artist must choose the colors, the textures, and execute his or her own style to create a great work. A teacher must be given direction and that direction should include what the students are expected to learn in the course. The direction should also include what attitudes the students should have when they complete the course. A teacher should be provided with materials needed to teach the course. However, the day-to-day classroom plans should be left up to the classroom teacher. The timing of tests, the number of activities, the type of activities, and the teaching style should be left to the teacher.

A curriculum is simply a guide and not the rule to a great teacher. The teacher-artist evaluates activities for their appropriateness and adds or subtracts parts or whole activities. The teacher-artist allows flexibility in the teaching schedule to treat a concept in more detail when the students show a specific interest. This is done extensively at the college level where the faculty develop their own courses.

During the 1950s there was a major push to develop curriculum that was "teacher proof." Of course, the major put-down to teachers was that the curriculum was written by college professors who felt they knew better what was needed than people in the field. The failure of "new math" was primarily due to the insensitivity of the college staff to the needs and abilities of younger students. There has been no shortage of time or money spent on curriculum development. In fact, over the past 40 years Americans have committed extraordinary resources to their schools. In the state budget, education is usually the largest single item. Student-teacher ratios have been lowered and teachers' salaries have gone up (although they may not have matched inflation). Despite all of this, the functional illiteracy rate in the United States is almost 20 percent.

The creativity in students will be fostered as teachers plan a variety of activities centered around the basic curriculum. For example, if the goal is stimulating interest in science, a teacher might plan a field day with science activity as the emphasis instead of regular athletic events. Instead of a final examination consisting of questions written by the author of the book, a teacher might find other ways of testing the students' knowledge of the subject. For example, a physics teacher might take his or her class to an amusement park and have them discuss the physics of several rides. That discussion might reveal far more about the students' knowledge of physics than a prepared exam.

Destroying Creativity by Restricting Freedom

A second reason that the students are not creative is because a creative spirit is never modeled by their teachers. For the students to be creative the teacher must be creative in the style of teaching. For a teacher to be creative there must be administrative support and confidence in the teacher. Yet, schools are moving away from placing confidence in teachers. In California after the passage of Proposition 13, the California Business Round Table convinced the governor to enact a major new education law. The state found $2.7 billion of new funding for education in a two-year period. The legislation was over 150 pages long and prescribed exactly what textbooks to use, what subjects students should be taught, and how many hours of instruction for each subject. In fact, almost anything that any teacher should be doing was spelled out in this document. In an era where we are moving away from regulation of employees, there is no other occupation that even comes close to the amount of regulation that teachers are subjected to. California is not unique in this regard. In New York the Regents' Action Plan and the Part 100 Regulations that are designed to implement that Action Plan demonstrates the same lack of confidence in teachers. In a profession where we need creative, bright young minds it seems that few would enter teaching if it is so restricted. Why should a creative young person enter a profession where there is so little opportunity to make professional decisions or to exercise judgment?

The contrast must be drawn to what has happened in American industry, especially the much maligned automobile industry. In the face of Japanese competition, Americans have taken a look at how to improve their own quality to meet the Japanese reputation for quality. What they have found is that Japan treats the workers differently. Every employee is actively trying to make the system of production better. MIT's Myron Tribus, writing in the spring 1983 issue of *New Management*, focused on Edward Deming's approach to being a manager.

> (He) believes that he and the workers have a natural division of labor: They are responsible for doing the work within the system, and he is responsible for improving the system. Under Deming's way the manager understands that he needs the workers not only to do work,

but to improve the system. Thus he will not regard them simply as flesh and bone robots, but as thinking, creative human beings.

In the application being made to teachers, the teacher should be responsible for the work done in the school, and policymakers should center their efforts on improving the system (which will never reach perfection).

In his book *The Making of a Profession*, Albert Shanker, the president of the American Federation of Teachers, tells the true story about a Ford small truck plant that was "so bad it was about to go out of business." Realizing this, the manager asked one of the workers on the line for his opinion on how to improve productivity. The man suggested;

> "There are really two things you can do. One is to put a little pedal under my foot so that every time I feel a crick in my neck I press the pedal and the assembly line will stop for a second; and as soon as I shake off the crick, I would tighten the bolt. Of course, it would mean that every six minutes or so the assembly line would stop for a couple of seconds, but you would get all the bolts tightened. And the other thing is—could you have me standing on top of the truck holding this tool down, because that would be a lot easier and a lot more natural than looking up and holding the tool up?"
>
> That's what the Ford management did in that plant. It went around to all the workers and sought their ideas about solving problems. And then Ford redid the entire plant in accordance with the wishes of the employees. The result was that the plant became the best in the entire Ford Motor Company anywhere in the country. It's a classic case.

The sad case is that very little of this type of thinking is happening in our schools. Where are decisions being made to change materials used in schools, the curriculum, or the organization of the schools? More often than not, these are being made by people far removed from classroom teaching. These decisions are being made by principals, superintendents, school boards, state education boards, and even by legislatures. The problem is that the people who govern schools believe their job is to have plenty of supervision over teachers so they can see who is good and who is bad. What is desperately needed is some freedom for our teachers to be involved in decision making. The teachers are the ones who know what works and what doesn't work.

Teachers at the high school level are usually capable of developing their own courses. The most popular course in my school is one that was teacher developed. Entitled "Science Seminar," we had three science teachers each develop one nine-week mini-course from an area in which they were particularly interested. Our earth science teacher developed a unit on field geology. Our chemistry teacher taught organic chemistry and I taught astronomy. We approached the principal with an idea. Our idea was to have a class that stressed doing science, not just learning about science. The principal knew that approval of any curriculum through the district was a long, involved process that included review from several committees and a pilot program. It would take at least a year to implement any new course. Also, there was a "hold" on any new courses at the time; thus, even if the process were followed, the course would not be approved.

We pointed out that there was one approved science class that allowed some curricular freedom. It was simply titled "science seminar" and was being taught in several high schools in the district. However, in every school it had a different form and there was no published curriculum guide from the central administration. The principal approved the teaching of science seminar on his own authority, without seeking approval from any higher office. Normally, any curriculum has specified textbooks that must be used. There were no textbooks specified by central administration for the seminar class.

The geology teacher put together a class with a field trip to a different geological area each week. To avoid problems in scheduling busses for the field trip he recruited several other teachers to be his drivers, using their own personal vehicles. The principal was very supportive and approved reimbursement for any miles driven.

The chemistry teacher happened to have a doctorate in organic chemistry and was teaching at the university each summer. He was able to use some equipment and borrow a few books so that he could structure a laboratory where students synthesized several chemicals.

I desperately needed a telescope to teach astronomy. I found that the students were interested in building a telescope. They were arranged in teams, and they chose various parts of the telescope to build. The team that worked on the base had two students who knew how to weld, a necessary skill for this team. Another group had a metal lathe available which one of the students knew how to use; they designed and built the drive mechanism that was necessary to compensate for the rotation of the earth. The team designing the telescope tube and mounts wanted it to look great, so one of the members of the team who had painted cars was chosen for this task.

Some funding was needed for this project, but since the budget for the school was approved over a year in advance, none was available. This turned out to be to our advantage, since the expenditure of more than thirty-five dollars would have required the approval of central purchasing. A purchase order required over two months to be approved and had to be sent out for competitive bids. Supported by the principal and department chairman, I decided to ask for some community assistance. The students spoke to the Rotary, Kiwanis, and Optimist Clubs. The $450 needed to purchase some basic materials was donated by the community, and construction of the telescope began thereafter. The task could not be completed within the school year, so the teams continued to work throughout the summer. Finally, one summer evening in mid-August all the teams met at my home and we assembled the telescope. They worked hours on the optical alignment and took their first look at the stars.

The telescope was used by classes that followed. The important lesson here is that there must be some flexibility in any school district so that teachers can be creative. If a teacher is expected to involve the students in learning, the school must not demand adherence to guidelines that make sure every school is teaching exactly the same thing. Uniformity will not lead to uniform excellence. Instead, it will lead only to uniform mediocrity. Standardization is usually achieved at the expense of creativity.

Too often, the teachers are not respected as professionals, even in my own school district. There has been a major push to implement a new "high tech" curriculum by our superintendent. The district has hired a person with no teaching experience to implement the curriculum. Each teacher who has carefully looked at the curriculum has recommended against its implementation. In spite of this, the school district has ordered that the course be taught in a "pilot" school. And the teachers in that school have been told that no matter what their opinion of the course, it will be expanded to other high schools the following year. It is this type of thinking that is destroying creativity in our teaching staffs throughout the nation. Teachers must be able to exert substantial control over their work environments. If they are unable to do this, they will not be effective teachers.

Even worse are the cases where teachers are told they have a voice, only to be ignored later. In *Free to Teach* Joseph Nathan tells the story of a school district textbook decision where a committee was established to make suggestions about which textbooks to adopt. The process took about one year and was done every five years. After meeting for months, the decision was made not to purchase any new books. But when some additional money became available, the decision was made to use the money to purchase out-of-date textbooks even though newer ones were available. Mr. Nathan summarizes;

> Thus, thousands of dollars were spent on five-year-old books when more up-to-date texts were available. The textbook-adoption process was designed to satisfy the community and its teachers. Sadly, this process ended up being counterproductive.

There has been a major push to improve teacher salaries to attract the "best and the brightest" to education. These efforts should be applauded and must continue. But even if the salaries do increase to the levels they need to be, the best and brightest will not work very long in schools as they are structured today, just as these people would not be attracted to traditional factory work. As Albert Shanker has said so well,

> (Teachers) will not work in a place where they are not trusted, where they are time-clocked, where they're supervised, where they're observed, where they are treated as people to be pushed around and instructed and regulated. . . . I am convinced that we will not attract the best and the brightest who are graduating today if teachers continue to be treated as they currently are, as workers in an old-fashioned factory who may not exercise judgment and discretion, who are supervised and directed by everyone from the state legislature down to the level of the school principal.

Destroying Creativity Through Textbooks

A third reason that creativity is limited in our classrooms is the overall poor quality of the curriculum. It amazes me that teachers are as creative as they are given the state of textbooks in this country. They are currently a national disgrace. We have allowed textbooks to be selected by school boards or at the state level instead of by professionals. The school boards have little or no knowledge about what needs to be in a good textbook. So they adopt rules. They look for short, easy-to-read sentences that can make a book so dull no one would ever want to read it. There is a required inclusion of all ethnic references, along with racial and gender references, so that no group is left out or offended. Naturally, evolution must be dealt with as demanded by the courts. There is no one who asks if students can learn from the textbook. Although there are defined, highlighted words on every page, no one even asks if students who have missed a class can gain insight on the lesson by reading the book. The number of illustrations is counted, but no one checks to see if the illustrations are captioned correctly or understandably. Every book must include questions, but those checking the questions have no idea if these are the questions that need to be asked or if they are at the appropriate levels. Wouldn't it be wonderful to see a school board ask a teacher to stand up and demonstrate what is right and wrong about a textbook? Much like a doctor or a lawyer standing before a group of laymen to explain the fine points of a case, a teacher could be so respected that he or she could stand before a group and discuss a textbook.

When a curriculum is evaluated for possible adoption, teachers should look for a flexibility in the materials that will allow a variety of teaching styles. There should be an abundance of resources and the curriculum should not depend on any one resource. Outlines with curriculum flow diagrams are very helpful, and there should be a division between essential concepts and optional concepts. Parents should exercise the same caution in searching out new materials. If the material has only a single learning path it should not be adopted.

Policymakers must use caution in funding the development of new curricular materials. Many of the more recent curriculum development projects have far too much educational jargon and far too little substance. All of the objectives and outcomes are stated and the material is so rigid that it cannot be adapted to individual needs. Before a curriculum development project is funded, it must be determined that a wide variety of materials will be developed that a teacher may pick and choose from rather than a single learning path. Single learning path materials destroy creativity in the classroom and may stifle even the most creative teachers.

Even the textbook manufacturers have little idea what is needed in a great textbook. Joseph Nathan has a description in his *Free to Teach* about how publishers have individualized instruction through textbooks.

> Individualized instruction was one of open education's fundamental ideas. This did not mean that students would move at their own pace through predetermined text material, but that students would use a wide range of material available in libraries, textbooks, and the world beyond the school to develop strong research, reading, and writing skills. Providing redesigned textbooks as the major source of knowledge for students reduced the amount of research for teachers and students. It also reduced the amount of learning and benefit which occurred.

The textbooks were rearranged to cover the material in a different way. However, students and teachers were not encouraged to bring in material from other sources. The question Joseph Nathan asked the textbook manufacturers was, "What about the teacher and student writing some of their own questions to research? What about encouraging teachers and students to bring in other source material to learn from, or to go into the community to look for answers to their questions?" The answer is that the manufacturers make money by selling textbooks, not by encouraging students and teachers to do their own research.

Inspiring Creativity Through Self-Confident Teachers

There is another means to foster creativity in our students. Students should be taught by self-confident teachers. In our schools we can help the teachers develop their confidence by supporting what they do well. Pick out those items and point them out to teachers. Parents are especially good at this. Typically, teachers believe them, and an easy place to do this is at parent conferences. It is easy for a parent to say thanks for a job well done to a teacher at a conference. Administrators can also be very effective in building teacher confidence. I am currently teaching in a school where the principal is a master of this. He greets teachers as they arrive each morning. He is often seen in the hallways or visiting classrooms. Often he will encourage with just a few well-timed words. However, most of the time administrators only deal with putting out fires. When a teacher is asked to come to the principal's office there is fear that rises from within. In our schools teachers are usually talked to by administrators only when there is a problem. Rarely will a teacher be called in and told what good things are happening in the classroom.

Immediate supervisors (principals in an elementary school or department heads in higher grades) should search for ways to reward good creative teaching. Many teaching awards are now available. Some can be given at the building level, some district wide, even some state and national awards. Most subject matter areas give awards to good teachers. It should be the goal of every school to see each of their teachers recognized. Most people are very aware of their weaknesses. Teachers, along with most other people, tend to overlook their strengths.

Encouraging Creativity Through School Organization

An efficient school organization will also encourage creativity in our schools. Although many teachers have a creative spirit to impart to the students, their time is often used up because of the inefficient organization of the educational system. Too many of our teachers are being used to lecture students. Instead, they should be actively coaching students or teaching thinking skills. They should be working to stimulate creativity, helping students to reason, argue, persuade. Lectures may be given effectively by skilled communicators over television to huge numbers of students, but no machine can replace the personal touch that a master teacher may give to students. Theodore Sizer, in his book *Horace's Compromise*, talks about the typical high school teacher who will teach 150 to 175 students each day. It is impossible for that teacher to assign very much written work and grade that work effectively. If the teacher spent ten minutes per student paper, marking the paper and going over it with the student, and if the teacher assigned only two papers per week, it would take a minimum of 3000 minutes (or 50 hours) per week to grade the papers. The dilemma the teacher faces is that if 50 hours are spent grading papers, then when is their time to plan creative activities? Technology has now reached a point where our schools could be arranged in a much more effective manner to utilize our physical and human resources.

Possible New Structures

Albert Shanker has proposed that there should be two levels of teachers which he calls "career teachers" and "idealistic transients." Using this proposal there would be several less experienced teachers working under a highly experienced career teacher. These novice teachers would be doing many of the things that all teachers do now. The career teacher "would be engaged not mainly in lecturing students but in actively coaching students, teaching thinking skills, stimulating creativity, working with students on rewriting papers, helping students learn to reason, argue and persuade. No machine can replace good teachers in these tasks; yet given the reality of life in today's public schools, the best teachers are left with too little time to perform them."

There are other structural changes that may prove of great benefit to freeing teachers to be creative. Many of the details of these plans require more attention, but allowing parents the freedom of choice to select their child's school seems promising; so do proposals to allow teachers to be in "private practice." In private practice, teachers would contract with schools for specific education services and guarantee specific results.

Education for the Future

Finally, to develop creativity teachers must recognize that their primary goal is the development of human beings that are productive and satisfied in our society. Knowledge of individual facts is not the primary consideration, although we often teach as though the knowledge is what makes a successful person. It is not the knowledge but what we do with the knowledge that can lead us to success or failure.

For example, if a teacher in 1950 had wanted to prepare his or her students for the future, she might have listed the courses that were essential for success in life. There would not have been any courses in computers, because there weren't any computers. There would not have been any electronics training in the auto shop, or adjustments of pollution control devices. Television repair would not have included transistors, and physics would not have taught semiconductors. This shows how impossible it is for our schools to teach us the facts or specific skills that we need for a job throughout most of our lives. Therefore, teachers who only teach facts that are useful or needed at the present time limit their students and make long-term success more difficult.

Teachers who are creative can influence character development using specific subject matter as the vehicle. Students need to learn the value of perseverance. They need to learn how to fail and be able to pick themselves back up and go on. They need to understand goal setting and reaching for a point that is higher than they presently are. Certainly the value of education and the importance of lifelong learning must be instilled in students. As Irving Kristol has stated:

> If we want our children to be neat, then there should be some kind of dress code. If you want them to be polite, you insist that they behave politely in school. If you want them to be respectful, you insist that they behave respectfully to their teachers. If you want them to exercise self-restraint, you give them homework. If you want them to be aware of their obligations, you punish them for an infraction of the rules. And, contrary to much current psychobabble, most young people actually feel more comfortable in such schools, more relaxed, more "at home." To put it another way: If a school has an ethos—a "way of life" within the school walls—youngsters are more likely to emerge with an ethic.

If students are taught the values of inquiry and self-discipline, they will become more creative. When a teacher realizes that the reason for homework is to develop these characteristics in students, the homework assignments will become more meaningful. Papers from students will be graded carefully, and comments will be made on the paper to help the students develop further. Much of this is not happening in our schools now. Indeed, work is covered in class with little thought of why it is even being taught. Students are asked to do assignments filling in blanks with no thought given. They take tests and are never again asked to use the material or show that they have really learned.

The Dangers of Unleashing Teachers

Naturally, this assumes that the teacher is an artist. Unfortunately, this is not the case in many of our schools today. Too many teachers are simply technicians. These teachers will never be great, no matter how much training they are given. This is because great teachers are great because of specific personality traits and a natural feeling for what they do, and it is very difficult to alter personality traits of existing technicians to make them into teachers. Administrators must carefully distinguish teacher-technicians from teacher-artists and only allow freedom to the true artists. In creating a positive environment to foster creativity an administrator should attempt to hire only artists. This is very difficult, because teacher unions are supported by the technicians and the unions place many barriers in the way of hiring quality teachers. Education policymakers should make sure the structure of the system allows administrators the freedom to hire the teachers that they need to form quality schools. Individual school districts will not be able to stand pressure from national teacher unions. Indeed, individual states may not be able to withstand the pressure from unions for job protection and security at the expense of quality teaching.

Pride in Teaching

So once again we come back to the students suffering through school as the creative spirit that they once possessed is repressed over and over. The questioning mind is taught not to question. Life has an order that is specified, and adults are so sure they are right in their description of the universe that we not only impose that order on our children but we specify how they will learn that order. Creativity in the classroom begins with the teacher. It is fostered by administrators and parents as they support even small journeys by teachers into real teaching, teaching that matters.

When teachers can be proud of being a teacher, then they will be creative themselves and thereby be able to produce creative students. Albert Shanker, writing in *The Making of a Profession,* tells the story of a professor of education at Vanderbilt University, Terrence Deal, discussing the difference between teachers and other employees. He says:

> He [Deal] walked into a nationally known cosmetics company, approached someone who turned out to be a secretary and asked, "What do you do here?" Instead of telling him about her job, she talked about what a wonderful company it was, how they were increasing sales, how they had opened a big Latin American branch and would move into the European market within two years. She was filled with enthusiasm and clearly felt she was playing a very important part in her company. Then Deal visited IBM and bumped into someone who was obviously cleaning the place. Again he asked, "What do you do here?" And this custodial fellow started talking about IBM, how it's the greatest company in the world, how they were going to be first with a new chip, and what sort of computer would be next. Clearly the man had a tremendous sense of pride and felt important and integral to the operation of IBM. Then Deal walked down a few blocks and into a local school. He approached someone and asked his question, What do you do here?" "Oh," said the person, "I'm only a teacher." We have to take the steps . . . so that when someone walks into a school and asks what a person does, no one will ever again reply, "I'm only a teacher."

In this nation we must make our teachers feel important. Judy Reznick, one of the astronauts killed aboard the space shuttle *Challenger* when it exploded in 1986, was speaking to a group of teachers who were finalists in the "Teacher in Space" program. In June 1985, she told this group that she was delighted to be able to speak to them because they were teachers and they "make a difference." If only the teachers could really believe that they do make a difference, then the creative fires of teachers, and thereby students, would glow again in our country.

People who care about the education of this nation's children can take many steps which are virtually cost free that would result in significant improvements in our schools. These steps begin when the teacher is respected as an artist. The improvements continue when students are respected and seen to have problems that may be beyond present psychological understanding and behavior modification. But learning is made exciting again when some positive steps are taken to unleash teachers from the yoke that now binds them. The stifling pressure of standardized curriculum must be removed. Teachers must be supported as professionals and confidence placed in their educational decisions. They must have some control over the education process, especially what happens in their classrooms. That control should translate into curriculum adaptation and textbook selection. New curriculum should be developed carefully so that teachers have a wide variety of strategies to choose from, including some suggestions on how to develop their own activities related to the printed materials. Administrators, parents, and the community should develop better policies for ways of recognizing and rewarding quality teachers. Finally, teachers should realize their primary goal is to develop quality human beings, not just machines who know a subject well.

The creative spirit within all of us may be unleashed once again through teachers who love learning and teaching.

REFERENCES

Adler, Mortimer. *The Paideia Proposal.* New York: Macmillan, 1982.

Kristol, Irving. "Schools Can Do This Much." *The Wall Street Journal*, Monday, September 8, 1986. (Mr. Kristol is the John M. Olin professor of social thought at the NYU Graduate School of Business and a senior fellow of the American Enterprise Institute.)

Nathan, Joseph. *Free to Teach.* Winston Press, 1984.

Shanker, Albert. *The Making of a Profession.* American Federation of Teachers AFL--CIO publication. April, 1985. (This booklet is an edited transcript of a speech before the Representative Assembly of the New York State United Teachers on April 27, 1985, in Niagara Falls, New York.)

Sizer, Ted. *Horace's Compromise.*

Tribus, Myron. "Deming's Way." *New Management*, Spring 1983.

Chapter 7

FROM ACCESS TO RETENTION: MINORITY STUDENTS IN HIGHER EDUCATION

Marvel A. Lang and Clinita Ford

The Civil Rights Movement of the 1950s and 1960s was in part a struggle to gain for minorities equal access to educational opportunities at the nation's institutions of higher learning. Yet, a quarter century later minorities are still disparagingly underrepresented, both as students and as faculty and staff at predominantly white colleges and universities across the country. The inequitable status of minorities in higher education continues to be a major concern and has generated considerable scholarly debate over the last few years.

Why does access to equal educational opportunity for minorities in institutions of higher education continue to be a problem? Why do the retention and graduation rates of blacks continue to decline while those for other minorities are improving? And, what are viable options for improving the access and retention of minorities in institutions of higher education? These are some of the major questions we address in this chapter. And though we do not pretend to have all the answers, we shall at least attempt to enlighten the intellectual debate on these crucial issues.

Minority Access: Some Historical Perspectives

When modern-day scholars debate the issues of minority access to higher educational opportunities, they do so without recognizing the reality that equal access to educational opportunity as a matter of national policy is a recent occurrence for minorities in the United States. In other words, scholars discuss the issues concerning minority access to higher educational opportunity as if minorities have had equal access from day one. However, it was only as recently as 1954 with the *Brown v. Board of Education* decision that the U.S. Supreme Court decreed that equal access

111

should be the law of the land. It was even more recently, in the late 1960s and early 1970s, after the passage of the Civil Rights Acts of 1964 and 1965 that de facto rights of admission to many institutions of higher education in this country, especially the predominantly white institutions, were granted to minorities. And, in most instances, only the most highly qualified minorities are accepted for enrollment at these institutions even today.

While black enrollment at colleges and universities grew rapidly in the years following the landmark civil rights bills, the nation reached its peak in black college enrollment in little more than a decade. For example, in 1977, 50 percent of all black high school graduates compared to 51 percent of all white high school graduates enrolled in college upon graduation. In 1981, the percentage of black high school graduates who enrolled in college had fallen to 40 percent, and by 1982 it had fallen to 36 percent (U.S. Bureau of the Census, 1986; National Coalition of Advocates for Students [NCAS], 1985). However, the percentage of other minorities enrolling in college has increased significantly.

By 1985, the percentage of blacks 18 to 25 years old who were enrolled in college was 26.1 percent, down from 33.5 percent in 1976. In absolute numbers, this meant that nearly 40,000 fewer blacks were enrolled in college in 1985 than in 1976. During this same period, however, the total college enrollments of all minorities had increased relatively significantly. At the same time, the number of black high school dropouts had decreased from approximately 1,024,000 in 1975 to approximately 789,000 in 1984. The number of blacks enrolled in graduate schools decreased by 19.2 percent, or 12,518, between 1976–77 and 1984–85, while the enrollments of Hispanics in graduate schools rose by 20.4 percent (4,128) and Asians by 54.4 percent (10,056) during this same period (Lang, 1988; U.S. Bureau of the Census, 1985, 1987).

While the access of minority students to higher educational opportunities has improved in general, the access of black students specifically has not. The question that must be raised is "Why has the percentage of black high school graduates who enroll in college declined during the past decade while the percentage of black youth who graduate from high school has increased significantly?"

The barriers to minority access to higher educational opportunities have been very well documented. The research literature in the field point to several factors that are consistently identified and summarized as barriers to minority student access and retention in higher education:

(1) the academic preparation of minority students for matriculation in higher education; (2) the availability of and decreasing financial aid resources; and (3) institutional barriers to minority student admission and enrollment (Lang, 1988; Christoffel, 1986). The following sections of this chapter shed some light on the impacts of these factors on black college enrollments.

Financial Aid

It was during the administration of President John F. Kennedy that significant moves were initiated in the provision of federal financial aid support for minority students to pursue a college education. During the early 1960s the federal government instituted such programs as the National Defense Education Act (NDEA), the National Defense Student Loan Program (NDSL) and other work-study programs that made it possible for minority students (especially blacks) to have the financial support necessary to attend college for the first time in the nation's history. Other programs followed in the mid and late 1960s such as the Basic Education Opportunity Grants Program (BEOG) and the Equal Education Opportunity Program (EEOP). Both of these programs provided direct loans or grants to low-income and minority students who qualified for college admission and enrollment.

It was because of these federal programs that low-income and minority students began to enroll en masse at colleges and universities across the country. With the financial barrier to college attendance diminished significantly if not totally removed, black students began to enroll in colleges in record numbers. It was the predominately black colleges and universities that initially felt the effects and reaped the benefits of these programs in their enrollments. In fact, by 1976, the enrollments of the historically and predominantly black institutions reached an all-time high, with the overwhelming majority of their students being supported financially by some form of federal financial aid (Turner and Rosen, 1979). The increases occurred also at historically white institutions as well. In fact, black enrollment across the country at predominantly black and white institutions reached its peak in 1980 (U.S. Census Bureau, 1986; Brown, 1987).

Prior to the late 1970s the majority of black students enrolled in college in the United States were enrolled at predominantly black colleges. Berry (1983), for example, points out that by 1978 a total of 866,315 black students enrolled in colleges; seven in ten were by then enrolled in predominantly white institutions—a drastic change from the previous decade. Even a few years earlier in 1973, 42 percent of all black college students were enrolled in 85 predominantly black colleges (Lang, 1986). Since 1980, this situation has changed dramatically and drastically.

The rapid increases in college tuition costs undoubtedly is a hindrance to the access of minority students to college entrance. An article in *The Chronicle for Higher Education* (Evangelauf, August 10, 1988) pointed out that with an average of 7 percent tuition increase for a nationwide sample of institutions, the rate of tuition increases has outrun the inflation rate for eight straight years. Coupled with the demise of state and federal student financial aid programs during the Reagan administration, more and more minority students are finding it extremely difficult if not impossible to afford college even if they are adequately prepared. Though the absolute numbers of black students in particular who enroll in predominantly white colleges have increased over the past decade, the numbers of those who drop out of college before graduation because of financial reasons have almost doubled.

Under the Reagan administration, the federal government began to withdraw support for social programs and education in favor of tax reductions and increased defense spending. Substantial reallocations have been made in federal student financial aid programs. These reallocations have had significant impacts on minority access to higher education, since the majority of minority students depended on some form of federal student financial aid to support their college education.

Although the data on the proportions and absolute numbers of minority students depending on and receiving federal financial aid support are scanty, the available data do give some insight into the dependence of low-income students on such aid and the recent impacts of federal reallocations on their access to college enrollment. The U.S. Department of Education (1987, p. 225) in its most recent report[1] sheds some light on this subject. It reports that in the 1981–82 academic year, 22 percent of low-income students attending four-year public colleges received grants and also received a loan. Similarly, 46 percent of low-income students[2]

---

1. These statistics are derived from the U.S. Department of Education, Center for Education Statistics Report, "High School and Beyond Survey" 1986. The data for this survey were collected in 1981–82, but the report was prepared in January 1986. No later comparable data have been tabulated. Thus, these are the latest statistics available.

2. Low-income status in this report refers to total family income of less than $12,000 annually (U.S. Department of Education, 1987).

attending private four-year colleges received grants and also a loan. On the other hand, during the same year 46 percent of four-year public college low-income students who received a grant and also applied for loans did not receive a loan, while 37 percent of those low-income students who attended four-year private colleges who received a grant and applied for a loan were refused.

Conversely, during the same academic year, 8 percent of low-income students who did not receive a grant received a loan to attend a four-year public college, and 23 percent who did not receive a grant but applied for a loan were refused. Likewise, 4 percent of low-income students who attended four-year private colleges who did not receive a grant received a loan, while 12 percent who did not receive a grant but applied for a loan were refused. Thus, we see the immediate impacts of the Reagan administration's reallocation of student financial aid funds on low income students which is a proxy for minority students.

Class Status

The decrease in federal support for student financial aid programs hurts the access efforts of minority students. The impacts of these cutbacks under the Reagan administration have had drastic effects on the college enrollments of lower-income students, especially given the generally lower socioeconomic status and lack of available financial resources of many minority families. While middle-class families may be able to re-mortgage their houses to pay for their children's collegiate education, this is not an option available to the poor who may not own a house. Approximately 31 percent of blacks and other minority families besides Hispanics in the U.S. live below the poverty level. Fifty-three percent of these minority families are female-headed. Similarly, approximately 28 percent of Hispanic families live below the poverty level and 51 percent are female-headed families (U.S. Bureau of the Census, 1985, 1987).

The statistics have serious implications not only for family resources available to support siblings' higher education but also for the preparedness of minority students to be successful in college even after they attain access. With minority families earning substantially less than white families, fewer family resources are available within minority families to provide the opportunities for exposure to as many learning and enrichment experiences for their children outside of school. When the generally poorer quality of public secondary schools in minority neighborhoods is considered, it is logical to deduce that minority students would not be as adequately prepared to score as well on college entrance tests as white students do, a fact that is seldom considered when scholars debate the lower level of minority students' performance on college entrance exams.

One result of the relationship between family resources and preparedness for college is the notion that college entrance scores are the best measures and predictors of intelligence and ability to succeed in college. The scores measure best what one has already learned and has been exposed to both in and outside of school, not one's intellectual capability or capacity to learn. There are sufficient data available to show that when the college entrance test scores of minority and white students of similar socioeconomic status and background are compared, their scores are relatively comparable. This fact substantiates that the lack of resources, family situations, and other social and economic environmental factors contribute considerably to lower levels of preparedness of minority students for college success.

Results of Weak Civil Rights Enforcement

In a recent report, Orfield and Paul (1988) concluded that there are four major issues that are clearly linked to the declining access of minority students to higher education. These issues are:

1. segregation in elementary and secondary schools;
2. increasing college costs;
3. inadequate assistance to unprepared students; and
4. lack of commitment to equal opportunity by institutions of higher education.

As a result of continuing high levels of segregation in elementary and secondary schools with large numbers of minority students, poorer quality of educational facilities are reflected in every aspect of the students' preparedness and consequently in every educational quality indicator. Orfield and Paul found, for example, that when predominantly white schools are compared to those where more than five out of six students are minority, the minority schools almost always have:

- more crowded classes;
- teachers with fewer advanced degrees, and degrees from less prestigious or less selective colleges;
- less resources for counseling those students who tend to rely more on counselors for course decisions and for making college choices; and
- wider differences in scores on achievement tests.

Continuing segregation in elementary and secondary schools, according to Orfield and Paul, also translates into widening of the gap between the learning experiences of minority students and their non-minority counterparts with each additional year of schooling. This results from tracking, less enriching curricula and academic programs, and ultimately less preparation and capability for entry to colleges.

Scholars generally recognize the deteriorating conditions of inner-city schools from which most minority students come. There is still generally an unspoken and unwritten agreement among selective four-year, higher education institutions (especially predominantly white ones) that this factor should not be considered when evaluating these students for admission. These institutions project a philosophy that if they can attract and admit the best prepared students they can find, then they will try not to uneducate them while they are there. Thus, these institutions look upon remediation and developmental programs or any other programs that will address the needs of underprepared students (and as basic skills tests across the nation reveal, many of these students are not minorities) as automatically lowering the standards, tarnishing the image, and damaging the reputations of their "fine" institutions. Community and two-year colleges are viewed as institutions designed to address these needs. Yet, community colleges far too often lack the necessary resources and the staff to adequately provide the development these students need. Consequently, few minority students who enroll in two-year community colleges successfully transfer to four-year institutions.

Admittedly, there is still a gross lack of commitment on the part of institutions, state and federal agencies, and higher education leaders to improving the opportunities for minorities' access to higher education. During the past decade there has been a noticeable decline in national sentiment toward equal opportunity, fairness and a commitment to the concerns of the disadvantaged and disenfranchised. As academic institutions are microcosms of the larger society, this demeanor has obviously trickled down to them. Practitioners of higher education administration and scholars alike know that the action within academic institutions permeates from the top downward. Thus, if the boards of trustees and chief academic officers at these institutions were to commit themselves to equal opportunity and direct their underlings to carry out their directives, minority access would improve virtually overnight. Because civil rights enforcement has become essentially non-existent in the 1980s, institutions sense this relaxed mood from the federal government as an endorsement of their non-commitment to equal access and equal opportunity for minorities. Orfield and Paul (1988) characterize this scenario perfectly by stating that "Where there is no commitment there can be only token response or none at all" (p. 61).

The Issues of Minority Retention

Gaining admission and financial aid to attend college has been only part of the problem. The problems of minority student retention, especially for black students, have become more recognized and pronounced in recent years. Data show that the proportions of blacks completing college have steadily decreased since the 1970s, although the numbers of blacks enrolling in colleges may have actually increased slightly, though still not matching their proportional share of the nation's population.

In too many instances minority student retention instantly provokes thoughts of remedial and developmental learning programs. While it is true that many minority students could benefit from such programs, far too many minority students drop out of college for reasons other than not being able to do the work. In fact, 85 percent of the students who drop out of college leave voluntarily and not because of reasons of academic failure or intellectual inability (Tinto, 1975; Berry, 1983; Clewell and Ficklen, 1986). This is as true for black students as for any others.

Still, the generally held perception of student retention centers around academic and financial problems rather than the social, psychological and programmatic needs of minority students that are not being met, especially on white college campuses. Yet, despite the large volume of research on minority student retention problems in recent years, these institutions continue to disregard the need to seriously address these problems or to allocate resources to increase the success rates of minority students.

In any case, too many institutions have no programs or inadequate programs to address either the academic or non-academic problems that cause minority students to leave college before graduation. The informed view, which is not the one held at most institutions and especially at predominantly white ones, is that minority student retention programs should be extensions and expansions of the process of educating. Student retention is not merely special programs to intervene in racial crises, as usually perceived. These programs should be intricate parts of the educating process.

The pertinent question then becomes, "How do we make retention programs extensions and expansions of the process of educating?" We begin by asking another question, "What do minority students need to make them successful in their educational pursuits?" If we are honest, our answer will be that minority students need the same amenities and opportunities as other students: good preparation, solid counseling, nurturing, mentoring, networking, encouragement to succeed, and the opportunity to fail and try again without being labelled as inferior and unworthy. In addition to these attributes, minority students also need to be made to feel that they are an integral part of the social and professional environment of the campus community and not socially isolated.

When these amenities are provided to minority students in the regular routine of doing business on a day-to-day basis on the college campus, then the retention program has become a part of the process of educating, which it should be, and there is no need for special retention programs. This process also encompasses acknowledging in positive ways the cultural differences and diversity that exist between minorities and their counterparts and using these differences as teaching opportunities to enlighten the different groups about each other from positive perspectives. This also means integrating the support services necessary to address the needs of minority students with those provided for the majority students so that one group does not perceive special services being offered to another at their expense. For example, there should not be a need for an Office of Minority Affairs and Counseling if sufficient minority counselors and student affairs personnel are hired as part of the staff of the Student Affairs and Counseling Office to adequately address the needs of the minority students. There should be no need for an office of Minority Student Financial Aid if the proper assurances are made to ensure that minority students' financial aid needs are adequately and equitably met in the Office of Financial Aid.

These processes are not impossible to put in place if there is a commitment on the part of the college administration. Realizing that administrative policies at institutions are executed from the top down, if chief administrators were to mandate that these changes be made, minority student retention would improve drastically within a year. But such commitments have not been made; thus most efforts we see toward minority retention are only token.

Remedying the Problems

It is unlikely that much will change regarding the access and retention of minorities in higher education until the pervasive attitudes of the systems that control higher education change. Part of the problem is that those who are responsible for instituting change are also partially responsible for creating the problems. Atwell (1988) has capsulized this idea, stating, "I propose that we acknowledge that many of the structures and values that we accept on our campuses are actually obstacles to the educational success of minorities" (p. 8). Another aspect of the problem that Atwell articulates is that much of what is needed to provide a genuinely hospitable, conducive and supportive environment for minority students is not provided for majority students. Hence, it may be farfetched to expect institutions to provide these for minority students.

When we think of addressing the needs for institutionalizing minority student retention and access, one possibility that arises is national legislation and policymaking. There can be stimulating debate both for and against this approach. But if diversity is truly one of the goals of higher education, then the need for change should first be realized by the institutions. While we can legislate actions, we cannot legislate attitudes and commitments. It is attitudes and commitments at institutions that need to be changed. Most institutions have had affirmative action and equal opportunity policies for more than 20 years. What they lack is the commitment to enforce these policies. Inroads into increasing minority participation will not occur until there are serious commitments made by institutions toward these goals.

Colleges and universities can begin to improve the access and retention of minorities in higher education by strengthening their linkages with elementary and secondary schools in inner-city areas where the greatest numbers and concentrations of minority populations reside. Atwell (1988) points out that higher education institutions must work with these schools, not to rescue them or to share great wisdom, but because their futures are inextricably tied to each other. When colleges and universities have exemplary programs to pilot, they invariably look to the suburbs where the better resources and facilities are already available for elementary and secondary schools. If these institutions would begin to look to inner-city areas to implement model programs, improvements could begin toward the preparation of minority students for college work from these initiatives.

Similarly, the transfer gap between two-year community colleges and four-year institutions must be narrowed for minority students. Several critical leakage points have been identified in the educational pipeline where significant numbers of minority students are lost in the educational process (Astin, 1984; Christoffel, 1986; Lang, 1988). One of those critical points is the transfer from community college to completing the baccalaureate degree at a four-year college. Since community colleges far exceed four-year colleges in providing access to and retention of minority students, they bear a disproportionate share of the burden of providing educational opportunity for these students. When it comes to providing access to the upper division programs, the four-year colleges often treat community college transfer students with disdain by not accepting all of their credits, by making them retake their general education courses even when they have earned passing grades, and by ignoring many of their major courses as well. The four-year institutions have an obligation to provide for smoother articulation with community colleges in order to assure that minorities gain access to all of the career options that are available to four-year graduates.

The ultimate fault is that too many higher education institutions (and the public resources to support them) exist for the elite upper classes, while too few exist for the masses. Because we fail to fully overcome the burden of historic exclusory and discriminatory racial practices in the education system, we have failed to fully utilize and develop our most valuable national resource: our human resource. In the end the total society will pay doubly.

Minority student access and retention should become integral parts of the overall education process rather than specialized programs that usually receive inadequate resources to be truly effective. Thus, the success of minority retention efforts should not be measured by the mere numbers of minority students being enrolled and graduated from college. But they should be measured by the structural changes in the institutions to accommodate the diversity of skills, cultural backgrounds, adeptness, and historical legacies that minorities bring to school with them. They should also be measured by the articulation and realization of the institutions' commitment to minority access and success at the institution.

Institutions across the country have developed and established specialized minority retention programs in recent years. At predominantly black institutions such programs are usually more integrated into the institution's regular institutional supportive services structures than at predominantly white institutions. Nevertheless, there are exceptions. At Kennesaw College just outside Atlanta, Georgia, for example, the president of the institution has mandated a campus-wide effort which involves each department separately and collectively in improving and being accountable for the recruitment and retention of minority students (Wilkerson, 1988). Likewise, the Boston University School of Medicine has developed an early acceptance program in conjunction with several predominantly black institutions whereby the minority students transfer to Boston University during their junior and senior years but receive their degrees from the black institution. This program helps to prepare them for admission to Boston's Medical School while helping them to become pre-adjusted to the social and academic climate of the university and community while still in undergraduate school (Culbert, 1988). Both of these programs have shown significant improvements in the access and retention of minority students at the institutions in only three or four years of duration. There are similar efforts underway at other institutions where serious commitments have been made to minority access and retention (Lang and Ford, 1988).

When we assess the role that academic institutions have played in the struggle for equality for minorities, we realize that they have not exemplified intellectual leadership, nor have they been role models for the rest of society. Rather, they have reflected the same prejudices and injustices that have been prominent among the unintellectual masses, despite their presumed harboring of information and their knowledge production. This truth is nowhere more substantiated than in their present handling of the minority access and retention issues. Equal access and retention of minority students are serious problems with very serious consequences for the welfare and tranquility of our nation. If our institutions of higher education cannot foster the production of knowledge needed to solve these problems, they can hardly be depended upon to solve the problems envisioned for the twenty-first century; problems that will be created by high technology and post-industrialization. We may need to urgently rethink our educational system's priorities.

REFERENCES

Astin, A.W. "Minorities in Higher Education." In *Equality Postponed: Continuing Barriers to Higher Education in the 1980's* (Adolphus, Stephens H., ed.). New York, NY: College Entrance Examination Board, 1984.

Atwell, R.H. *Minority Participation in Higher Education: We Need a New Momentum.* Washington, D.C.: American Council on Education, 1988.

Berry, M.F. "Blacks in Predominantly White Institutions of Higher Learning." In *The State of Black America* (Williams, James D., ed.). New York, NY: The National Urban League, 1983, pp. 295–318.

Brown, S.V. *Minorities in the Graduate Education Pipeline.* Princeton, NJ: Educational Testing Service, 1987.

Christoffel, P. "Minority Access and Retention: A Review." In *Research and Development Update.* New York, NY: The College Board, October, 1986.

Clewell, B.C. and Ficklen, M.S. *Improving Minority Retention in Higher Education: A Search for Effective Institutional Practices.* Princeton, NJ: Educational Testing Service, 1986.

Culbert, A. "Early Acceptance and Institutional Linkages in a Model Program of Recruitment, Retention, and Timely Graduation from Medical School." In *Black Student Retention in Higher Education* (Lang, Marvel and Ford, Clinita A., eds.). Springfield, IL: Charles C Thomas Publisher, 1988, pp. 13–22.

Evangelauf, D. "Tuition Rises 7 Percent, Outruns Inflation for 8th Straight Year." *The Chronicle of Higher Education.* Vol. 34, No. 48, (August 10, 1988), pp. 1 and 26.

Lang, M. "Black Student Retention at Black Colleges and Universities: Problems, Issues, and Alternatives," *The Western Journal of Black Studies,* Vol. 10, No. 2, 1986, pp. 48–54.

Lang, M. "The Black Student Retention Problem in Higher Education: Some Introductory Perspectives." In *Black Student Retention in Higher Education* (Lang, Marvel and Ford, Clinita A., eds.). Springfield, IL: Charles C Thomas, Publisher, 1988, pp. 3–12.

National Coalition of Advocates for Students (NCAS). *Barriers to Excellence: Our Children at Risk.* Boston, MA: January 1985.

Orfield, G. and Paul, F. "Declines in Minority Access: A Tale of Five Cities," *Educational Record,* (Fall 1987 – Winter 1988), pp. 57–62.

Thomas, G.E. *The Access and Success of Blacks and Hispanics in U.S. Graduate and Professional Education* (A working paper). National Research Council, Washington, D.C.: National Academy Press, 1986.

Tinto, V. "Dropout from Higher Education: A Theoretical Synthesis of Recent Research," *Review of Educational Research,* Vol. 45, 1975.

Turner, W.H. and Rosen, N.L. *Traditionally Black Institutions: A Profile and an Institutional Directory.* Washington, D.C.: National Center for Educational Statistics, 1979.

U.S. Bureau of the Census. *Statistical Abstract of the U.S., 1986* (106th Edition). Washington, D.C.: U.S. Government Printing Office, 1985.

U.S. Bureau of the Census. *Summary Characteristics of the Black Population for States and Selected Counties and Places: 1980.* Supplementary Report PC 80-51-21, Washington, D.C.: U.S. Government Printing Office, 1987.

U.S. Department of Education. *Digest of Education Statistics 1987.* Enter for Education Statistics, Washington, D.C.: U.S. Government Printing Office, 1987.

Wilkerson, D.W. "The Black Collegian Advisement Program at Kennesaw College: A Comprehensive Black Student Retention Model." In *Black Student Retention in Higher Education* (Lang, Marvel and Ford, Clinita A., eds.). Springfield, IL: Charles C Thomas, Publisher, 1988, pp. 35–41.

Chapter 8

ASSESSING COLLEGIATE OUTCOMES

Edward A. Morante

Introduction

A well-accepted notion, at least in theory, is the need to assess or evaluate what is being attempted. Many individuals periodically, and almost always informally, assess their behavior and how they are perceived by others. What did you think of that (performance)? How did I come across? What did so and so say about what I said (or did)? We use this as feedback in modifying and hopefully improving our performance or appearance.

Assessment is also carried out, of course, in more formal ways: applying for a job, for entrance into an institution, annual performance evaluation, tests and grades. What important text or theoretician does not recommend integrating evaluation into any program design? The reality that evaluation is too often a rare component of most programs is *not* a reason for concluding that evaluation is unimportant or extraneous.

One factor in avoiding assessment or evaluation is fear of what the results might show. It takes a certain strength of character and purpose to seek such feedback. For some, having evaluation data as an aid in decision making is counterproductive to the "freedom" to make decisions without such information. These individuals would prefer to act without regard to facts which might be used by others to judge the quality of their decisions.

Another reason in avoiding evaluation is the inherent difficulty of taking on extra responsibilities. It *is* more work! And when you consider the problems of differentiating between extraneous and relevant information, it is little wonder that some question whether the effort is worth undertaking.

Institutions frequently react much in the same way as individuals. Meaningful assessment takes commitment. When an institution needs to concern itself with other priorities like attracting sufficient students, seeking appropriate funding resources, or responding to the needs of alumni, assessment is frequently viewed as one more burden and not given a high priority. Of course, survival is more important both for individuals and institutions. But even when survival is not the issue, too many other concerns compete for attention. Something that is uncomfortable, like assessment, will rarely be a focus. Still other institutions are not merely seeking survival; they have *arrived.* They are successful. And, like individuals with supremely confident egos, these institutions perceived themselves as already being successful. Why, then, should they commit themselves to assessment?

The Need for Assessment

The National Commission on Excellence in Education in 1983 issued *A Nation At Risk* which decried the mediocrity of our nation's educational system. This report, more than any other in the past fifty years, stirred a national debate on how to improve our country's schools. A myriad of reports have followed, some further elaborating on the extent of the mediocrity, some offering suggestions on how to improve. It was not unexpected, therefore, to find similar reports and concerns about higher education.

Involvement in Learning, issued in 1984 by the National Institute of Education, called for increased focus on undergraduate teaching, learning, and accountability both in stating goals and standards and in determining how well these have been achieved. Numerous reports from a variety of sources (see reference list at the end of this chapter) have indicated a variety of concerns about the United States's higher education, including:

1. Many students come to our college ill-prepared to handle college-level work;
2. General education is often a chaotic distribution of political compromise;
3. Institutional missions and goals are frequently ill-defined and all-encompassing;
4. Too many students graduate without cultural literacy;
5. There is an overdependency on careerism;
6. Undergraduate teaching and student learning are too often given low priority; and
7. The setting of curriculum, standards, and grading are overly dependent on the individual faculty member and too closely related to the low proficiencies of students.

Assessment is needed to improve our efforts; it can identify our strengths and weaknesses and can serve as a basis for reform and renewal. Demonstrating problems is not the sole or even the most important rationale for assessment. Of course, no institution is perfect and it is unlikely that any institution can remain at its best without periodic renewal. Assessment can provide the information needed to better understand where renewal must take place. In addition, assessment can meet needs for both improvement and accountability. Indeed, assessment can lead to demonstrating success—even bragging about it. And, what is perhaps most exciting, faculty and administrators who have become engaged in assessment activities have had intellectually stimulating discussions over the meaning of higher education.

External Forces

Despite the potential for renewal and excitement, very few institutions have, of their own accord, chosen assessment as a high priority—beyond the internal process of grading students and evaluating faculty. And yet, can assessment be successful if both the objects of the assessment and the assessors are the same? The question is not whether self-assessment is helpful, even important, but whether it is sufficient.

Accreditation agencies have traditionally served the role of external evaluators. Periodically, institutions or specific departments or programs get geared up through a series of committees and, for a year or two, become feverish over writing a report for accreditation. Many times these activities raise important questions; fewer times are the questions answered. Too often, the report sits on a shelf collecting dust. Too often, the institution settles in with limited, if any, change, waiting for the next round of accreditation. Assessment needs to be ongoing; questions need to be answered; renewal needs to be institutionalized.

Some wonder whether the accreditation process itself needs reform. Except in the relatively few instances where an institution is near collapse, are the accrediting agencies or the study teams providing meaningful assessment? Are peer evaluations too geared to the status quo, too tied to being responsive to the requests of the institution under review to be objective? Several accrediting agencies have begun, at least in writing, to add outcomes assessment or a focus on results to their procedures. The federal government (see regulations) has attempted to add teeth to these endeavors. More time and experience is necessary to determine whether such requests for outcomes information is real or rhetoric.

In the meantime, states and their agents have begun to look at higher education. In this chapter, we will explore why states have become so interested, what several states have already done, and what role a state can play in assessing higher education. Included will be suggestions as to what should be included in a successful, comprehensive outcomes assessment program.

State Focus on Accountability

State government plays many roles in the lives of its citizens. Ensuring a quality education for each child is one of its preeminent responsibilities, more often than not built into its constitution. In higher education, too, the state has an obligation to ensure high quality and standards. While a state's constitution may not explicitly require the same assurance in higher education for each citizen as it does for elementary and secondary education, the need for oversight is clear including fiduciary and consumer protection.

This obligation for monitoring will vary among the different states and can take numerous forms. Granting a charter to operate, providing licensure and program approval, requiring periodic program review, and carrying out assessment are all appropriate forms of fulfilling the obligation to ensure quality. Of these various forms of overview and monitoring only outcomes assessment goes beyond examining the process and the structure and takes results into account. Looking at the structure, the input, the resources, the processes are all important but incomplete and insufficient. Quality control must examine the product, the results, the *outcomes* to be complete. States that do less are not fulfilling their role to their citizens—nor to the very colleges they are supposed to be monitoring.

In recent years, governors, state legislators, and coordinating boards have begun to focus on accountability in higher education. These state leaders have been the principal leaders in assessment activities in higher education. Despite claims about the need for a grass roots approach to assessment, there is to date no state where a majority of institutions have developed an outcome assessment program from the demands of faculty or staff, individually or organized, or which came from a groundswell of local institutions demanding assessment activities. While few would request a "top-down" approach to state government, it is clear that without state leadership little has been accomplished beyond the efforts of a relatively small number of isolated institutions. The current forces and customs of higher education make the probability of many institutions carrying out assessment on their own very unlikely.

Why have states become so interested? Several factors have played a role:

1. **Economic Competition.** Over the past decade there has been a widespread recognition of the role of education, including higher education in a competitive marketplace. A growing number of state leaders believe a state (or a country) will not be able to compete for the jobs of the future without a well-educated work force. Industry has joined in this effort as they scramble for trained and educated workers. It also makes good economic sense from industry's perspective to have the state focus on improving quality rather than increase the billions of dollars already spent by industry on education. Whether this recognition has come about by deductive reasoning based on strong evidence or because higher education has convinced many decision makers that they are capable of playing this role can be debated. Suffice to say that state leaders increasingly believe this and want to improve the quality of education received by its citizens.

2. **Changing Demographics.** The data is convincing (see Hodgkinson, 1987) that within a relatively short period of time the term "minorities" will need to be reconsidered. A combination of blacks, Hispanics, Asians, and immigrants will soon make for a majority in many states, especially in the public schools. In addition to ethical and moral reasons, our country can no longer afford, economically, politically, or socially, to preclude these traditionally underrepresented segments of our society from access to the opportunities of higher education. (In this regard, access is not merely entrance but quality as well. Indeed, access without quality is not access but chicanery in raising false expectations.)

In the past, our society could survive without active participation of "minorities," and jobs were available and success possible without higher education. The sheer numbers of individuals as well as the increasing level of skills required preclude this from continuing into the next century. Those traditionally left out must be brought in. There are not enough "non-minorities" to adequately fill the jobs that will be available. Our country will at best stagnate without actively including those left out in the past. The numbers alone will force participation or, like the Roman Empire, the "have-nots" will cause its destruction. States recognize their need for access to education including a college education.

3. **Funding Accountability.** Over the past twenty-five years, increasing

numbers and percentages of students have entered higher education. To meet these increasing demands many states have increased their budget allotments to higher education. New colleges, especially community colleges, have been created. Narrowly focused institutions, such as teacher education colleges, have become comprehensive colleges or universities. State-funded research universities have grown to meet increasing demands and expectations. Many states have recognized the importance of private institutions for education in their state and have provided increased funds for that sector. Finally, many states have increased financial aid appropriations to replace the significant decline in support from the federal government in more recent years. These funding increases have led to increasing attention on higher education, on how effectively the money is being spent, and on how effective the institutions are in providing a variety of services.

4. **Consumer Protection.** As the number and percentage of constituents attending higher education and the amount of money spent by students and their parents have both increased significantly, the number of individuals seeking protection and assistance from the state has also increased. State leaders who survive do not ignore such concerns.

5. **Reform.** Although the notion of reform can be traced throughout the history of education, the issuance of *A Nation At Risk* in 1983 dominates the current movement. Decrying the mediocrity of our educational system, this report and the many that followed have documented significant declines in standards, quality, and levels of aspiration. Not unexpectedly, a number of reports followed which focused on higher education, calling for reform in addressing concerns about underprepared students, general education, careerism, and so on.

Many state leaders, truly motivated by seeking improvements in education, frequently do not differentiate between K–12 education and higher education. And, of course, different forces in different states have and will lead to various responses.

Whatever the specifics, there appears to be a growing recognition that higher education is no longer merely a matter of individual choice by students and parents to improve their own personal life. Increasingly, the state is perceiving the need for higher education as a requirement for economic growth, for political and social stability, and for improvements in the quality of life. A desire for improving access and quality and a concern about appropriate use of funds combine with a dissatisfaction with a "trust me" attitude on the part of higher education and a lack of confidence in the traditional "old boy" school of accreditation. State leaders are increasingly looking for more appropriate forms of accountability, information that is understandable and useable. How institutions and specific states respond to such calls will greatly influence the direction, the amount of local control, and the success of accountability efforts. While accountability can mean different things, outcomes assessment offers the best method to provide meaningful data to state leaders.

What is Outcomes Assessment?

Outcomes assessment is *not* basic skills assessment; basic skills assessment should take place before students begin college-level courses. Outcomes assessment is *not* program review, although program review could include outcomes assessment. Program review is traditionally a focus on process and resources such as curriculum, facilities, and background of faculty. Most accreditation has been focused on program and institutional *process* and *facilities.*

Outcomes assessment is an evaluation of results, an examination of the products, an assessment of what happens with students or with programs or with institutions. Outcomes assessment, in fact any assessment of higher education, must include an examination of multiple variables. Reliance on one or two indicators opens the assessment to valid criticisms at best and invalid conclusions at worst. While any single indicator might be flawed, the combination of several key indicators enables construction of a powerful examination which can be useful in planning and decision making.

Reliance on the traditional admissions criteria tells little of the effectiveness of a collegiate institution. The mean SAT/ACT scores of entering freshmen will provide information about the quality of the *entering* student body as well as some indication of the competitiveness of the admission process at the institution. These data alone, however, will do little to inform as to how many students stay at the institution and receive a degree. Nor will they indicate what or how much students learn while studying at a particular college or university.

Similarly, the number of books in the library may impress prospective students and their parents but say little of the quality of the collection, much less how often the library is used by undergraduate students. The degrees of the faculty, while one important indicator of academic preparation of the faculty, say little of the quality of teaching or research at that institution. For example, if undergraduates are taught by graduate assistants in lecture halls containing hundreds of students, some of them watching on television, can we demonstrate how well students are learning based on the percentage of faculty doctorates?

This is not a treatise on the quality of American higher education but rather a brief rationale that outcomes assessment is necessary for appropriate understanding of what is happening in our colleges and universities. The historical methods, while frequently informative, are inadequate in determining the *results* of the efforts of colleges and universities.

State-Level Leadership

States have both a right and an obligation to assess outcomes. A principal role of the state is to determine budgets and to provide oversight over those expenditures. At what point does oversight, monitoring, and assessment become intrusion and therefore counterproductive? Like beauty being seen in the eye of the beholder, the line between appropriate oversight and intrusion is perceived differently depending upon which side of the line one is standing when making the judgment.

What is leadership is an equally perplexing question. Does leadership by the state mean careful monitoring of all expenditures and all decisions? On the other hand, does leadership imply complete confidence in an institution's appropriate use of funds (at least until some reason becomes evident for further investigation)?

While different state systems work in different ways, the absence of assessing outcomes in higher education is not only an absence of leadership but a failure to carry out the traditional roles of the state. These roles include ensuring appropriate use of funds; determining acceptable levels of achievement of goals; and protecting the broad interests of the citizens of the state. The level of monitoring, the amount of common definitions and assessment techniques, the length of time, and the freedom of self-assessment can all differ with judgment of state leaders, but the failure to assess outcomes of institutions can no longer be acceptable to appropriate state management. The state has an obligation in ensuring quality of services by monitoring the results or outcomes of its system of higher education. Resources, facilities, and reputation are no longer sufficient to ensure quality.

Unique Missions

In the United States, the concepts of autonomy and diversity are paramount in higher education and frequently used as examples of strength. Every institution of higher education in the country is unique. It has its own mission, faculty, student body, resources, etc. No institution is exactly like any other institution. Unfortunately, institutional differences are all too often used as excuses for avoiding external review, accountability, and ultimately improvement. In fact, much of higher education overlaps across a wide spectrum of colleges and universities. How would joint community college-senior college programs, articulation agreements, or transfer from one institution to another be possible without some commonalities? Indeed, could our country have a higher education system that met the needs of the country and its citizens without sharing at least some common goals?

Missions, goals, and objectives of American undergraduate institutions have sufficiently common features to be able to be defined and characterized as seeking many common goals including student learning. For example, which colleges or universities don't have a faculty or utilize faculty? Which institution doesn't care about its retention rates? About its students' ability to write or think critically? Or what happens to students after they graduate? While each institution might be described as having a unique combination of factors, each institution also has, to a greater or lesser extent, common areas of overlap with other institutions. It is these common areas of overlap that can be commonly assessed. It is these common indicators that should be included in an outcomes assessment program even when the definitions of the indicators are different. The state can play a leadership role in identifying or helping to identify which areas of an institution's efforts need to be assessed, which areas are common across institutions that all colleges and universities need to assess, and even which indicators can be commonly defined.

There is an important distinction that must be made between common areas to be assessed and indicators that can be commonly defined. For example, general education is a common area that all colleges and universities should include in their assessment activities. But the nature of general education is such that each faculty and institution must define for itself the components and emphasis it chooses to provide to its students. Thus, general education is a common area of assessment but one that allows an individual definition for each institution. ("Allows" rather than "requires" because institutions may choose to define general education in a sufficiently common way with other institutions to be able to use a nationally or state-developed common assessment instrument.)

There are, however, some indicators (e.g. retention) that can and should be defined commonly across institutions in a state system or even nationally. The current situation of multiple definitions (the word "multiple" doesn't adequately describe the current chaotic system of definitions) of an indicator like retention provides little understanding of either the term or the data. A knowledgeable and reasonable interpretation of current data on higher education, including retention, cannot be made without asking many questions regarding definition, cohort, time sequence, population, and so on. A cynic might conclude that the current system of keeping multiple definitions for all indicators is intended to preclude meaningful interpretation. Lack of coherence enables "freedom of choice" in making multiple interpretations. Lack of commonality also allows game playing rather than accountability or improvement.

This does not mean to imply that any definition need be simplistic or easily agreed upon. A common definition must include sufficient flexibility to account for the wide variations in the goals of higher education. Not every student who comes to an institution seeks a degree, so a definition of retention must be devised at least according to the initial intent of the student. But this does not preclude a definition of retention for a particular group such as "first-time, full-time, degree-seeking students." While specific refinements can always be made, the point is that common definitions can be reached. (It should *not* be construed that common definitions should lead to common comparisons. Private and public institutions, two-year and four-year institutions, and open access versus restricted research institutions, among others, have sufficiently different missions that such comparison would be fraught with misinterpretations. But this doesn't preclude comparisons among members of a sector of institutions such as community colleges or research universities, assuming comparable mission and reasonably similar student bodies.)

This process of having institutions select areas of assessment according to mission and priorities as well as identifying common areas for assessment, leaving most definitions of indicators to the local institution, allows for meaningful assessment without interfering with the diversity of our higher educational system. The balance between common definitions, common areas of assessment, local control, and diversity of programs and processes is essential for a strong higher education system within a reasonable level of accountability. Indeed, this reasonable balance, rather than the acceptance of "total uniqueness," enables a state to provide increased support and assistance for institutional improvement. How would an institution, much less a state agency, know how well it was performing if no comparisons could be made on any indicator? Comparisons need to be made either with similar institutions or against some standard; data in isolation is meaningless. The essence of an effective state program of assessment is to understand and use an appropriate balance between commonality and diversity.

Important Indicators in Outcomes Assessment

The following areas have been the focus of statewide and institutional assessment efforts.

A. Student Learning

The most important outcome of undergraduate education is student learning. It is not surprising, therefore, to conclude that the heart of any outcomes assessment program in higher education must be an evaluation of what and how well students learn. While other indicators (the kinds of students enrolling, their beginning strengths, how many stay and graduate, what happens to them after they leave an institution) are all important, student learning must be the prime focus for an outcomes assessment effort.

Assessment of student learning has been ongoing for as long as higher education has been in existence. Grades, awarding degrees, course and department tests, licensure and other standardized tests, portfolio analysis, and external examiners are all methods used by colleges and universities to assess student learning. Some of these methods are direct measures and some are indirect.

Retention rates, student satisfaction, graduation rates, and alumni survey are all indirect measures of student learning. The assumption is made that if you stay in college or get a degree or get a job, then the student has learned at a certain level. It seems that these are reasonable assumptions that something has been learned or accomplished, but what or how much is rather tenuous to conclude. Indeed, the meaning or value of receiving a degree in terms of student learning is one of the areas now being questioned by government and industry leaders.

Another indirect measure of student learning is course grades. Many in higher education and out assume that the reception of a high grade translates into learning. But how much is learned and on what standard? Different institutions, of course, have different grading patterns and standards but so do different departments at a college. Different faculty members in a department even when teaching the same course have different grading standards. How can anyone know how much or what a student has learned by such a system?

Not only are comparisons impossible, but grades are not necessarily based on proficiency or what is learned. Students who miss assignments, papers, classes, or tests often receive lower grades regardless of their proficiency at the end of the course. In addition, marking on the curve is widespread which means that many grades are awarded based on the skills and knowledge of the students *in that section* of a course (occasionally across multiple sections of a course). Thus, grading is frequently based on very local group norms, not on some external or predetermined standard of proficiency or knowledge.

While a grade point average (or GPA) frequently helps to adjust for some idiosyncratic differences in course grades, the standards for an institution as a whole are not easily assessed and the adjustments made by GPA need not be sufficient to handle the various patterns of individual faculty. In addition, GPA, based as it is on grading in individual courses, does not assure *integration of knowledge* across courses. How many students erroneously conclude that at the conclusion of a particular course or area of learning, knowledge or proficiency in that course is no longer needed and can therefore be forgotten? How much is forgotten anyway based on the content or the methodology used to teach the course? Reception of a degree needs to translate into something more than successfully completing a series of courses.

Examples of direct assessment of student learning include: departmental and comprehensive exams, senior thesis, project, or portfolio analysis, and standardized tests used to receive a license or certification. (While the latter may not be sufficient to assess what faculty members want their students to learn at any particular institution, these kinds of tests are *direct* measures of student learning.)

While indirect indicators of student learning help to understand the effectiveness of programs/institutions, an outcomes assessment program which does not include direct assessment of student learning cannot be an effective program. The key aspects of student learning include:

1. General Education

This includes those aspects of a college education, whether at a two-year or four-year institution, which all students are expected to learn as decided by the faculty and the institution. The assessment should focus on the outcomes of this general education program—what common knowledge and proficiency should students gain at a particular institution.

General education can be divided between general intellectual skills (i.e. critical thinking, problem solving, quantitative reasoning, and speaking and writing) and content. Ideally, the general intellectual skills build upon basic skills, are embedded in all or nearly all courses including courses in the major, and continue to be developed throughout life. Indeed, it is these general intellectual skills that can probably best be described as those aspects of general education most likely to be expected of students across all institutions of higher education regardless of institution, major, or program.

General education also includes content which is much more idiosyncratic to an institution, the *what* that all students should learn as decided by the institution. Of course, the general intellectual skills and the content aspects of general education need to be integrated within courses and within an agreed-upon curriculum (including principal areas and electives).

In reality, at many institutions, the general education curriculum has been determined long ago by a set of criteria modified over time by concerns about faculty lines, student enrollment, and similar internal political-economic criteria. On many campuses this has led to a free-wheeling smorgasbord of available courses chosen by students more on the basis of strengthening strengths and preconceived interests and avoiding perceived weaknesses. The assessment of general education can serve as a rationale for examining current programs and patterns, reviewing and where necessary revising the goals and objectives of general education at that institution. Given this process, essential to defining and assessing outcomes, the determination of how well students achieve the desired outcomes becomes almost secondary. Analysis of the results, especially over time, can be used by faculty to modify curriculum, policies, and course content and methodology.

2. The Major

The major or area of specialization is in a number of ways similar to general education, in that it is an essential component of higher education and consequently outcomes assessment. The outcomes of a particular program or major are idiosyncratic not only to an institution but to a particular department within an institution. Too often, the specific courses taught, required or not, are determined by the interests and expertise of individual faculty members, at any particular time. In an attempt to reach harmony and consensus, tenured faculty, especially full professors in the department, often teach what they want, both as to the courses and as to the specific content of those courses. While much can be said for flexibility and freedom of choice, does this lead to the best possible educational system? Does this freedom overly rely on the maturity, self-assessment, and careful planning of the student? Should there be some common theme or thread of what a major ought to be at least within a discipline, or a program/department?

Outcomes assessment provides the spur to examine these questions. What do we as a faculty in this department expect students to know, expect students to have proficiency in before we award that student a degree? Further, how well are we helping our students achieve what we have agreed they should know or have proficiency in?

3. Student Personal Development

Students learn outside the classroom and they learn more than facts or the ability to think. They develop as human beings, learning about themselves and others, how to relate to a variety of people, develop values and attitudes, construct a philosophy of life, make career choices, and become involved in a wide variety of activities. Clearly, much of this happens despite a college education and well after a person leaves an institution. But what is also clear is that a college or university can and does impact a student's life. While the goals may change from institution to institution, the impact is there. How effectively are goals achieved? What is the impact of an institution on the personal development of its students? Residence life; cultural, social, athletic, and career activities; and campus environment all play significant roles in the lives of students. Enrollment, retention, and student learning and development are all impacted by these campus activities. Colleges and universities need to assess their effectiveness in these areas.

B. Institutional Effectiveness

The direct assessment of student learning, what and how well students learn, must be seen in the context of the kinds of students attending, remaining, and graduating from an institution, as well as what happens to them afterwards. While these indicators are not sufficient to assess an institution's effectiveness in educating its students, they are necessary for understanding how many and what kinds of students have been educated.

For example, a college or university can have very restrictive admissions standards or a very low rate of retention so that an assessment of those students who remain may not accurately reflect either what those students have learned (compared to what they brought with them) or how effective an institution is in the broader sense of educating citizens. In a comprehensive assessment program, each of the following indicators should be included:

1. Access

What kinds of students are recruited, admitted, and enrolled? What are the demographics, backgrounds, proficiencies, and intents of the entering students? Outcomes can only be understood in the context of the types of students an institution has enrolled and what they bring to the institution.

Access is especially important for public higher education and crucial for open-access institutions. How well does the student body match the population served by the institution for relevant demographic subgroups? If a college or university maintains a very selective admissions policy, how well is that institution meeting the needs of its constituency or the goals of the state? Different institutions have differing responses to these questions, depending upon their mission.

2. Retention and Completion Rates

How many students stay in college and graduate have become increasingly important questions for most colleges and universities. Not only do these factors help pay the bills, but they are increasingly seen as measures of effectiveness, used both to recruit new students and to demonstrate a successful program or institution. For some, this is a change in tradition, since it has been argued in the past that a high attrition rate is a standard of high quality. This position, however, places most of the burden on students to perform. An institution shares heavily in the performance of its students through quality teaching, adequate support services, and a campus climate conducive to student learning and development.

On the other hand, an institution which admits everyone who applies, retains all students, and awards a degree to everyone who enrolled will probably have a difficult time maintaining a reputation for high standards of student learning. But is this appropriate? Why can't an institution have as a goal the successful achievement of a degree by each student it admits, especially if it can be shown that each degree recipient has achieved an acceptable level of proficiency? In fact, the combination of providing access, retaining students and demonstrating directly and indirectly that students are learning makes for a powerful demonstration of institutional effectiveness.

3. Post-Collegiate Activities

What happens to students after they leave (not only graduate) can provide invaluable information about the effectiveness of an institution. Further education, career choice and success, and satisfaction with the institution can give insights for improvement in programs and services.

C. Faculty Activities

Almost every college and university has a faculty who are generally expected to serve four broad types of activities: teaching, research, community services, and services to the institution such as advising and participation in committee work. Outcomes assessment programs which focus on the effectiveness of an institution should also include components which examine the impact of faculty.

D. Impact on Community

The very existence of an institution in a community has an impact on that part of society. Thus, a comprehensive outcomes assessment program should include an examination of the impact of an institution as a whole on its local community and the society at large. Some of these are intended according to the mission of that institution; examples include pre-college courses, cultural and athletic events, continuing-education courses and extension services, and counseling and health services. Some impacts occur without being planned and, although they cannot easily be altered, need to be understood for planning and decision making; examples in this area include economic impact, housing, property values, and taxes. Finally, some impacts are neither planned nor wanted but affect a community: increased fire and police protection, transportation, congestion, noise, and so on.

Understanding the kinds of impacts on a local community can be important in improving an institution, since the quality of life on both the campus and in the surrounding community are frequently interrelated and dependent upon decisions made by an institution. The effectiveness of an institution in its broadest sense is frequently impacted by these decisions.

Implementing a State Effort

There is no way to implement a state role in outcomes assessment. Much depends on the forces within each state including the ability and willingness of state leaders to play a leadership role. It is unlikely that a majority, much less all, of the institutions in a state will place outcomes assessment as a priority without strong intervention and leadership by the state. This is not to condone in any way a top-down autocratic approach which is likely to be short-lived at best and counterproductive at worst. There are, however, several factors that states have used to increase the probability of institutions undertaking meaningful outcomes assessment programs. These include:

1. **Collaboration.** Probably the best method of producing an effective program and to encourage commitment and institutionalization is to work collaboratively with a broad range of representatives. This encourages more cooperation and involvement and increases the likelihood of creating a workable professional system. State leaders may set the parameters, but they do not have all the ideas nor the answers to all problems.

Collaboration means active participation in statewide assessment planning by representatives of the colleges and universities. Simple, occasional review creates a showcase of periodic advisory meetings but rarely leads either to commitment or to the construction of the best possible system.

In a meaningful collaborative model, participants are asked to understand the concerns and interests of their constituents and institutions but to "vote their conscience." Participants do not represent some group in the traditional sense but rather reflect their group's questions and ideas. They are able to largely set aside local conflicts for the common good. They vote for the best possible system, not necessarily according to directions from back home. Thus, care is taken in selecting participants to a statewide committee or task force who can contribute expertise, understanding of local and state concerns, an open-mindedness to the ideas of others, and a willingness to vote for the common good. To do otherwise increases the probability of not reaching consensus, multiple minority reports, or agreement on the lowest common denominator of self-interest.

2. **Building Upon Existing Systems.** The construction of effective state-wide systems takes advantage of existing statewide structures and procedures wherever feasible and builds upon the activities in place on the various campuses. For example, outcomes assessment components are added to degree program review processes and time lines already in place. Similarly, assessment programs make use of ongoing regional and specialized accreditation activities. In this way new assessment activities can be more systematic and can encourage reorganization and consolidation if necessary to fill in the gaps between existing efforts.

3. **Allow Time.** Probably the greatest thing that is feared by most people is change itself—regardless of what the change is. Effective assessment efforts have recognized this while not giving in to it. They have allowed sufficient time for change to take place (getting started and organized, venting of feelings, discussing and debating, collecting information, revising, piloting, sampling, and so on). They have used calendars and time lines to provide balance. They have, of course, also avoided open-endedness which might encourage delay and stonewalling in the hope that this change or demand will go away.

Perseverance and Patience. These go together and are essential in producing the kinds of assessment programs and the types of changes hoped for. A "quick and dirty" program is usually exactly that, producing little or no long-range improvements. State leaders need to have the patience to lead and to allow institutional change; commitment and involvement takes much longer than does mere compliance. In this regard, both state and local leaders need to make a commitment for the long-term; perseverance over the long run is essential. Frequent changes, short-term decision making, stops and starts, inadequate support and leadership give inappropriate messages. They have avoided the trap of following unreasonably short time lines which might have been set to meet the political needs of state leaders and that might have lead to simplistic solutions and compliance rather than careful deliberation. With a view of change as being systemic and long-lasting, they have taken the time to do it right (with, of course, a balanced wariness about procrastination).

4. **Provide Help.** Outcomes assessment does not need huge sums of new money. When an institution establishes outcomes assessment as a high priority, funding sources are found. Examples include: recharging existing committees; reassigning existing staff; providing for released time for key faculty leaders; using staff development funds by tying

assessment to the teaching/learning process; seeking grants, and additional funding from both state and local sources; sharing information and work load with other institutions; using sampling procedures and multi-year time lines; building on existing assessment, review, and accreditation processes rather than creating entirely new systems, programs, or committees; and calling upon the state to provide consultation and technical assistance. Still, assessment does take some additional resources, mostly people and some money. The provision of additional state funding to aid institutions to begin and to strengthen assessment has been an essential element. This funding needs to be long term and as much a part of the regular budget base as the state wants assessment to be a regular part of the institution.

In addition to direct funding, some states provide leadership in coordinating activities, hiring consultants for multiple institutional use; creating manuals, data bases, and information; encouraging sharing of information; organizing workshops, seminars, teleconferences, newsletters, and similar information-producing activities; and training staff to become consultants and technical advisors to the state's institutions.

State Models

Four states, Florida, Tennessee, Virginia, and New Jersey, provide different models of statewide assessment activities. All four can be characterized by leadership from a central source, although the amounts of involvement with common assessment indicators and definitions varies, as does control from local institutions. Florida's model can best be described as focused on a sophomore-level standardized test of basic skills that students must successfully complete to achieve an associate degree or to continue on to the junior year. In Tennessee, the assessment effort centers on a budget enhancement program which allows institutions to earn extra funds when achieving certain prescribed levels of improvement. Virginia has called for assessment plans at each of its public institutions and is relying, with some central oversight, on local initiatives to assess the outcomes of each college and university. The outcomes assessment effort in New Jersey is probably the most complex and comprehensive in the country, combining local initiatives with commonly defined indicators including a common statewide assessment of general intellectual skills. Each of these programs are now described in more detail.

Florida

In the late 1970s, political and educational leaders were expressing concern about the proficiencies of students in college and especially those leaving two-year colleges, many of whom were transferring to four-year institutions. Florida decided to create a competency testing program similar to that put into effect for high school graduation. As part of a broader program (called the "Gordon rule" where students are required to take a minimal number of college math and English courses and to write at least 24,000 words in the first two years of college), all students in public institutions (those receiving financial aid at independent colleges are included as well) must pass a test to receive an associate degree or enter the third year of a four-year college or university. This test, called the College Level Academic Skills Test (CLAST), measures reading, writing and mathematics. The test was first administered in 1982, with students first required to pass in 1984. Standards were set to be fully in place by 1989, but, because of concerns about high numbers of students not passing, especially among minority group members, the standards were being phased in. In the mid-1980s, Florida added a basic skills testing component for entering freshmen.

Higher education institutions have reacted in a variety of ways in Florida. All of them have added math and English courses to the curriculum; writing across the curriculum is common, and there has been a significant increase in focus on reading, writing, and mathematics. Many colleges have begun courses and other efforts to help students to pass the CLAST. A number of people have expressed concern about the numbers of students, especially minority students, who are predicted to fail the CLAST if the standards are fully implemented.

Presently, only Georgia has a similar "gateway" or "rising-junior" testing program which requires students to pass a test before continuing their education. Texas is scheduled to join this group in 1989.

Tennessee

The program in Tennessee has been characterized as an incentive-funding assessment program. Begun in the early 1980s, it was designed to improve the quality of higher education by providing opportunity to receive funding additional to the normal formula budget process if certain program and process improvements were made. A structured system including a manual was created which described the kinds of activities, efforts, and accomplishments that were needed to earn additional dollars. During the first five years (1981–1986), the emphasis was on achieving program accreditation, setting up assessment efforts, and testing students. Tennessee revised the program, issued a new manual, and required higher standards and more emphasis on results and improvement of results. For example, the ACT–COMP (a nationally standardized test of general education) was merely required of graduating students in the first phase while achievement of certain scores and increases in scores are now required if additional funding is to be earned.

Institutions across Tennessee have received millions of additional dollars to their formula funding by carrying out a broad series of behaviors and programs. The University of Tennessee at Knoxville has played a leadership role, both in its state and nationally, in developing a comprehensive assessment effort.

More recently, some concerns have arisen about the implementation of the additional funding. These concerns have centered around interpretation of the regulations and questions about the fair use of data and statistics.

New Jersey

In its College Outcomes Evaluation Program (COEP), New Jersey has probably the broadest assessment program of any state in the country. Created by its Board of Higher Education in 1985, COEP is a program of improvement and accountability. It uses a broad-based collaborative model of decision making with a balance between locally defined and assessed indicators and those defined centrally. With a goal of having outcomes assessment become institutionalized at each public college and university, with independent colleges voluntarily incorporating parts of the program, some additional seed money has been provided either directly or through grants.

COEP focuses on the following areas of each higher education institution: student learning and development, faculty activities of research, scholarship, and creative expression, and institutional impact on a community. In student learning, institutions need to define their own goals in general education, all majors or areas of concentration (phased in at 20% per year on a five-year cycle), and personal development of students by June 1989. A year later, assessment plans must be formulated and then the results need to be reported by September 1991. In addition, through a Student Unit Record Enrollment (SURE) System located in the Department of Higher Education, various cohorts of students will be followed to study retention and program completion rates, grades, credits completed, and licensure/certification exam results.

An important component of assessing student learning is the development of a statewide test of general intellectual skills, the ability to gather, analyze and present information. These are the skills that faculty expect to be learned by all students at all institutions. An attempt is being made to develop an assessment instrument based on extended tasks rather than on multiple-choice questions.

In assessing the impact of faculty activities in research, scholarship, and creative expression, COEP is attempting to look beyond the traditional methods of counting the number of publications, citations, and research grants and to examine the *outcomes* of various faculty activities.

The final area covered by COEP is assessing the impact of an institution on society or a community in such areas as: access (to courses and services), economic impact, human resource development (meeting the labor needs of industry and government), and the post-collegiate activities of former students, as well as those areas defined locally by an institution as part of its mission.

In coming years, it is expected that institutional profiles will be developed for each college and university describing the kinds of students who enter and leave, what and how well they learn, what happens to them after leaving, and the impact of its faculty activities as well as the impact of the institution as a whole. Comparisons will be made with students entering and graduating, with institutional changes over time, and with similar institutions where feasible and reasonable.

Virginia

Virginia began its statewide assessment effort following the passage of legislation. While assessment at each public institution is mandated, the characteristics of that assessment effort has been left up to the local campus to define. Each college and university was asked to submit assessment plans by June 1988. These were reviewed by the staff of the state's higher education coordinating board with the help of out-of-state consultants. All of the institutions in Virginia submitted plans and most were accepted with varying degrees of suggested modifications. Several statewide conferences and workshops have been sponsored by the state and varying amounts of state funds have been allocated to pilot projects at several conferences. The largest allocation was given to James Madison University to serve as a model for other institutions in Virginia.

All of the institutions of higher education in the state are currently implementing their local assessment plans. Virtually all of the effort has concentrated on assessment of student learning. Among the community colleges, the assessment plans have focused on basic skills, general education, and post-collegiate follow-up including data on career placement and alumni surveys. At the four-year colleges, focus has been centered on general education and the major. There are currently no plans in Virginia for any common statewide assessment or testing, nor any common definitions or indicators.

Final Remarks

Outcomes assessment in higher education is a relatively new but rapidly growing phenomena. While a small handful of institutions have embraced assessment activities of their own accord, most of the impetus has derived from state leadership. A combination of factors including economic competition, changing demographics, and needs for accountability have led state leaders to call for improved results from higher education. These changing conditions are also related to a growing awareness that quality in higher education is a necessity for survival and growth of a state and not merely an individual's choice for self-improvement.

These factors offer important opportunities for higher education but also contain some possible risks. Stonewalling or providing persistent resistance on the part of higher education may succeed in weathering what some perceive as a passing fad. The risk is that accountability is not passing but growing, and state leaders may take increasing interest in monitoring higher education out of necessity and lack of trust. This course increases the probability of inappropriate state interference, enlarged bureaucracy, and loss of diversity and autonomy.

On the other hand, an institution that plays a proactive role in state efforts will increase the probability of having an impact on state initiatives. As state leaders formulate plans, cooperating institutions have more chances to set the model, the tone, and the details than do those perceived as difficult to relate to. This cooperative course tends to increase support and trust with state leaders that institutions are serious about accountability and improvement. In turn, this trust translates into greater flexibility in constructing a sound professional system that maintains and strengthens autonomy and diversity while meeting the accountability needs of the state.

Including assessment as a priority at a local institution has implications, of course, beyond the needs of the state. As one dean reported at a state meeting, "We see assessment as a chance to combine renewal, strategic planning, faculty development, reform, and accountability all in the same program of activities." This attitude leads to involvement, commitment, and institutionalization. Assessment is not seen as meeting state reporting questions nor as a giant research project nor as a report to be placed on a shelf, but rather assessment can become an integral part of the teaching and learning that takes place on a campus. The results can be used systematically to determine goals and achievement of goals. Indeed, the level of integration between assessment efforts and teaching and learning is directly related to the level of usefulness of outcomes assessment. This should be the real goal of outcomes assessment, both at the state level and at each institution.

Chapter 9

EMPOWERING EDUCATION THROUGH PARTNERSHIPS

Benjamin D. Stickney

Introduction

As education has assumed a preeminent position on the nation's political agenda, one has increasingly heard the word "partnerships" employed as a description of some form of collaboration between the schools and other societal institutions. Used traditionally in reference to fostering the critical linkage between home and the school, "partnerships" in recent years has come to label the relationships between the business community and education and the cooperative endeavors between higher education and the K–12 grade levels. In addressing the partnerships phenomenon, this chapter will establish a rationale for partnerships, review various partnership activities and discuss the policy implications of educational collaboratives.

THE RATIONALE FOR PARTNERSHIPS

If there is a common denominator to the recent educational reform movement, it is that schooling should make significant improvement in increasing the scholastic performance of pupils. Whether one entitles it "back to basics," "educational excellence" or "cultural literacy," the dominant theme of the 1980s reform initiative is unmistakenly achievement oriented. According to most reformers, the schools have done a poor to mediocre job teaching children fundamental academic knowledge and should change their means of delivering educational services. Among the reform recommendations has been increasing graduation requirements, strengthening the core curricula, lengthening the school year, improving teacher training and copying the Japanese. With the exception of increasing the number of school days, numerous states and innumerable school districts have adopted these and many other recommendations associated with the improvement of achievement by the strengthening of standards. Laurence Marcus, in this volume, chronicles many of the reform initiatives that have taken place "Far From The Banks of The Potomac."

Paralleling the changes in the schools has been a rather dramatic increase in partnerships, principally between the schools and higher education and the schools and business. Traditionally, the reasoning behind the establishment of educational partnerships has involved such endeavors as collaborating on research, the receipt of foundation grants and the training of school district personnel. These and other components of the rationale will be addressed later in this section. However, given the growing concern with the strengthening of America by scholastically reforming the schools, the primary focus in this chapter is on the foundation for partnerships as it relates directly to improving the academic performance of pupils.

The Schools and Academic Achievement

School reformers have based much of their assumptions about the relationship of schooling to achievement by their reading of the effective schools' research. Although quantitative surveys from the mid-sixties and early seventies by Coleman (1966) and Jencks (1972) found that educational processes had little to do with variations in pupil achievement, studies generating from the mid to late 1970s provided the impetus for a rejuvenated acknowledgment of the influence of schooling. Collectively, these investigations have found that such variables as a school's commitment to establishing high academic standards, its employment of a principal as an instructional leader, its constitution of a caring and orderly atmosphere, and its housing of teachers who create high academic engagement and structured lessons have a good deal to do with improving pupil performance (Rutter et al., 1979; Edmonds, 1979; Rutter, 1983; Rosenshine, 1986; Berliner, 1987). Unfolding as a climate providing greater opportunity for scholastic learning, Denham and Lieberman (1980) and Walberg and Shanahan (1983) have found that at both the elementary and secondary levels academic learning time or quantity of academics has a relatively strong relationship with pupil achievement.

Given the relationship between an academically purposeful educational climate and student achievement, the reformers' call for greater attention to time on task (i.e. more requirements in science and math) and the promotion of higher expectations for pupils (i.e. stronger standards) appear to be empirically sound recommendations. There is also some data suggesting that the reform movement school initiatives may be paying dividends by contributing to the improvement in pupil achievement in many states (U.S. Department of Education, 1989). But there has also been, during the 1980s, a growing feeling that the recommendations of the many "mediocrity" reports are too narrowly focused by their ignoring such allegedly needed institutional changes as fundamental alterations in school structure. Moreover, there has been some acknowledgment that most reform recommendations are targeted at simply changing the schools and that the educational enterprise needs to extend its base. In recognition of the assumption that the schools need to establish partnerships to broaden their influence, John Goodlad (1983), in the concluding chapter of *A Place Called School*, sounds the following warning:

> To continue with the myth that schools alone can provide the education we need is to assure their continued insularity and probably their ultimate irrelevance. This need not be the scenario we follow.

A scenario Goodlad advises is one that promotes our "develop[ing] an understanding of education as a community-wide rather than only a school based activity." Moreover, the contention that reformed schooling by itself can contribute to the necessary increases in educational attainment is not supported by most empirical inquiry which has attempted to measure school effects. Indeed, the research from Coleman's 1966 survey to the present has found little evidence that schooling can completely compensate for the totality of environmental condition. Released shortly after Coleman, the Plowden Report (Peaker, 1967), an English study of the effects of the environment and schooling on achievement, found out-of-school factors more related to learning than in-school factors. In addition, a review of 28 schools input-output survey by Bridge, Judd and Moock (1979) found socioeconomic status, rather than schooling, the significant achievement indicator.

Depending on the kind of analysis employed, more recent studies have reached different conclusions on the effects of schooling, but even the most optimistic acknowledge the important role of family and socioeconomic status. For example, Coleman is now very much aware that his earlier findings underestimate the powers of schooling, an acknowledgment that goes beyond his 1981 report on the alleged potency of private schools (Coleman, 1982). It also involves his contention that, at least in some Third-World nations, schooling processes have a *greater* effect on achievement than do socioeconomic factors (Coleman, 1985). This finding was reiterated by Walberg and Shanahan (1983), who found that among high school seniors the quantity of instruction (completion of academic courses such as English, mathematics, history, science and foreign language) had a slightly higher correlation with achievement than did home environment. However, the important words here are "greater" and "slightly higher" regarding schooling effects, leaving considerable room for the significance of out-of-school factors. Sociocultural conditions may have an even greater effect on younger students. In an analysis which includes elementary schools, Jencks (1972) concludes that only approximately 15 percent of the total variance in pupil achievement can be explained by differences in schooling processes. Combining Jencks's findings with an analysis of sixth grade achievement in 405 California schools, Rowan, Bossert and Dwyer (1983) estimate that "school level properties" explain only 4.5 percent of the variance in individual pupil achievement.

It is important to recognize that surveys like Jencks's and like Rowan, Bossert and Dwyer's report only what schools *are* doing, not what they are *capable* of accomplishing. Nevertheless, it can be argued that the influence of schools is likely to be strengthened if they develop well-formulated partnerships with other educational entities and with other institutions. Goodlad has devoted considerable attention to cultivating partnerships between the schools and higher education. Acknowledging that the schools have not successfully traveled alone, many institutions of business have also initiated collaborations with education.

Given the paucity of empirical data on the scholastic benefits of specifically school-university and business partnerships, the rationale for these alliances remain largely theoretical. However, within the effective schools research, there are considerable data in support of coordinating components *within* schools and of linking the schools with the community of parents. One of the most comprehensive and scholarly reviews of the effective schools' research is a publication by Purkey and Smith (1983). In addition to identifying such organizational and process variables as strong principal leadership and an overall climate of academic purposefulness, Purkey and Smith identify the components of staff stability (which includes the fostering of good interpersonal relationships and shared goals of school improvement), collaborative planning and collegiality as constituting organizational and process variables evident in effective schools. In addition, parent involvement (involving an awareness of school goals, student responsibility, homework assignments and the means to reinforce such expectations) comprises an important component of the Purkey and Smith composite. Teacher collegiality in support of pupil achievement is also a principal component of the Herbert Walberg (1986) prepared U.S. Department of Education report, *What Works: Research About Teaching and Learning.* In addition, a recent U.S. Department of Education review of exemplary Chapter 1 programs has identified coordination of effort and parent involvement as variables correlating with achievement effectiveness (U.S. Department of Education, 1988).

Economic Security and Competitiveness

Aiding and abetting the theoretical and empirical rationale for educational collaboration are profound national security concerns, particularly as they relate to work force training and economic competitiveness. A 1987 meeting of thirty-seven college and university presidents and chancellors provides testimony to this national attention (Kennedy, 1987). Gathering at the Spring Hill Conference Center near Minneapolis, the representatives of higher education met "to discuss how we might help in the improvement of our nation's schools." In a letter mailed to higher education presidents and chancellors throughout the country, Stanford University president Donald Kennedy, on behalf of the thirty-seven meeting participants, appealed for a national commitment to the fostering of school-university partnerships.

> We must all think more deeply about the manifold connections between our institutions and the schools, and act together as persistent and passionate advocates for reform. . . . We say this because our future as a nation depends more critically than ever before upon the quality of what and how we teach our children.

According to the thirty-seven presidents and chancellors, higher education must go "beyond speaking out *about* issues facing the schools, we must make a new commitment to working *with* schools on many issues of mutual interest." Accordingly, the Spring Hill meeting called for the establishment of "partnerships," which would be based on the recognition "that we are engaged in a common profession—the profession of teaching." Interestingly, this composite—several of whom represented major research universities such as Stanford and the State University of New York—stated that "Teaching is the first business of our universities, just as it is the first business of the primary and secondary schools across the country." Therefore, the "recognition of that deep community of profession should . . . underlie all our efforts." Included in this collaborative focusing on teaching is a commitment to "enhance teaching as a career, to improve teacher preparation," to possibly appoint " 'master teachers' " to adjunct university positions and to publish inventories of existing partnership activities.

If business has not embraced alliances with education to strengthen the national interest, there is strong evidence suggesting that the increasing attention business is paying education has much to do with protecting business interest. In order to be both internationally and nationally competitive, business needs better educational workers. This need has intensified in the 1980s, partly due to the decline in the number of eligible employees. Principally caused by the termination of the baby boom, the number of workers annually entering the labor force decreased from approximately 2.5 million in the 1970s to an estimated 1.5 million in the late 1980s. Given the smaller labor pool and the fact that a larger percentage of workers are coming from historically underachieving populations, business is now more inclined to develop partnerships with schools to aid and abet the training of prospective employees (Spring, 1984). Accordingly, this new interest has included business working with schools to lower dropout rates and improve the education of low-income and minority children. Indeed, in this volume House Education and Labor Committee counsel Jack Jennings has observed that 1987 marked the first time in congressional history that representatives from business testified in favor of greater funding for federal aid to education.

In the minds of many business people, education's failure to properly educate the work force has forced business to assume costly educational training of ill-prepared employers. David Kearns (1988), chief executive officer of the Xerox Corporation, states the dilemma bluntly:

> If current demographic trends continue, American business will have to hire a million new workers a year who can't read, write or count. Teaching them how—and absorbing the lost productivity while they are learning—will cost industry $25 billion a year for as long as it takes. And nobody I know can say how long that will be. Teaching new workers basic skills is doing the schools' product recall work for them. And frankly, I resent it.

Steve Schuck (1989), a Colorado land developer and former gubernatorial candidate, echoes this theme by chastising the "atrocity" that is American education's teaching of the work force's required skills. In response, Schuck has initiated an "Action Tank" to generate demonstration "models to improve the delivery of educational services." Privately funded, this proactive think tank is given virtually free reign to experiment with structural change." States Schuck,

> Our objective is not to tinker marginally with education but to initiate fundamental change. Education must be driven by the consumer, not the provider, and by directing marketplace courses into the delivery system. It is critical that we improve our work force, but the old system is antiquated and unproductive. In partnership with business, education can substantially improve its effectiveness. In so doing, the concerns of society in general and employees in particular will be addressed.

By the mid-1980s, the industry-based system of education had become a nearly $30 billion annual enterprise, with much of its expenditure being targeted for supplementary employee training. Indeed, only $1 billion of the total went directly to educational institutions and a mere 3 percent of the $1 billion was directed at pre-collegiate education. Noting that 97 percent of corporate America's direct support of education went to higher education, Manuel Justiz (1983), former director of the National Institute of Education, lamented that "business grants . . . help *only the survivors* of the public schools."

In addition to empirical-theoretical and security concerns is a current political climate which appears to be conducive to collaborative educational endeavors. In moving toward greater decentralization and teacher empowerment, there has been increasing attention given in the schools to developing site-based management and collegiality. Although often interpreted as principally a local control initiative, site-based management has the potential for the fostering of cooperation. Regarding the call for greater school-level democratization and building-level autonomy, Ann Lieberman (1988) emphasizes the importance of professional educators, parents and students collectively meeting to establish the school's operational goals and "the general means of running a school." According to Lieberman, an outgrowth of this greater autonomy at the building site should be the greater benefits from collegiality: an establishment of greater trust, professional dialogue, cooperative planning and participatory decision making. Beyond the building level, Kenneth Sirotnik and John Goodlad (1988), in an accounting of the "flood of 'partnerships' cover[ing] the educational landscape," contend that "the politics of educational reform have created the need for at least symbolic associations between educational stakeholders." They offer the example of businesses establishing "adopt-a-school 'partnerships' " and universities creating an array of collaborative endeavors with the K–12 public schools as indicative of this "flurry of activity." Education is a hot ticket and nearly everyone wants a piece of the action.

In summary, much of the effective schools research and the political climate underlying many reform initiatives provides theoretical testimony to the significance of educational partnerships both (1) within the educational arena and (2) between education and other major societal institutions. The forthcoming section will describe collaborative initiatives in each of two partnership areas: (1) the schools and higher education within the arena of education and (2) education and business within the category of education and other societal institutions.

PARTNERSHIP ACTIVITIES

The School and Higher Education Connection

A Historic Overview

In a review of school-university partnerships, Kenneth Sirotnik and John Goodlad (1988) note the historic rarity of institutional collaboratives "between *equal* partners working together" to solve problems. There have been, however, several coalitions which have ranged from symbolic to formal associations in our nation's past. Interestingly, one of the most publicized historical references to educational reform is also associated with one of the earliest calls for collaborations between the university and the schools. In 1892, at a National Education Association meeting in Saratoga Springs, a group which was to be entitled "The Committee of Ten," was initiated by NEA's National Council on Education (Button and Provenzo, 1989). Under the chairmanship of Harvard President John Eliot, the committee was determined to "broaden the channel" from high school to college by structuring the secondary school curriculum more in line with an academically oriented and mentally disciplined college preparatory program. According to Clark (1988), among the committee recommendations which would hopefully lead to a better integration of the academics was

> a conference of school and college teachers of each principal subject which enters into the programs of secondary schools ... to consider the limits of its subject, the best method of instruction, the most desirable

allocation of time for the subject, and the best methods of testing the pupils' attainment therein.

As a result of this recommendation, a conference of 47 higher education representatives and 42 school officials was convened which collaborated on the calling for greater cooperation between the schools and the universities. The participants addressed the improvement of teacher preparation, the fostering of critical thinking and strengthening of disciplinary integration. In accomplishing such cooperative endeavors, it is Clark's observation that higher education had to transcend the confines of the ivory tower and "take more interest than they have heretofore done, not only in the secondary, but in the elementary schools.... " Accordingly, higher education should concentrate on improving schools in their respective localities and in contributing to the thorough discussion of all questions affecting the welfare of both the elementary and secondary schools.

Essentially, the Committee of Ten called for a greater standardization of the high school curriculum to better prepare students for the rigors of academia. Accordingly, in 1894 Charles Eliot initiated the creation of the College Entrance Examination Board by calling for a systematic means for examining admissions to higher education (Clark, 1988).

Also initiated by the NEA was the influential bulletin entitled *Cardinal Principles of Secondary Education,* a 1918 publication of the commission on the Reorganization of Secondary Education (VanScotter et al., 1985). Called "perhaps the most widely accepted list of educational aims in the twentieth century ... ," the *Cardinal Principles* — by its emphasis on the teaching of such areas as health, worthy home membership, vocational education and the worthy use of leisure in the secondary schools — stood in fundamental contrast to the recommendations of the Committee of Ten (Ornstein and Levine, 1984). Although less extensive in its school-university collaboration than the Committee of Ten, the *Cardinal Principles* have been viewed as strongly affecting the kind of student entering college throughout much of the twentieth century. Chastised by E. D. Hirsch (1987) in *Cultural Literacy* as driving "the shift from subject matter to social adjustment ... ," the *Cardinal Principles* are viewed as contributing to the "fragmented curriculum" which has ill-prepared high school students for meeting university standards. According to Allan Bloom (1987) in *The Closing of the American Mind,* this demise of a coherent academic purposefulness (i.e. "the great revelations, epics and philosophies as part of our natural vision") has also permeated higher education. Accordingly, two of the most influential reports initiating the recurring debate over the need for greater curricular homogeneity or heterogeneity were the products of school-university partnerships.

Furthering the heterogeneity that became known as progressive education was another principal school-university collaborative that unfolded in the 1930s. Initiated by the Progressive Education Association, the Eight-Year Study examined the effects of variations in secondary school curricula on pupil success in college (Aiken, 1952). In conducting the study, colleges and universities throughout the country agreed to reduce admission standards so that the investigation could assess the effectiveness of high school progressive education. Furthermore, according to Aiken, "everyone involved in the study was convinced that some means should be found by which teachers in the schools and professors in the college should work together in mutual respect, confidence and understanding."

Another early example of school-university collaboration were so-called "networks"—loosely structured, largely symbiotic associations typically involving school district administrators who had attended the same institution of higher learning with similar faculty sponsors (Clark, 1988). Because many big city superintendents of the early twentieth century were educated at prestigious universities like Columbia, Stanford and Chicago, there existed a commonality of higher education experience which both laid the groundwork for networking and for school district similarity. These professor-student relationships often produced research surveys which served the mutual benefits of providing honoraria and with assistance recruitment for the university professors in exchange for credited experience and prestigious affiliation for the school-based students.

While early, collaboratives tended to focus on entrance requirements, curricular community, research and individual aggrandizement, more recent partnerships—although often incorporating the tenets of the past—have endeavored to amplify these foundations by broadening and formalizing the associations. The listing below gives example to principal partnership actions spanning the last twenty years.

Broad-Based Alliances

The Southern California Partnership's (SCP) existence can be credited principally to John Goodlad, who initiated this equal partnership venture as an organized outgrowth of his earlier research and collaborative experience. Goodlad's principal partnership endeavor was his 1966 design of The League of Cooperating Schools, a relatively formalized network of 18 schools in 18 school districts. According to Goodlad (1988), the key elements included in the network of schools were "the individual school as a center of change, . . . a long-term commitment signed and approved by each district's superintendent and board, a rather substantial supporting 'hub' independent of the districts and loosely connected to a major university and a data gathering process capable of providing useful information for formative evaluation at both the school and network level." According to Goodlad, the primary focus throughout the League's six-year history was the school as the center of change "and of individual and institutional renewal." The semi-autonomous HUB aided and abetted the schools' problem-solving process as it incorporated this renewal process.

Fundamental to SCP is Goodlad's (1988) viewing the schools as a change unit and the reflective inquiry associated earlier with the HUB. According to an analysis by Paul Heckman (1988), "Instead of imposing an alien paradigm of generating and using knowledge onto the schools, he [Goodlad] advocated the idea of involving people in their own knowledge-generating process, in the cultural context of their work." An anticipated outcome of this knowledge generation was SCP-designed activities to challenge the educational order ("extant knowledge must be brought to bear of extant practice"). It is Heckman's observation that more fundamental to this partnership paradigm "was the idea that theory and practice would share a common source—the real world of schooling." Accordingly, "the SCP . . . would eschew the separation of thinking and doing, and encourage the idea of reflective practice."

Essentially, the principal challenge to the sound orchestration of the SCP was the use and generation of time for collaborative endeavors. University faculty have the available time but must devote considerable energy to research and publication. Contrariwise, public school personnel have little time to pursue scholarly activities, and the gaining of release time, to design research studies and analyze data, is typically foreign to the school-based order. Emergent activities that helped overcome the confines of time and other obstacles to collegialism included meetings of discipline-alike groups, a curriculum task force which focused on theory and practice and collaborative research projects in such areas as cooperative learning (Heckman, 1988).

In his analysis of the SCP's successes and failures, Heckman, its executive coordinator for five years, points to (1) "world view" differences between conventional school-based "administrania" and that represented by the SCP; and (2) university faculty reluctance to become engaged in K–12 partnership activities. The latter problem centered around the rather rigid cultural regularities of a major university which mitigated against conducting applied research and practical discourse. The former involved a conflict between the prevalent top-down management style of many Southern California school districts and the more egalitarian philosophy of the SCP. Difficulties such as these, in combination with the exodus of John Goodlad, Heckman and several other SEP affiliated staff from UCLA in 1985, precipitated the demise of the Goodlad-envisioned Southern California partnership.

Collaborative experiments in other parts of the country have assumed similar SCP ambitions and have faced similar problems. Another major educational partnership, New York's Metropolitan School Study Council, has assumed collaborative ambitions similar to SCP in its attempt to target research as a principal component of Columbia University's affiliation with New York City area school districts. Under the nearly ten-year leadership of Ann Lieberman, its executive secretary, MSSC challenged the common university tenets that faculty responsibility was not primarily school related and that research "emanated from the professorate, not from the field" (Lieberman, 1988). A former affiliate of John Goodlad with the SCP, Doctor Lieberman set her sights on tackling the cultural differences incorporating the worlds of public schooling and university academia.

Faced with "doing something" to break down the practitioner's hostility toward the alleged irrelevance of university-generated research, in 1977 the MSSC initiated the recruitment of school teacher fellows, who, as doctoral students, were instrumental in cultivating a linkage between the K–12's education and that of higher education. Through the use of doctoral students' study of school cultures and a series of workshops involving school district and university staff, the MSSC began to break the barriers and generate an agenda for mutual trust and productive growth. Within two years, the MSSC had grown from 9 districts to 25 and was gearing itself to undertake collaborative research which would involve scholars and practitioners in endeavors to *improve* the process of schooling. By 1988, the school improvement agenda had attracted 48 urban and suburban districts to the MSSC consortium (Lieberman, 1988).

According to Lieberman, "As an organization that stands between two cultures, a school-university collaboration must create a culture of its own." Similar to Goodlad's semi-autonomous "hub," the mechanics of the collaborate "Administrania" needs to constitute a culture "that is important to both institutions, but one that stands independently as something unique and different." This independence is critical to transcending the institutional rules and vested interests governing the communities of practitioners and scholars.

Robert Sinclair, a principal actor in the Massachusetts Coalition for School Improvement, echoes the "partnership built on parity" dictum of the California and New York based partnerships. In an accounting of the coalition's activities, Sinclair and Harrison (1988) recall the common obstacles to collaborative reform: the reluctance of university "experts" to tackle problems of the schools and the reluctance to identify teachers as the principal decision makers in the generation of change. Often, university professors feel they have all the answers and "are unwilling, unable, or unaccustomed to participating as equals with elementary and secondary school colleagues. . . . " Regarding the involvement of teachers, the top-down decision-making design confronted by SCP can be a fundamental negation of developing effective parity for school improvement. Simply stated, if the goal of a coalition is to improve student learning, teachers — as the primary disseminators of information — must buy in to any changes in curriculum and methodology. That buy in is best attained if there is, within the coalition, the inclusion of teachers to democratize of the decision-making process.

Such is the stuff of good theory, but how does the Massachusetts Coalition for School Improvement attempt to attain the desired collegiality and democratization among the University of Massachusetts and the 26 schools incorporating the consortium? According to Sinclair and Harrison (1988), essentially, this is attained by several professional groupings beginning with school building level "improvement" teams (which include the principal and at least four teachers) to identify needs and action priorities, "study" teams (composed of teachers, school administration and university personnel) to generate information instrumental to school improvements, "staff development seminars" on critical educational issues and pertinent research findings, and a "school's council" (consisting of member district superintendents, principals and teachers plus the university chancellor or designee, the dean of the School of Education and the director of the Center for Curriculum Studies) which creates policy and facilitates collaboration. Other groups include "evaluation" teams and "inquiry" teams, which include administration, university staff and teachers in data collection and data analysis.

While the coalition's efforts appear to have successfully developed greater cooperation among professionals *within the schools* in the fostering of school-based improvement initiatives, it seems that changes at the university level are less likely to occur. Like Heckman's (1988) observation on the rigidity of higher education in California ("cultural regularities promoting the status quo in a major research university were much tougher nuts to crack than those in the local districts and schools"), it is Sinclair and Harrison's (1988) observation that "for the most part . . . colleges of education are slow to engage in critical inquiry into the appropriateness of their own practices." One powerful, contributing factor to the reduction of university faculty to involve themselves in K–12 activities is the unwillingness of major research universities to give substantive reward for community service. Currently, the principal incentives for university faculty's involvement in the school remain financial, i.e. the traditional consulting capacity which mitigates against organizational parity.

Academic Alliances

According to Martin Friedman (1989), Director of College-School Collaboration for the New Jersey Department of Higher Education, the principal collaboratives of California, New York, and Massachusetts are unrealistic attempts to nurture the parity of school-university partnerships. Echoing the conclusions of Heckman, Lieberman and Sinclair and Harrison, Friedman contends that the independent nature permeating the university culture contributes to an entrenched isolation. Accordingly, only a relatively small cadre of faculty with the "intrinsic" motivation to involve themselves in schools are willing to form the nucleus of school-university partnerships.

Friedman argues for the vitality of "academic alliances," collaborative interactions of faculty members in schools and colleges. Rather than attempt an integration of the rather distinct institutional cultures of the university and the schools, academic alliances typically constitute a relatively simple sharing of information within particular disciplines. According to Claire Gaudiani (1987), there are more than 180 academic alliances spanning at least 40 states. At last count, approximately three thousand faculty members from the schools and higher education were meeting regularly to discuss academic content and institutional methodology in the disciplines of chemistry, physics, math, English, history, geography and geology (Wilbur, Lambert and Young, 1988). Gaudiani contends that two paradoxes currently afflicting American education provide an impetus for the establishment of alliances. The first is that "those who spend the most time developing our children's minds are not encouraged to develop their own." The second is that those who have been encouraged to develop their minds have isolated themselves from those minds most in need of development. Additionally, it is often assumed that those who teach best know least and those who teach worst know most. Therefore, it is important to diffuse such paradoxes by the sharing of research findings and pedagogical strategies.

Typically, academic alliance meetings include the reporting of research findings, the discussing of disciplinary change and the sharing of curricula and learning strategies. Incentives for participation include receiving in-service, recertification and academic credit for school-based faculty and the providing of "service" credit for university-based teachers (Gaudiani, 1988).

In many institutions of higher learning, incentives for participation in an alliance program involve the recruitment of students. A collegial collaboration involving faculties from Texas Tech University and the Lubbock Independent School District provide examples of the recruitment buy in (Ishler, 1987). Strongly endorsed by the president of Texas Tech, 141 faculty "adopted" a Lubbock public school classroom during the 1986–87 school year. Available on an average of once a week, university faculty have served as resource persons, have engaged in teacher exchanges and have familiarized high school students with university life. According to Texas Tech School of Education Dean Richard Ishler, a substantial number of university faculty who volunteered gave recruitment of students— particularly minority students—as their principal reason for their involvement. Unfortunately, the 141 who originally volunteered for the project have recently dwindled to about 55. Interestingly, only 10 of the approximately 55 university faculty are from the School of Education (Ishler, 1987).

While most "academic alliances incorporate a relatively egalitarian university and school faculty sharing, a more common collegiality appears to be a university centered collaboration which brings teachers to the higher education institution as fellows and research associates." Vivian (1985) describes the Yale-New Haven Teachers Institute as "empowering teachers as colleagues during their five-month tenure at Yale." As Yale fellows, approximately 80 New Haven school teachers become "full" members of the Yale community as evidenced by their listing in the university directory of faculty and staff. The teachers' study at Yale focuses on seminars and workshops "intended to stimulate thinking and discussion and to point up interdisciplinary relationships in scholarship and teaching." In another university-based faculty partnership, Porter (1987) reports on Michigan State University's Institute for Research on Teaching (IRT) which has brought select East Lansing area teachers to collaborate in the research process. Supported by an NIE grant, the university buys teacher release time to the tune of approximately $20,000 annually for their half-time work with the university. Such collegiality allows university educators to focus on the real problems of school and permits school faculty the time to reflect upon and critically examine their own practices.

Although "academic alliances" appear to be the term encompassing the largest collaborative endeavors among school and university personnel, the *National Directory of School-College Partnerships* identifies several additional categories such as the "instruction of pre-college students," the attraction of "minority, disadvantaged, and 'at-risk' students," the "preservice/training of new teachers," the training of administrators and the adoption of schools (Wilbur, Lambert and Young, 1987). Nearly as widespread as academic alliances, pre-college student instruction exists in nearly two hundred institutions of higher learning. The fundamental purpose of these collaboratives is to allow high school students to "test the waters" by enrolling in college-level courses. These partnerships are intended to "smooth the transition from school to college, shorten the time needed to earn an undergraduate degree, avoid unnecessary duplication of curricula, and improve the study habits, general academic readiness and academic options for all college-bound youngsters. College-coordinated enrichment programs for gifted and talented students are a common extension of pre-college student instruction. At the other end of the continuum, more than 100 colleges and universities have reported collaborating with the schools on serving the educational needs of "at-risk" students. These programs typically incorporate improved counseling, special remediation and employment opportunity. Regarding teacher training, a natural area for school-college collaboration is in the preparation of prospective teachers. Beyond the traditional coordination of field experiences, teacher training institutions and the schools are now exchanging faculty and sharing material resources. Also popular are higher education coordinated training programs for school administrators, which typically unfold as academics or institutes designed to make the educational manager an educational leader. Additionally, approximately 30 institutions of higher learning have formalized their involvement with schools by "adopting" one or often coordinating with business. These colleges and universities commonly adopt secondary schools with sizable percentages of "at-risk" youth to exchange resources, coordinate academic training and improve job placement (Wilbur, Lambert and Young, 1987).

There are obviously many benefits to school-university partnerships which go beyond the educationally sound dictum that coordination of the schooling environment can enhance student learning. The common ground attracting institutional collaboration is fundamental. An example of this is Paul Heckman's (1988) observation that "universities prepare many of the educators that work in public schools and these educators, in turn, prepare many students for post-secondary teaching." For higher education, more mundane benefits include recruitment (including minority students), improved relationship with the community, greater access to school-related research and, of course, a closer pulse on reality. For the schools, the benefits include a greater familiarity with college academic criteria, the access to university expertise, the opportunity to gain credited experience for furthering graduate degrees or recertification, and, of course, the opportunity to think more empirically and critically.

Although the benefits abound, the jury is still out on whether school-university collaboration, in any enduring formal capacity, is the wave of the future or a passing fancy. Historically, it has involved collaborative research, reports, fellowships and consulting. Only relatively recently has it involved a more comprehensive parity of institutional relations envisioned by Goodlad, Lieberman and Sinclair. According to Sidney Trubowitz (1987), a principal coordinator of Queen's College's affiliation with New York's Louis Armstrong School, school-university partnerships are a fluid process with professors exiting, because there are no reward systems for "field work," and school professionals leaving because of personnel turnover. Accordingly, it would appear there needs to be a greater institutional commitment to dealing with such reward system obstacles and teacher release time that go beyond the continuation of a semi-autonomous "hub" with relatively little administrative clout.

Unfortunately, the institutions of higher and K–12 education can be cumbersomely bureaucratic. According to longtime partnerships observer

Phillip Schlechty (1987), "In some respects . . . working with a university, a large school system, and a well-organized teachers association is like trying to get dinosaurs to do a ballet." As noted earlier, higher education is probably even more intransigent than the K–12 system, in part because of its "collection of 'fiefdoms' " mitigate against unified action to implement policy. Given these institutional rigidities among education in general and higher education in particular, the more modest association such as academic alliances appear to be more realistic educational collaboration than the cultural integration associated with the more comprehensive partnership endeavors.

The Education-Business Connection

A Nation At Risk signaled a call for action—educational initiatives which would maintain and increase our "slim competitive edge we still retain in world markets." Accordingly, education, as a contribution to this malady, must unleash its chains of mediocrity and embrace excellence to revitalize the nation. The University of Cincinnati's Joel Spring (1988) has observed that "the picture painted in *A Nation At Risk* is that of a tired giant losing a global trade war because of the failure of its public schools." Continues Spring, "The solution to the problem in international trade, according to the report, is the reform of its public schools."

Although Spring may have taken some liberty with the commission's viewing the schools as the nation's salvation, there is little question that *A Nation At Risk:* (1) pointed to education's failure as a principal culprit in weakening the nation and (2) saw education as the promising means for strengthening the nation. Viewing American strength in economic terms, a well-educated public was indispensible to the maintenance of preeminence on the world market.

Given the shrinking work force, the changing demographics of our youth and the approximately 25 percent secondary school dropout rate, industry has begun to give greater attention to investing in pre-collegiate education. Although the degree of current interest by business is unprecedented, the involvement of business in pre-collegiate education is not without precedent. Initiated by the Christian organization, Young Life, New York City's Harlem and Lower East Side "street academies" sprouted in the early 1960s which provided educational intervention for economically disadvantaged youth (Justiz, 1983). In funding these academies, Young Life relied almost exclusively on the private sector with contributions by American Airlines, IBM, Union Carbide, McGraw-Hill and

First City National Bank. Viewed as institutions capable of "turn[ing] failure into success for significant numbers of dropouts," it is Justiz's observation that these novel public-private partnerships were the fore-runners of much of today's "alternative delivery of social services to alienated urban youths." The alternate delivery advocated by Justiz is an intervention that "bring[s] a community's human service agencies and its businesses."

A principal representation of Justiz's definition is the Washington, D.C. based Cities in Schools project which now exists in 25 American cities. Led by Atlantic Richfield (which put $2 million into the project), more than 50 private sector institutions have collaborated with social service agencies, other community resources and urban public schools to remediate the academic and job skill deficiencies of "at-risk" students.

A review of additional school-business collaborations by Hahn and Aaron (1988) includes an identification of higher education's role in the partnership activities. For example, The Boston Compact, which began as an agreement between the city's school system and business commu-nity in 1982, has grown to incorporate area colleges and universities. Zeroing in on improving the performance of underachieving students, the compact's business component offered summer jobs and priority full-time hiring to students from schools showing significant increases in the scores and attendance and commensurate decreases in the percentage of dropouts. Since 1982, area higher educational institutions have targeted a 25 percent admissions increase of Boston's public school graduates as institutional goals. In support of this impressive goal is an even more impressive $1 million of college and university funds for pupil scholar-ships. A national extension of similar partnership activities is represented by Career Beginnings which enrolls more than 5,000 low-income stu-dents in over 25 institutions of higher learning. Supported by several corporate foundations, this collaborative features work experience, career planning and remedial education for each college enrollee. In conjunc-tion with public school professionals, area colleges and businesses pro-vide individualized academic and vocational guidance for each Career Beginnings' student.

Additional partnerships include the broad-based New York City School and Business Alliance and New Futures, a five-city business-school consortium. Targeting all 112 New York City high schools, the alliance principally involves area business in cultivating the critical linkage between the school and the job. Business interest in these job placement activities has been supported to the tune of $5 million. The New Futures collaboration is funded by the Annie E. Casey Foundation, which is investing $10 million in each of several cities to pump up local initiative in combatting social maladies associated with at-risk youth (Hahn and Aaron, 1988).

More narrowly based involvement include such ventures as businesses "Adopting Schools" and even creating their own. The adoption movement may have been launched by New York industrialist Eugene Lang by his 1981 declaration that he would offer college scholarships to all sixth graders at his elementary school alma mater in Harlem who graduated from high school. Given Lang's success (50 of the 54 students finished high school and a good majority went on to college), corporations have followed suit. In Dallas, for example, the city's 200 public schools have been adopted by more than one thousand businesses. In Los Angeles, Arco Oil and Gas Company employees have "adopted" the Tenth Street Elementary School. Indeed, in 1988 125 Arco employees were serving as classroom aides in the academic tutoring of minority students. More direct still is a venture by a Chicago business consortium (including McDonald's and Borg Warner) that has launched the private Corporate Community School of Chicago. Tuition free and providing nursery school through the eighth grade, the corporate school is described as an "action laboratory" addressing the deficiencies of socio-disadvantaged youth (Howe, 1987).

The partnerships that have been described typify the alliances between business and schools currently operating in the nation. While some collaborative activities may be more symbolic than substantive, many persons associated with the business community are so concerned about the work force's productivity that many partnerships intend to go well beyond political image building. When Xerox Corporation's David Kearns (1988) states that "education is the cornerstone of every civilization, including our own" and thus "business will have to force the agenda for school reform . . . or see its own agenda," it signals a worry that places portions of the private sector into an intricate association with education. This attitude is further communicated by a 1988 *Business Week* magazine's "special report" which headlines the "need for human capital" to "regain the productivity lead lost to foreign competitors" (Nussbaum, 1988).

Business Week credits the work force superiority of the U.S. in the mid-nineteenth century and of Japan today with the productive power these nation's enjoyed in two historic periods. Since "the evidence is overwhelmingly that people, not machines, are the driving force behind economic growth" and since "America(s) scrimping on human capital . . . is already haunting the business community," the educational investment in people is "the only way" to reverse America's economic decline. This message has been reiterated by former President Reagan's Secretary of Labor Ann McLaughlin (1988) who stated that "our nation's economic strength, our productivity and international competitiveness depend on our capacity to build and maintain a quality work force." Accordingly, the Federal Departments of Labor, Commerce and Education have "one common agenda—building a quality work force to meet the needs of a new technological society."

POLICY IMPLICATIONS

Given the strong relationship between the total environmental structure and scholastic learning, the assessed value of educational partnerships will be judged upon the degree to which they constitute a quality coordination of the environmental structure. The key concept here is unity. If the alleged malaise of our educational state is to be effectively tackled, a "united front" incorporating the entities of education with each other, with business, and with other institutions must be developed. It is irrelevant at this point to wrestle with the question of whether the school environment or the out-of-school environment has the greater effect on learning. The fact is that the total environment (including the schools) profoundly affects learning, and, thus, it is theorized that the greater the scholastic coordination of the total environment, the greater the scholastic learning that will take place.

Historically, most partnership activities—whether school-university based or education-business based—have not involved an institutional integration constituting significant structural change. Collaboration on grants, on teacher training and on curricular design can be accomplished by establishing little more than a task force and a partnership committee. Such modest associations can, however, set the stage for more comprehensive collaboration and thus provide a foundation on which to build. The Southern California Partnership and the Metropolitan School Study Council grew out of smaller, less formal associations between the respective universities and the neighboring school districts. Accordingly, those persons who wish to pursue productive partnerships with and within the educational arena would do well to familiarize themselves with academic alliances and adopted schools.

Meaningful Partnerships

Given the contention that the schools should ideally be intricately interwoven with a total environment which reinforces scholastic learning, what kind of educational enterprise should exist? In addition, within education, what policies should be fostered to create an environmental influence most conducive to promoting scholastic learning? The following policy recommendations may be instrumental in creating a model educational enterprise:

1. **Strong Leadership From The Top.** If there is an educational crisis in the nation, the nation should lead the way in overcoming this malaise. This requires the president, in conjunction with the fifty governors, creating a sense of urgency about educational reform and how to best accomplish it. Coordination at the bottom is best accomplished through leadership at the top. A school environment fostering academic purposefulness should be permeated by a nation committed to academic purposefulness. This coordinated direction should unfold from both national and state capitals and include, in its educational emphasis, the promotion of school-university and business partnerships.

2. **Educational Partnerships Should Be Community-Wide Initiatives Linking The Schools, The Businesses And Higher Education.** Within most metropolitan areas in America, there are schools, businesses *and* at least one institution of higher learning. Rather than a university or business "adopting" a school or contributing to a single research project, there should be broad-based collaboration which involves the entities of the schools, the university and the businesses in educational reform. The Southern California Partnership and the New York Metropolitan School Study Council are noble attempts to link a major university with several school districts on numerous cooperative endeavors. More impressive still are the Boston Compact and Career Beginnings in New York, which integrate business with both the schools *and* higher education throughout much of the Boston and New York areas.

3. **Educational Partnerships Should Integrate Resources In A Manner Which Provides Optimal Opportunity For Pupil Learning.** Since opportunity to learn (quantity of instruction, time on task) is the educational variable correlating most strongly with pupil achievement, it is important that the various partners in instruction coordinate their efforts to

maximize learning time. International educational studies have suggested that the instructional time and study time of American students is considerably less than in most countries. In Japan, for example, students average 240 days of schooling (versus 182 in the United States), and at the secondary level, most Japanese students receive additional instruction from tutors. As cited in an earlier chapter in this book, the amount of time allocated to academic learning has changed very little over the last few years, despite repeated calls for lengthening the American school day and school year. Accordingly, through partnerships with higher education and businesses, the schools can coordinate an extension of learning time without formally extending their own instruction. Colleges and universities can offer Saturday workshops and summer enrichment programs to better prepare students aspiring for higher education. Similarly, industry can provide after-school, weekend and summer job experience that is coordinated with students' courses of study.

4. **Educational Partnerships Should Incorporate Family, Social Services Agencies And Other Community Resources.** Finally, collaborative endeavors should go well beyond the typical narrowly focused school university or school business partnership and serve as a catalyst for integrating the institutions and entities of the entire community. Ideally, this would mean the incorporation of government, social service agencies, charitable organizations, volunteer associations and parents with the partnerships of schools and universities and businesses. This association should not be a loosely structured consorsium but a well-defined collaboration with identified goals and a means to attain them. The partner members should be engaged in participatory decision making, with each entity representing an equal stake in building a consensus.

A consorsium which approximates the aforementioned model is currently under operation in Newark, New Jersey. The Newark Education Council (NEC) includes the school superintendent, the Board of Education, the City Council, community leaders, business leaders, higher education representatives, union officials and parents. Intricately involved in the collaborative, representatives from higher education sit on the steering committee and attend council meetings. In fact, Saul Fenster, the president of the New Jersey Institute of Technology, is one of the founders of the council. According to Fenster, "Anyone who wants to participate can be involved. It is not a blue ribbon panel, but an inclusive body of stakeholders." According to management consultant David

Straus, the NEC operates by the adage that "by working together and reaching agreement each step of the way, a sense of ownership develops." Continues Straus, "The people who ultimately are responsible for plan implementation—the major stakeholders—are all part of the process. When the NEC comes up with a series of recommendations, they are, in effect, recommendations to themselves."

New Jersey Bell, as another principal founder of the Newark Education Council, contends that "the realization that no one group can impact education to the extent necessary to impart strong, effective and meaningful change has caused these groups to direct their efforts to partnerships." Terming "the issues of education [as] bigger than any of us individually," New Jersey Bell President, Anton Campanella, says that NEC plays a "cooperative role in the improvement of our public education system. Each of us (business, government, public education, community organizations and parents), no matter which components of the partnership we represent, has an overwhelming interest."

The changes targeted by the NEC include measurable improvement in academic performance, dropout prevention and job placement. NEC director, Regina Marshall, also identifies "the harnessing of social services and businesses to generate productive employment training" as another goal. Adopting components from the "cities in schools" model, Marshall emphasizes the importance of extending classroom learning by "focusing on after-school training and summer employment." This collaboration also focuses on readiness for higher education and the development of productive citizenship. Further recognition of the importance of out-of-school factors is the council's establishment of an "outside influence task force" which "examines environmental obstacles that impede the education process and makes determinations of the approaches which could best reduce these negative environmental influences."

Like other relatively broad-based educational consortiums, the Newark Educational Council grew from a less comprehensive collaboration. For example, for fifteen years, the New Jersey Institute of Technology has received private and public funding for its programs to augment the education of pre-college students. Attracting approximately 2500 students from urban public and parochial schools, NJIT offers academic enrichment during the after-school hours, on Saturday and during the summer. Under NJIT's leadership, the pre-college program became the impetus for the Consortium on Pre-Collegiate Education which includes NJIT, Rutgers University at Newark, Essex County College and the

University of Medicine and Dentistry of New Jersey, with significant funding provided by the New Jersey Department of Higher Education.

The significance of relatively narrowly focused partnerships can increase markedly by incorporating the breadth of the community for emphasis and action. Educational partnerships may not be able to compensate fully for the environmental whole, but they are an important step toward transcending the confines of the classroom. By meaningful integration of varying components of the environment one can strengthen the influence of the environment. And it is total environmental change that is needed to profoundly improve achievement and to markedly strengthen the nation. Accordingly, the more that the schools are in partnership with higher education, with business, with government, with other social agencies and with parents, the greater the chance that the schools may have of "making a difference."

REFERENCES

Aiken, W. M. (1952). *The Story of the Eight Year Study.* Cited and quoted in School-University Relationships: An Interpretive Review. In Kenneth A. Sirotnik and John I. Goodlad (Eds.), *School-University Partnerships In Action.* New York, NY: Teachers College Press, 44.

Berliner, David C. (1987). But do they understand? In V. Richardson-Koehler (Ed.), *Educators' Handbook: A Research Perspective.* New York: Longman.

Bloom, Allan. (1987). *The Closing of the American Mind.* New York: Simon and Schuster.

Bridge, R. G., Judd, C. M., and Moock, P. R. (1979). *The Determinants of Educational Outcomes: The Impact of Families, Peers, Teachers and Schools.* Cambridge, MA: Ballinger.

Busby, Alta. (1987). Personal Communication.

Button, Warren H. and Provenzo, Eugene F. (1989). *History of Education and Culture in America.* Englewood Cliffs, NJ: Prentice-Hall, pp. 95–96.

Business Week. (1988). "Business is Becoming A Substitute Teacher." In *The Generational Journal,* 1, 46–47.

Clark, Richard W. (1988). School-university relationships: An interpretive review. In Kenneth A. Sirotnik and John I. Goodlad (Eds.), *School-University Partnerships in Action.* New York, NY: Teachers College Press.

Coleman, James, Hoffer, T. and Kilgore, S. (1982). *High School Achievement: Public, Catholic and Private Schools Compared.* New York: Basic Books.

Coleman, James S. et al. Equality of Educational Opportunity. Washington, D.C. (1966): U.S. Government Printing Office.

Denham, C. & Lieberman, A. (Eds.). (1980). Time to learn. Washington, D.C.: National Institute of Education.

Edmonds, R. R. (1979). Effective schools for the urban poor. *Educational Leadership*, 37, 15–27.

Fenster, Saulk and Straus, David A. (1988). Newark's Collaborative Education Reform Process Could Become a National Model. *New Jersey Bell*, 7, 1–10.

Finklestein, Martin (In Press). Faculty development in higher education. In Laurence Marcus and Benjamin Stickney (Eds.), *Politics and Policy in the Age of Education*. Springfield, IL: Charles C Thomas, Publisher.

Friedman, Martin. (1989). Telephone interviews, June, 1989.

Gaudiani, Claire. (1985). Local communities of inquiry: Penn's academic alliances program. In W. T. Daly (Ed.), *College School Collaboration: Appraising the Major Approaches*. San Francisco, CA: Jossey-Bass.

Goodlad, John. (1983). *A Place Called School.* New York: McGraw-Hill.

Goodlad, John. (1987). School-university partnerships for educational renewal: rationale and concepts. In Kenneth A. Sirotnik and John I. Goodlad (Eds.), *School-University Partnerships in Action.* New York, NY: Teachers College Press.

Hodginson, Harold. (1985). *All One System.* Washington, D.C.: Institute for Educational Leadership.

Hahn, Andrew B. and Aaron, Paul. (1988). *Social Policy*, Winter, 32–36.

Heckman, Paul. (1988). The Southern California Partnership: A Retrospective Analysis. In Kenneth E. Sirotnik and John I. Goodlad (Eds.), *School-University Partnerships In Action.* New York, NY: Teachers College Press.

Hirsch, E. D. (1987). *Cultural Literacy.* Boston: Houghton Miffin Co.

Ishler, Richard E. and E. C. Leslie. (1987). Bridging the gap between a public school system and a university. *Phi Delta Kappan*, 69, 615–16.

Jencks, Christopher et al. (1972). *Inequality: A Reassessment of the Effect of Family and Schooling In America.* New York: Harper Colophon Books.

Jennings, Jack. (In Press). Economic competitiveness: The Sputnik of the eighties. In Laurence Marcus and Benjamin Stickney (Eds.) *Politics and Policy in the Age of Education.* Springfield, IL: Charles C Thomas, Publisher.

Justiz, Manuel. *Phi Delta Kappan*, Jan., 1987.

Kearns, David T. (1988). An Educational Recovery Plan for America. In Fred Schultz (Ed.), *Education 89/90.* Guilford, CO: The Dushkin Publishing Group, Inc., 6–10.

Kennedy, Donald. (1987). A letter to higher education presidents and chancellor. Mailed from Stanford University, October 5, 1987.

Lieberman, Ann. (1986). Collaborative Work. *Educational Leadership*, 43, 4–8.

Lieberman, Ann. (1988). Expanding the Leadership Team. *Educational Leadership*, 45, 4–8.

Lieberman, Ann. (1988). The Metropolitan School Study Council: A Living History. In Kenneth A. Sirotnik and John I. Goodlad (Eds.), *School-University Partnerships in Action.* New York, NY: Teachers College Press.

Marshall, Regina. (1989). Personal Communication.

National Commission on Excellence in Education. (1983). *A Nation At Risk: The Imperative for Educational Reform.* Washington, D.C.: U.S. Government Printing Office.

McLaughlin, Ann. (1988). Building a quality workforce for America. *The Generational Journal,* 1, 47–48.

Nussbaum, Bruce. (1988). Needed: human capital. *The Generational Journal,* 1, 42–43.

Peaker, Gilbert F. (1967). *The Plowden Children Four Years Later.* Slough, England: National Foundation for Educational Research, 1971.

——. "The Regression Analysis of the National Survey." In Central Advisory Council for Education, Children and Their Primary Schools, vol. 2, appendix 4. London: Her Majesty's Stationery Office.

Pritzen, Jackie. (1987). Personal Communication.

Purkey, S. C. and Smith, M. S. (1983). Effective Schools: A Review. *Elementary School Journal,* 83, 427–452.

Rosenshine, Barak. (1986). Synthesis of research on explicit teaching. *Educational Leadership,* 43(7), 60–69.

Rowan, Brian, Bossert, Steven and Dwyer, David. (1983). Research on effective schools: A cautionary note. *Educational Researcher,* 12, 24–31.

Rutter, M., Maugham, B., Mortimore, P., Ouston, J., & Smith, A. (1979). Fifteen thousand hours: Secondary schools and their effects on children. Cambridge, MA: Harvard University Press.

Sinclair, Robert L. and Harrison, Anne E. (1988). A partnership for increasing student learning: The Massachusetts Coalition For School Improvement. In Kenneth A. Sirotnik and John I. Goodlad (Eds.), *School-University Partnerships in Action.* New York, NY: Teachers College Press, 87–105.

Sirotnik, Kenneth A. and Goodlad, John I. (Eds.). (1988). *School-University Partnerships in Action.* New York, NY: Teachers College Press.

Spring, Joel. (1984). Education and the Sony War. *Phi Delta Kappan,* 66, 534–537.

Stickney, Benjamin and Plunkett, Virginia. (1983). Closing the Gap: A historical perspective on the effectiveness of compensatory education. *Phi Delta Kappan,* 65, 287–90.

Schuck, Steven. (1989). Personal Communication.

Trubowitz, Sidney. (1987). Stages in the Development of school-college collaboration. *Educational Leadership,* Vol ?, 18–21.

U.S. Department of Education. (1986). *What Works: Research About Teaching and Learning.* Washington, D.C.: U.S. Government Printing Office.

U.S. Department of Education. (1988). *Effective Compensatory Education Sourcebook, Vol. IV: Project Profiles.* Washington, D.C.: U.S. Government Printing Office.

U.S. Department of Education. *The Condition of Education, 1989,* Vol. 1. Washington D.C.: U.S. Government Printing Office, 11.

Van Scotter, Richard D. et al. (1985). *Social Foundations of Education.* Englewood Cliffs, New Jersey: Prentice-Hall.

Vivian, James R. (1985). Empowering teachers or colleagues. In William T. Daly (Ed.), *College-School Collaboration: Appraising the Major Approaches.* San Francisco: Jossey-Bass, 79–89.

Walberg, Herbert and Shanahan, Timothy. (1983). High school effects on individual students. *Educational Researcher,* 12, 4–9.

Walberg, Herbert. (1985). Synthesis of the Research on Teaching. In M. C. Wittrock (Ed.), *Handbook of Research on Teaching* (3rd Ed.). Chicago: Rand McNally.

Wilber, Franklin P., Lambert, Leo M., and Young, M. Jean. (1987). *National Directory of School-College Partnerships.* Washington, D.C.: American Association of Higher Education.

Wilson, Reginald. (In Press). The impact of demographic changes on future educational policy. In Laurence Marcus and Benjamin Stickney (Eds.), *Politics and Policy in the Age of Education.* Springfield, IL: Charles C Thomas, Publisher.

PART III

Sustaining the Drive Toward Excellence

Chapter 10

TWO DECADES OF GALLUP POLLING: MAJOR FINDINGS AND POLICY IMPLICATIONS*

Stanley Elam and Benjamin D. Stickney

One of the prime functions of the Gallup/Phi Delta Kappa polls of the Public's Attitudes Toward the Public Schools is to identify and report national trends in public opinion on questions and issues of interest to education policymakers. Because certain questions have been asked repeatedly in this twenty-year series, we now have a data base that allows education leaders to study opinion trends and relate them to political, social, cultural, and economic events of the recent past.

This chapter focuses on public reactions to just three questions of special interest to policymakers. In each case, the question has been asked in the annual poll repeatedly, so that trend lines are firmly established.

Let us start with a caveat, one that George Gallup Sr. often expressed: the figures presented in these poll reports are relatively accurate for the *nation as a whole* at the time of polling. Local opinions may be similar to national opinions—or they may be wholly at variance with them. For this reason, persons considering local policy changes with public attitude components should consider taking their own local polls. Phi Delta Kappa leaders have long been aware of this crucial point. They therefore developed a package of materials that make it possible for persons with no experience in scientific polling to secure valid results from local, area, or state surveys. A brief description of these materials, called PACE (Polling Attitudes of the Community on Education), with instructions for obtaining them, appears in Appendix II of this volume.

---

*The first section of this chapter, entitled "Major Findings of the First Twenty Polls," is written by Stanley Elam and is taken from the *Phi Delta Kappa* book, *The Gallup/Phi Delta Kappa Polls of the Public's Attitudes Toward the Public Schools: A 20-Year Compilation and Educational History.* The second section, entitled "The Polls and Educational Policy," is authored by Benjamin Stickney.

Another emphasis of this chapter is examination of public attitudes toward new ideas in education or the revival and extension of old ones. Are policymakers too timid about the introduction of innovations because they fear public disapproval? The summary of findings on some 50 questions related to change in the schools will surprise some observers.

Finally, in this chapter we shall describe what we regard as the major lessons of the poll for education policymakers. For public education in America to flourish—indeed, if it is to survive as a vital instrument of success for the people of a democratic state—we will have to apply these lessons with increasing skill and determination.

I. Three Benchmark Questions

Public Perceptions of School Problems

We start with the only question that has been asked in all 20 polls: "What do you think are the biggest problems with which the public schools of this community must deal?" The following chart summarizes answers to this question for the 1969–1988 period. More complete reports of these findings appear in subsequent chapters.

While it is difficult to tabulate the answers to an open-ended question of this kind—and no summary does them full justice—there are very good reasons for using this one in open-ended form. Chief among these reasons is the fact that respondents' true feelings leap to the surface, uncontaminated by the views of people (chiefly educators) who devise poll questions. Uninformed, superficial, and unsophisticated though the answers may be, they constitute the opinion reality with which school people must deal.

Consider, for example, the "problem" that has been mentioned most often in 16 of the first 20 polls: discipline. Educators themselves, in several polls asking the same question, hardly mention discipline, which they generally regard as symptomatic of more basic problems. Educators tend to see the "problems" in Gallup's list as a mosaic of sometimes direct, sometimes intricate interrelationships of cause and effect. For example, "difficulty of getting good teachers" is directly related to "lack of financial support" and less directly but definitely related to "overcrowding," "parents' lack of interest," and "lack of support for teachers."

Poll planners have developed a series of questions that probe the public's concept of discipline as a school problem. The first of these, asked in 1973 and 1982, was "When we talk about 'discipline,' just what does this mean to you?" Most of the respondents said discipline is a matter of obeying rules; respecting views of parents, teachers, and others in authority; and being considerate of fellow students who wish to learn in a peaceful atmosphere. Gallup observed, "While law and order have become almost code words for the conservative viewpoint in politics, the basic concept is held in high regard by the public. In fact, in the 1972 survey, when asked to choose from a list of nine goals of education, the public placed teaching students to respect law and authority as its top goal for students in grades 7–12."

It is important to note that few people blame the schools directly for student behavior problems.* A 1983 question asked respondents to identify "best explanations" for disciplinary problems in the schools. "Lack of discipline in the home" (72%) and "lack of respect for law and authority throughout society" (54%) led the list. "Punishment is too lenient" was a distant seventh with 39%.

Since 1986 another behavior problem—another law and order crisis, if you will—has replaced discipline in public perception as the number one public school problem. It is the use of illicit drugs by students. Ironically, overall drug use by young people is in gradual decline, according to the University of Michigan's Institute for Social Research. Increasing alarm over a declining problem is a conundrum I shall not attempt to solve.

In interpreting the tables that appear in this chapter and later, it is well to remember that a change of one percentage point, assuming that the survey sample is representative, means a change of attitude or opinion by at least one and one-half million persons. Changes of only a few percentage points may seem trivial until they are translated into numbers of people. Then they may be startling.

Table I suggests considerable stability in the public's perceptions of the major problems in their local schools.· The same problem areas tend to appear in about the same sequence every year. The high point for the leading problem, "lack of discipline," came in 1982, when 27% of all respondents noted it. That figure is not greatly different from the low point reached in 1976: 22%. An exception to this general stability can be found in the public's perception of racial desegregation as a problem for the schools

---

*Note that only problems mentioned by at least 10% of the respondents appear in this table. The one exception is "teacher lack of interest," which reaches the 10% level when added to "teacher," which is shorthand for "difficulty of getting good teachers."

(combined with busing for desegregation after 1975), which trended downward from a high of 17% in 1970 to a low of 4% in 1988 (see Chapter 21). What does this mean? Certainly not that schools are now successfully integrated by race or even that controversy over busing for desegregation has disappeared. Perhaps it only means, as was speculated in "Impressions of a Poll Watcher" (September 1983 KAPPAN), that early hopes for the schools as society's best tool for integrating the races have largely evaporated.

The People Rate Their Schools

In 1969, 42% of education survey respondents admitted that they knew "very little" about their local public schools. Only 18% claimed to know "quite a lot."* When a similar question was asked 18 years later (1987), the response was almost identical. Numerous poll questions have confined these self-evaluations. For example, in 1979 people were asked if they knew how much it cost to educate a child for one year in their local public schools. Only 12% thought they knew or ventured a guess, and of these 85% were wildly wrong (see Chapter 12). From such data we can infer that perhaps 1% of the public has accurate, detailed information of the kind that should undergird judgments about the schools.

In view of these facts, why ask people to grade their schools on the typical school A–F scale? How can you give a grade if you know very little about the thing you are grading? The answer, of course, is that you *can't* give an intelligent or informed grade. But this doesn't deter people from assessing the schools and making judgments. On the average, less than 18% of Gallup survey respondents refuse to grade the schools, locally or nationally. And public perceptions matter, faulty as they may be; educators and school policymakers must bear them in mind, seek to understand their origins, try to correct them, and consider them in making policy decisions.

The ratings question serves as a national barometer, telling us about fluctuations in approval of the public school system as a whole. These fluctuations have been considerable, as Table II shows. Ratings were comparatively high in 1974, then comparatively low in 1983, when the survey was made just after publication of the highly critical government schools report, *A Nation at Risk.* Since 1984, ratings have stabilized near 1970s levels.

---

*And this 18% undoubtedly includes most educator respondents, who make up some 2.5% of the U.S. adult population.

Table I

Items Most Frequently Cited as Biggest Problems in Local Public Schools (in Percentages)

1969

		%
1.	Discipline	26
2.	Facilities	22
3.	Teachers	17
4.	Finances	14
5.	Integration	13

1970

		%
1.	Discipline	26
2.	Integration	22
3.	Finances	17
4.	Teachers	14
5.	Facilities	13
6.	Drugs	

1971

		%
1.	Finances	18
2.	Integration	17
3.	Discipline	17
4.	Facilities	12
5.	Drugs	11
6.	Teachers	11

1972

		%
1.	Discipline	23
2.	Finances	19
3.	Integration	18
4.	Teachers	14
5.	Facilities	5

1973

		%
1.	Discipline	22
2.	Integration	18
3.	Finances	16
4.	Drugs	13
5.	Teachers	10

1974

		%
1.	Discipline	22
2.	Integration	18
3.	Finances	16
4.	Drugs	13
5.	Teachers	10

1975

		%
1.	Discipline	23
2.	Integration/busing*	16
3.	Finances	13
4.	Teachers	13
5.	Size of school/class	11
6.	Drugs	

1976

		%
1.	Discipline	22
2.	Integration/busing	15
3.	Finances	14
4.	Poor curriculum	14
5.	Drugs	11
6.	Teachers	11

1977

		%
1.	Discipline	26
2.	Integration/busing	13
3.	Finances	12
4.	Teachers	11
5.	Curriculum	10
6.	Drugs†	7

1978

		%
1.	Discipline	26
2.	Drugs**	13
3.	Finances	12
4.	Integration/busing	11
5.	Curriculum/standards§	10
6.	Teachers	7

1979

		%
1.	Discipline	25
2.	Drugs	13
3.	Finances	13
4.	Curriculum/standards	13
5.	Teachers	12
6.	Integration/busing	9

1980

		%
1.	Discipline	26
2.	Drugs	14
3.	Curriculum/standards	11
4.	Finances	10
5.	Integration/busing	10
6.	Size of school/classes	7
7.	Teachers†	6

1981

		%
1.	Discipline	23
2.	Drugs	15
3.	Curriculum/standards	14
4.	Finances	12
5.	Teachers	11
6.	Integration/busing	11

1982

		%
1.	Discipline	27
2.	Finances	22
3.	Drugs	20
4.	Curriculum/standards	11
5.	Teachers	10
6.	Teachers' lack of interest	7

1983

		%
1.	Discipline	25
2.	Drugs	18
3.	Curriculum/standards	14
4.	Finances	13
5.	Teachers	8
6.	Teachers' lack of interest	8

1984

		%
1.	Discipline	27
2.	Drugs	18
3.	Curriculum/standards	15
4.	Finances	14
5.	Teachers	14
6.	Teachers' lack of interest	8

1985

		%
1.	Discipline	25
2.	Drugs	18
3.	Curriculum/standards	11
4.	Teachers	10
5.	Finances	9

1986

		%
1.	Drugs	28
2.	Discipline	24
3.	Finances	11
4.	Curriculum/standards	10
5.	Teachers	9

1987

		%
1.	Drugs	30
2.	Discipline	22
3.	Finances	14
4.	Teachers	9
5.	Curriculum/standards	8
6.	Large schools/overcrowding	8

1988

		%
1.	Drugs	32
2.	Discipline	19
3.	Finances	12
4.	Teachers	11
5.	Curriculum/standards	11
6.	Pupils' lack of interest	7

*"Forced busing for racial integration" became a focus of concern in this and following years.

**"Alcohol" began to be listed as a separate problem in 1978, with mention by 1 to 3%.

§"Poor standards" was added to "poor curriculum" in 1978.

†If one adds "teachers' lack of interest" to "difficulty of getting good teachers," this category ranks third with 12%.

The following table reports answers to the question, "Students are often given the grades A,B,C,D, and FAIL to denote the quality of their work. Suppose the public schools, themselves, in this community were graded in the same way. What grade would you give: the public schools *here*... the public schools *nationally*. (National ratings were begun in 1981.)

Table II Public School Ratings

	1974 Local %	1975 Local %	1976 Local %	1977 Local %	1978 Local %	1979 Local %	1980 Local %
A	18	13	13	11	9	8	10
B	30	30	29	26	27	26	25
C	21	28	28	28	30	30	29
D	6	9	10	11	11	11	12
FAIL	5	7	6	5	8	7	6
DK	20	13	14	19	15	18	18

	1981 Local %	National %	1982 Local %	National %	1983 Local %	National %	1984 Local %	National %
A	9	2	8	2	6	2	10	2
B	27	18	29	20	25	17	32	23
C	34	43	33	44	32	38	35	49
D	13	15	14	15	13	16	11	11
FAIL	7	6	5	4	7	6	4	4
DK	10	16	11	15	17	21	8	11

	1985 Local %	National %	1986 Local %	National %	1987 Local %	National %	1988 Local %	National %
A	9	3	11	3	12	4	9	3
B	34	24	30	25	31	22	31	20
C	30	43	28	41	30	44	34	48
D	10	12	11	10	9	11	10	13
FAIL	4	3	5	5	4	2	4	3
DK	13	15	15	16	14	17	12	13

Without some understanding of historical context and demographics, it is easy to misinterpret survey findings of this sort. Let us examine in greater detail the decreases in public approval of local schools between the peak in 1974 and the low in 1983. First, convert the A–F scale to a numerical one, with A equalling 4; B, 3; C, 2; and F, −1. Then calculate the average 1974 rating. It turns out to be 2.63, or B−. The same figure for 1983 was 1.72, or C−. Expressed in percentages, this was a horrendous 35% drop in approval. Now look at some of the demographics. Between 1974 and 1983, the percent of Americans with children in school fell from 39% to 27%. Gallup's 1974 sample included 770 parents, whereas the 1983 sample included only 416. Significantly, all of the polls confirm that parents with children in public school give their local public schools considerably higher ratings than do non-parents. The decrease in parent ratings between 1974 and 1983 was from 2.61 to 2.15; *non-parent* ratings went from 2.54 to a dismal 1.50. Had the percentage of parents been the same in the two years we are comparing, the overall approval rate would obviously have fallen much less precipitously.

As children of the baby-boom generation swell the nation's elementary schools in the years immediately ahead, ratings will probably rise. There are two reasons for this prediction. First, parents give their local schools high grades, as we have noted. Second, elementary schools seem always to get higher ratings than secondary schools, and the coming population bulge begins, of course, in the lower grades.

Gallup was careful to point out in most of his annual reports that persons with the best access to firsthand information about the public schools (e.g. parents) are much more likely to give high grades than are people who depend on secondary sources, such as the media. The very highest ratings are given schools attended by a parent's oldest child. In 1985 and 1986, when these ratings were first obtained, a remarkable 70% plus of parents gave the schools their oldest child was attending an A or B rating. The importance of such findings can hardly be overstated. Xenophobia, chauvinism, a bad press, and lack of proprietary interest have much to do with low grades given the schools nationally — or even across town. The schools people know best, because their own children bring home firsthand information, fare very well in the Gallup polls.

Raising Taxes to Improve the Schools

On nine occasions poll planners have asked people if they would approve tax increases specifically for their local public school. Not surprisingly, given Americans' perennial resistance to tax increases, the idea has never been overwhelmingly popular. Even among those who say they would approve, there is a considerable difference between telling a pollster yes to such a question and casting a favorable ballot in a school bond election. Historian John Lukacs has pointed out the difference between "public opinion" and "public sentiment."[*] Public opinion, he says, is the formal remarks that folks make to pollsters. Public sentiment is the private set of beliefs and biases that people are often embarrassed to disclose. Approving higher taxes for the benefit of schools may be an example in which one's public opinion differs from his private sentiment.

In any case, educators can take some comfort from responses to a very special question asked in 1983 and 1988: "Would you be willing to pay more taxes to help raise the standard of education in the United States?" In 1983, 58% of the public said yes to this question vs. 33% who said no and 9% who were undecided. The affirmative vote had risen to 64% by 1988 and the negative had shrunk to 29%, with 7% abstaining.

The tax question most often asked in the Gallup polls, however, was a bit different, and that difference no doubt explains a less favorable reaction. People were asked, "Suppose the local public schools said they needed much more money. As you feel at this time, would you vote to raise taxes for this purpose, or would you vote against raising taxes for this purpose?" Note the modifier "much more" and the fact that it was the "schools"—a word respondents probably translated to "school people"—who were asking for money, and without saying what it was for. Had the purpose "to raise standards" been given, would many more people have said yes? Probably.

Here are responses, from 1969 to 1984, to the second question above:

	1969 %	1970 %	1971 %	1972 %	1981 %	1983 %	1984 %
Would vote for	45	37	40	36	30	39	40
Would vote against	49	56	52	56	60	52	41
DK	6	7	8	8	10	9	12

Among the many other questions that have dealt with school finances and taxation over the 20-year poll history, one of the more useful was this, asked in 1986: "Many states have recently passed school improvement legislation that requires additional financial expenditures. If your state needed to raise more money for the public schools, would you vote for or against the following proposals?"

Six forms of taxation were offered. The public approved increased alcoholic beverage taxes for education (79% for, 18% against), state lotteries for education (78% for, 10% against), and increased cigarette and tobacco taxes (74% for, 22% against). They opposed increased local prop-

---

[*]As quoted by Fred Barnes in "Campaign 1988: A Fine Romance," *The New Republic,* July 11, 1988, p. 10–12.

erty taxes (33% for, 60% against), increased gasoline taxes (28% for, 67% against), and increased income taxes (27% for, 66% against).

At least 15 other questions—not dealing with taxes or school finance— have been asked three or more times in the poll series. In the chapters that follow, trend lines in opinion on these questions can be studied.

II. Does the Public Approve of Change in the Public Schools?

Throughout the history of the poll, the public has indicated a willingness to accept new ideas or to have old ones revived in the hope of improving public school effectiveness.* Table III shows that, in more than 40 representative instances, a majority of respondents have approved proposals for change, often by large margins. During the same 20-year period, a majority disapproved of suggested changes in only about a dozen cases. Educators will note that the poll reports public approval of several recommendations of the National Commission on Excellence (in *A Nation at Risk*) and of other reform-minded bodies and agencies. In a few instances, changes that were once disapproved became acceptable a few years later. In still others, support has dwindled.

Proposals intended to improve the quality and effectiveness of teachers head the list of approved changes. People would like to give prospective teachers basic competency tests before they begin teaching. A majority would require experienced teachers to take periodic competency tests or state board examinations in their specialty. A majority approves the idea of career ladders for teachers and even (by a smaller margin) merit pay. A majority would retain teachers on the basis of performance, not seniority. More people than not would give higher pay for teachers in such shortage areas as math and science. A majority favors a year of internship at half pay for prospective teachers before certification. Finally, a majority favors a national set of standards for the certification of public school teachers.

Gallup questions have examined the acceptability of several ideas for school improvement that have already been adopted in many public schools. Approval for such ideas has often been registered in more than one poll. For example, people have said on four different occasions (1975, 1980, 1981, and 1987) that they would like more emphasis on ethical and moral education. In 1987 a majority also said they thought it

---

*In this connection, results of two early poll questions (1970 and 1974) should be noted. Essentially, each asked whether local schools were trying too many or too few innovations. Nearly as many respondents said "too many" as "too few," and still more (32%) said "just about right."

possible to develop courses in ethics that would be acceptable to the people of their communities.

Sex education, which many school authorities are hesitant to add even to the high school curriculum because of community opposition, real or imagined, has been approved by a public majority in six different surveys. Over the years majority approval has gradually increased until in 1987 it was 76% vs. 16% (for high school) and 55% vs. 37% (for elementary). In 1988 a majority was even ready to have the public schools teach "safe sex" for AIDS prevention. The vote was 78% for, 16% against.

The idea of using standardized national tests for high school graduation, unworthy as it may be (in the eyes of professional educators), has been approved by the public in six different Gallup polls (including one, in 1958, before the current series was started). Table III shows approval rising from 50% in 1958 to 73% in 1988.

Would fewer innovations have been approved had a price tag been part of the question? We do not know, but it seems very likely. Many proposed innovations would be expensive to implement. Examples: good job-training programs (approved by a margin of 86% to 11%) and special schools to teach English to non-English-speaking immigrants (approved by an 82% to 13% margin). Also, if a merit pay system (approved by a majority) is to be fair and workable, it requires enormous commitments of both time and money.

Finally, when interviewers begin to probe, as was done on the topic of sex education in 1981, they sometimes find that answers seeming to express overall approval actually conceal rejection of some aspect of a proposal. In 1970 the public approved sex education by a margin of 65% to 28%. But when in 1981 pollsters asked first about sex education in the elementary school, they discovered that slightly more respondents opposed the latter (48%) than favored it (45%). Also, as the full report shows, only certain sex-related topics gained majority approval for school instruction, even in high school. Considered taboo or questionable were abortion, homosexuality, and the nature of sexual intercourse.

Inspection of Table III reveals many other interesting instances of public acceptance of change in education. These findings suggest that public opinion favors venturesomeness in the schools, and there is no reason for believing that private sentiment is different. However, the cautious policymaker may well wish to conduct a local survey before initiating an important change or one on which the public has strong feelings.

Table III
Public Attitudes Toward Change and Innovation in Education*

Suggested Change	Approve %	Disapprove %
More career education (1973)	90	7
(1976)	80	5
Basic competency tests for teachers before hiring (1985)	89	6
State board exams in speciality before teacher certification (1984)	89	7
National standards for teachers (1988)	86	9
Periodic testing in specialty to retain certification (1979)	85	10
(1985)	85	11
(1988)	86	11
High school credit for community service (1978)	87	8
(1984)	79	16
Work-study programs for students uninterested in school (1974)	86	9
Parents confer with school personnel at start of each semester (1980)	84	11
Job-training programs for out-of-work youth, age 15–18 (1975)	86	11
Special schools to teach English to immigrants (1980)	82	13
Computers for instruction (1983)	81	10
Evening classes to teach parents how to help child in school (1971)	81	13
(1976)	77	19
Tax-supported kindergarten for all who wish it (1986)	80	13
More emphasis on moral/ethical education (1975)	79	15
(1980)	79	16
(1981)	70	17
Course credit for community service (1984)	79	16
Retaining teachers on basis of performance, not seniority (1981)	78	17
Constitutional amendment to permit prayer in public schools (1974)	77	17
Early graduation (1980)	77	19
(1977)	74	22
(1987)	68	26
High school credit for volunteer work by students not interested in school (1974)	77	17
Grade promotion only if student can pass test (1978)	68	27
(1983)	74	20
(1984)	71	25
Standardized national tests to compare local with other students (1970)	75	16
(1971)	70	21
(1983)	75	17
(1986)	77	16
(1987)**	70	14
(1988)	81	14

Suggested Change	Approve %	Disapprove %
Liberal arts degree before teacher training (1987)	72	17
Compulsory kindergarten (1986)	71	22
Nongraded (continuous progress) schools (1972)	71	22
(1975)	64	28
(1980)	62	30
(1984)	54	39
Standardized national test for high school graduation (1958)	50	39
(1976)	65	31
(1981)	64	26
(1984)	65	27
(1988)	73	22
Compulsory national service for unemployed youth (1979)	67	27
Parents' right to choose public school their children attend (1986)	68	25
(1987)	71	20
Constitutional amendment to equalize per-pupil spending (1974)	68	25
Sex education (1970)	65	28
(1981) high school	70	22
(1981) elementary	45	48
(1985) high school	75	19
(1985) elementary	52	43
(1987) high school	76	16
(1987) elementary	55	37
Job placement by schools for recent graduates (1980)	64	30
Alternative schools (1973)	62	26
Girls participating with boys in noncontact sports (1974)***	59	35
Merit pay for teachers (1981)	58	36
Fundamental (back-to-basics) schools (1975)	57	33
(1977)****	34	5
Year of internship for teachers at half pay before certification		
(1980)	56	36
(1988)	51	41
Rewarding schools for improving achievement of minorities (1988)	53	34
Year-round schools (1970)	42	49
(1972)	53	41
Constitutional amendment to permit government financial aid to		
parochial schools (1974)*****	52	35
Mainstreaming for the physically handicapped (1979)	53	36
Higher pay for math, science teachers than for others (1983)	50	35
Preschool child care as part of the public school system (1976)	46	49
(1976)	46	47
Same question, somewhat different wording (1988)	70	23
Tax-supported child care for latch-key kids in public schools		
(1985)	43	45

Suggested Change	Approve %	Disapprove %
Voucher system (1970)	43	46
(1971)	38	44
(1981)	43	41
(1983)	51	38
(1985)	45	40
(1986)	46	41
(1987)	44	41
Providing instruction in student's native language (1988)	42	49
Extend school year by 30 days (1982)	37	53
(1983)	40	49
(1984)	44	50
	40	53
Lengthen school day by one hour (1982)	37	55
(1983)	41	48
(1984)	42	52
Start school at age 4 (1972)	32	64
(1973)	30	64
(1986)	29	64
Conduct vocational education outside the public school system		
(1978)	32	53
More independent study (1971)	31	22
Raise college entrance requirements (1984)	27	59
Constitutional amendment to prohibit forced busing for		
integration (1974)	18	72
Home schools (1984)	16	73
(1988)	28	59
Mainstreaming for the mentally handicapped (1979)	13	77

* For more details on each change, see complete poll reports in later chapters.
** The question was worded slightly differently in this poll.
*** By 1985 a majority approved of having boys and girls participate on the same teams in tennis, swimming, and track but not in basketball, baseball, football, or wrestling.
**** In the 1977 poll only 41% had heard of the term "back-to-basics." Of these, 83% approved of the concept and 11% disapproved, resulting in these low percentages.
***** But in 1981, when asked whether some tax money should be used to help parochial schools, only 40% of respondents favored the idea and 51% opposed it.

Lessons from the Polls

The first 20 Gallup education polls have considerable potential for helping school authorities and policymakers improve American public education. Their prime function, of course, has been to provide a kind of topographic map of public opinion on a variety of education questions and issues. As I have just shown, this map indicates rather clearly what kind of changes are most acceptable to the public. Professional educators agree with the public on a majority of these questions. There is also disagreement on a number of important issues; for example, the need for better financing of public education. These disagreements define a future agenda for the profession. Where the public is plainly uninformed or in error, educators and their professional associations should muster the best communications resources at their command to set the record straight or explain their position. Organizations like the National School Public Relations Association can help with techniques for this public relations effort, but the first problem is one of educator consciousness raising. Few educators have a sophisticated understanding of the relationship between public opinion and the health of the schools, and many do not even appreciate its importance. So far as the public is concerned, poll after poll has shown that familiarity breeds respect for the public schools, and public respect is what we must have.

One of the immediate, concrete steps school leaders can take in this connection is to make sure that every required course in government features a unit on American public education. Such courses can overcome at least some of the ignorance about our education system revealed in the polls. Too often, educators take it for granted that, because a majority of the people spend at least 12 years in the public schools, they understand the schools' purposes, how they are organized, and how they are financed and controlled. Because we know how few facts taught in government classes stick in students' memory, people should be exposed to a variety of refresher courses after leaving school. These can come partly from the schools themselves, in the form of bulletins and flyers, fairs and open houses, citizens' advisory committees, much more complete report cards for students to carry home, and the like. But educators also need to enlist the help and cooperation of the media. Many enlightened editors are beginning to recognize the thirst for more and better coverage of school news. Some of them have seen results of the two polls (the first and the 20th) which indicate (1) that people recognize their own ignorance about the schools, (2) that they depend heavily upon newspapers and radio and television for information about the schools, and (3) that a solid majority want more information. For editors who aren't familiar with these findings, educators might arrange an introduction. Editors who aren't aware of it should be informed that the number one concern for Americans in 1988 (according to a Roper poll conducted in April) was the education of children.

On three occasions Gallup education polls have asked, "How important are schools to one's future success—extremely important, fairly important, not too important?" The results:

	1973 %	1980 %	1982 %
Extremely important	76	82	80
Fairly important	19	15	18
Not too important	4	2	1
No opinion	1	1	1

Obviously, the American public has overwhelming faith in the power of education, and it did not diminish between 1973 and 1982. A similar question was asked about college education in 1978 and again in 1983. Belief that college is "extremely important" to success grew from 36% in 1978 to 58% in 1983. People remain convinced that the schools, if only they were better organized or staffed or supported, could somehow take on any task.

In fact, this is part of the problem; the public has shifted or tried to shift too many problems to the schools, and educators have been unwilling or unable to resist.

In this connection it is instructive to examine answers to a question the poll asked in 1980: "How much confidence do you, yourself, have in these American institutions to serve the public's needs?" Among eight institutions listed, respondents placed public schools second only to the church. Then why, one might ask, isn't the public willing to leave moral and ethical instruction to the church, since morality and ethics would seem to be the church's prime concern? Why do people favor, four to one, having the schools take on this herculean task? For the same reason, one supposes, that the public believes that America's strength in the future depends on developing the best educational system in the world: education has almost magical power. (Eighty-four percent of the respondents in 1982 and 88% in 1988 said this is "very important," while only 47% in both 1982 and 1988 regarded "building the strongest military force in the world" as very important.)

If others will not explain to the public what the schools can do best with the limited resources they are given, then it is up to educators themselves to do so. The very fact that many people view their schools as needing improvement gives rise to the hope that more support will be forthcoming in the years ahead. Properly conceived, the combination of strong public faith in education as the answer to society's ills, willingness to accept change in the schools, and a continuing crisis in the financing of education constitute a magnificent opportunity for a triumph of educational leadership.

THE POLLS AND EDUCATIONAL POLICY

Although there is no definitive evidence that disclosure of the public's opinions, as measured by the Gallup/Phi Delta Kappa education polls, has *caused* changes in educational policy, there is some correlation between poll findings and recent educational reform initiatives.

Prior to the release of *A Nation At Risk* in 1983, a substantial majority of poll respondents supported retaining teachers on the basis of performance, agreed with standardized testing for high school graduation, and supported grade promotion on the basis of standardized tests. In addition, a majority of poll respondents approved of merit pay for teachers and wanted greater emphasis on "the basics."

At the same time these attitudes were being revealed, the polls also showed a decline in approval of the public schools. Far fewer people gave their local schools an A or B grade in 1983 than gave those grades five or ten years earlier. While a demographic change—the decreasing percentage of adults with children in school during the 1974–1983 period—may account for much of the declining grades the schools received, public dissatisfaction with educational policy may have also contributed to the lowered ratings which were at an all-time low in 1983. Interestingly, the 1984 poll marked a reversal of this trend; there was a significant increase in the percentages of A's and B's given in the schools. A further increase in the percentage of A's and B's given in both national and local schools was recorded in 1985, after which ratings leveled off. In essence, despite the continuing demographic change, the schools have been graded more favorably from 1984 to 1988 than from 1981 to 1983.

What may have been the role of the educational reform movement in the generation of more positive public attitudes about the state of the nation's schools? *A Nation at Risk* was released April 26, 1983, only a few weeks before the 1983 Gallup education poll was taken in early May to early June. Given the extraordinary press coverage of the report's conclusions regarding "the imperative of educational reform," it is not surprising that the 1983 poll showed a drop in ratings. Indeed, between 1982 and 1983 the six-point drop (37 to 31) in the percentage of A's and B's given local schools represented the sharpest *annual decline* in the history of the Gallup/PDK education poll. The following May, however, we find the greatest single increase (31% to 42% for local and 19 to 25 for national) in the public's grading of the schools in poll history. (Grading the schools was started in the 1974 Gallup/PDK poll and has been repeated in each subsequent poll.)

Interestingly, this relatively dramatic upward shift corresponded with the circulation of an often overlooked publication entitled *The Nation Responds: Recent Efforts To Improve Education.* Released by the U.S. Department of Education in May 1984, *The Nation Responds* provides a fascinating chronicle of reform initiatives which allegedly unfolded from April 26, 1983 to early April 1984 (U.S. Department of Education, 1984).

The document begins by noting the extraordinary attention given *A Nation At Risk*, during "12 short months." Following its release, an estimated 570,000 copies of *A Nation At Risk* were circulated, and uncounted millions of readers had access to the report through "extensive excerpts" in such newspapers as *The New York Times, The Washington Post,* and *The Oregonian.* Indeed, in just the first four months (May to September 1984), a review of 45 different newspapers counted more than 700 articles relating to the National Commission on Excellence in Education Publication. Regarding the reforms themselves, *The Nation Responds* provides a state-by-state and District of Columbia summation of "recent initiatives," in accordance with *A Nation at Risk* recommendations, that were either under consideration or approved. With the exception of Colorado, New Hampshire, and Maine, every state and the District of Columbia reported the enactment of one or more initiatives related to *A Nation at Risk*'s recommendations. Forty-seven states had strengthened or were in the process of strengthening high school graduation requirements, 41 had increased or were increasing student evaluation and testing, 37 had increased or were increasing instructional time, 30 had developed or were developing master teacher/career ladder formulas, and 44 had reported initiating curriculum reform (which involved essentially a tightening of academic standards).

It is impossible to assess to what degree the aforementioned reforms may have generated a better public grading of the schools. It would appear, however, that there has been, during the 1980s, a rather *strong* relationship between public opinion and educational policy. A reading of the public's attitudes toward education was surely not lost on Terrel Bell and the "excellence" commissioners when constructing *A Nation At Risk.* It is probable that they knew the report would strike a responsive chord. What appears to have surprised them is the magnitude of the response. What *A Nation At Risk* seems to classically exemplify is the manner in which a national report—appropriately timed and skillfully written—can capture the public's thought, amplify its voice, and generate an action. The action that unfolded was educational reform policies, generated in large part, perhaps, by public opinion, that in turn affected public opinion. It is interesting that lengthening the school day and school year, two of the *A Nation At Risk* recommendations which have had a minimal effect on policy (U.S. Government Printing Office, 1984; Laurence Marcus in this volume), were among the few suggested reforms which have been generally opposed by the public. In 1982 longer school days and a school year were opposed by margins of 53% to 37% and 58% to 38%, respectively. In 1984, the opposition margin was somewhat weaker at 50% to 44% for a longer school day and 52% to 42% for a longer school year. The latest (1989) poll (Elam and Gallup, 1989) marked the first time that the national totals favored increasing student time in school. But the approved margin was a modest 48% to 44%. If support for lengthening schooling continues to grow, one cannot help but wonder whether changes in policy will follow suit.

The 1989 poll, twenty-first in the series, revealed an approval rating which matches the record high 1985 and 1987 levels (43% A or B) for *local* public schools. This represents a three-point increase over 1988. In this volume Laurence Marcus (see "Far From The Banks of The Potomac") provides an analysis of state and local educational reform initiatives that continued throughout the middle and late 1980s. From reading his review, one can conclude that the reform movement has continued well beyond the year or so following the publication of *A Nation At Risk*. Accordingly, it is suggested that the continuation of school reform is partly responsible for the continuation of favorable local ratings.

In grading the *nation's* schools, however, as opposed to *local* schools, the public seems less impressed by reform reports. There was even a slight decline in A and B percentages, from 23% in 1988 to 22% in 1989. Given the expressed concern in the 1989 poll about the alleged deterioration of inner-city schools, it is conceivable that this impression affected the image of the schools as a whole. (Some 57% of those polled stated that inner-city schools have gotten worse, vs. 12% gotten better, over the last several decades.) Combined with increasing concern about the abuse of drugs—which since the 1986 poll has been the most frequently identified problem facing local public schools—it is reasonable to suspect that the grading of and opinion on the nation's schools in general, and inner-city school in particular, may continue to decline.

Aside from its relationship with the public's impression of schools, the public's attitude toward substance abuse may provide further testimony to the hypothesized relationship between public opinion and educational policy. According not only to the most recent Gallup education poll but to the most recent Gallup polls on domestic issues of May 17, 1989 and September 11, 1989, drug usage is identified as both the most serious educational problem (34%) and the number one domestic problem (27%) in responses to open-ended questions (Gallup News Services, 1989). The Drug Free Schools and Communities Act of 1986, one of the very few federal educational initiatives of the Reagan administration, stands symbolic of this national concern. More comprehensive endorsement of a "war on drugs" was provided by President Bush in a September 1989 televised message to the nation's schoolchildren, during which he outlined his recommended policies. Given the findings of the Gallup education and domestic polls, it is fitting that the president chose the classroom as the forum for executive action.

How Accurate Is Public Opinion?

Interestingly, the generation of educational policy may have little or nothing to do with the findings of behavioral science. According to the U.S. Department of Health and Human Services in 1989 and the U.S. Department of Education in 1986, abuse of drugs by high school seniors has dropped moderately since 1981, when it reached a reported high of 65.6% who had ever used these illegal substances. Since 1981 there has been a downward trend every year in the reported usage, decreasing to 53.9% in the last recorded year, 1988. Frequency of use has also declined; the percentage of seniors who had used drugs in the last 30 days dropped from a high of 38.9% in 1978–79 to a low of 21.3 in 1988. Even the use of cocaine has dropped yearly by "ever" and "frequent" users from respective highs of 17.3% and 6.78% in 1985 to 12.1% and 3.4% in 1988. Alcohol abuse declined by only a single percentage point (93.2 to 92.0) between 1978 and 1988; yet in the "frequent user" category, (i.e. the number who used alcohol in the last 30 days), it appears to be down significantly, from 72.0% in 1980 to 63.9% in 1988 (U.S. Department of Education, 1989).

Although these statistics have been widely circulated annually in the U.S. Department of Education's *The Conditions of Education*, growing public concern about substance abuse would appear to be a principal promoter of governmental policy. Indeed, former Secretary of Education William Bennett is currently overseeing the "war on drugs." In the public mind, drug use may be strongly associated with the growth of crime and poverty, which in turn are viewed as major domestic problems by Gallup poll respondents (Gallup News Services, September 11, 1989). Moreover, the fact that public opinion differs from scientific assessments does not necessarily mean that the public is wrong. There is more to drug abuse than the percentage of high school seniors who say they use illegal substances, which is the only barometer of the problem employed by the National Center for Educational Statistics.

There is also a good deal more to the state of education than standardized test scores. However, it can be argued that in the early 1980s the public's declining approval of the schools, as revealed in the letter grades given in the Gallup/PDK polls, had little relationship to empirical inquiry. With the principal exception of declining SAT scores, the scholastic data collected during the 1970s and early 1980s suggests that the schools were improving. At three different testing periods (1970–71, 1974–75 and 1979–80) during the 1970s, the National Assessment of Educational Progress (NAEP) reported increases in reading skills attainment by 9- and 13-year-old children (Forbes, 1981). Moreover, the reading achievement increases for historically underachieving pupils (i.e. minorities, urban residents, impoverished rural residents) was most impressive. Particularly encouraging was the performance of black 9-year-olds from 1970 to 1980; they outgained their white counterparts by percentage increases of 10 to 3 on NAEP's standardized reading test. Despite such reports—and others from Title I and compensatory preschool programs which suggested similar improvement—public opinion seemed to suggest that something was awry. Although in the early to mid-1980s a substantial percentage of educators seemingly held the belief that the state of education was good, the release of several international comparisons, which showed American pupils at or near the bottom of the scholastic pile, provided some testimony to the validity of public impressions.

Thus public opinion, regardless of its agreement with social science investigation, may be both a primary ingredient for change and a statement of relative truth. Perhaps no institutional entity is as familiar with life in America as the people who reside here. Accordingly, their sampled opinion should be respected both politically and academically.

REFERENCES

Elam, Stanley M. and Gallup, Alec M. (1989). The 21st Annual Gallup Poll of the Public's Attitudes Toward the Public Schools. *Phi Delta Kappan,* 71: 41–54.

Gallup News Services. (1989). From telephone conversations with the news information desk, September, 1989.

U.S. Department of Education. (1984). *The Nation Responds: Recent Efforts To Improve Education.* Washington, D.C., U.S. Government Printing Office.

U.S. Department of Education. (1989). *The Condition of Education 1989,* Volume 1. Washington, D.C., U.S. Government Printing Office, 116.

Chapter 11

PUBLIC SUPPORT AND
THE QUEST FOR DOLLARS

Kenneth S. Burnley, Jr.

D uring the current worldwide, techno-economic revolution, public education, as with many other American institutions, must forge a new strategy or continue losing ground. A nation hungry to regain preeminence must be the driving force behind this new strategy. A hungry nation will sacrifice to achieve its goals.

There are many throughout the world and in this country who maintain that the United States and its institutions have lost their worldwide preeminence. Some even say that American institutions, among them public education, are in crisis. When the Chinese write the word crisis they use two characters, one meaning danger and the other meaning opportunity. For those who may agree with the crisis notion, the gradual decline of the United States may be underway. On the other hand, for those who believe problems are disguised as opportunities, the best for the United States may be yet to come!

However, before we can take advantage of the opportunity to forge a new strategy, we must first understand where public education is now, where it needs to go, and how to get it there. It is only through knowledge and comprehension of the past and present that we can best forge a new strategy for the future, regain full public support for education and win the quest for dollars.

COMPETITION FOR THE SHRINKING DOLLAR

We are experiencing some of the most difficult times in American history for the funding of public education. There are many reasons for this phenomena. Educators are better organized and have done a great deal to improve their wages. This is augmented by a general awareness that teachers do deserve a better living standard. Associations and unions have become more aggressive in assisting communities throughout the country to come to this realization. As a result of salary increases and other expenses of doing business, educational costs have increased substantially in recent years and will continue to do so.

Parents with children in the public schools have become a new minority in America. Between 70 and 75 percent of the taxpayers no longer have children in the public schools. Yet, these same taxpayers are continually asked to pay more and more for schools their children no longer attend. Schools, on the other hand, have not done a very good job in building bridges between the schools and the "shareholders." Since most of these unconnected taxpayers get their information about schools from the mass media, one can readily see where the problem lies.

With the phenomena of the "Graying of America" and more citizens living longer on fixed incomes, taxes have become an ugly word. Very often taxpayers cannot do anything about federal income taxes, sales taxes, etc. Yet, they do vote most often at their local level on: (1) millage which generates money for the operation of the schools, and (2) millage which supports the bonds necessary to build and upgrade facilities. Without feeling obligated to "support their schools," no votes often represent the only way people have to show their displeasure with taxes. So, throughout the country the schools are caught in a "tax revolt."

Because schools have not been able to develop comprehensive efforts for public relations, they have not done a good job of marketing their services, thus enabling communities to understand that: (1) public education is the backbone of a democratic society; (2) the quality of life of a community is directly related to the quality of its schools; (3) everyone has a stake in the public's "community schools" which everyone can use to meet individual and group needs; (4) someone paid the bill when they attended school; and (5) our economy depends upon an educated and highly skilled work force. Since the schools have not been successful enough in taking this approach, the community is feeling "estranged" from what was once the center of their life, the public school.

THE COMPETITIVE FACTOR: RESISTANCE TO CHANGE

Philip Kotler, in *Marketing for Non Profit Organizations,* writes, "Organizations come into being to accomplish some purpose. The founders are clear minded about the organization's mission and they often pursue it with single-minded dedication. A new hospital is organized to serve the sick; the public schools to provide education and job skills to the young; the new church to administer to the spiritual needs of the community. The original founders are spirited, dedicated and customer oriented."[1] Kotler does a very thorough job of comparing organizations in their early responsive years to the later, generally less responsive years.

> The organization that meets the needs of its customers grows and prospers. As it grows, it becomes more complexed and multi-purpose. It takes on additional responsibilities to its customers, employees, agents, suppliers, and other publics. The organization has to serve well not only the original client group that prompted its creation but also the various internal and external groups that derive their income or symbolic status from the organization. Interest groups form around the organization. Top management faces the task of harmonizing often incompatible goals and interests. Much of its energy turns inward. But here comes the weakness. The world and the markets are continually changing while the organization stands still. New needs emerge, new interest groups appear, new stages are reached in the economy, law, technology, and culture. The organization becomes increasingly maladapted to its environment. It appears to its publics to be increasingly unresponsive to their needs. There's a creeping tendency towards organizational un-responsiveness.[2]

To paraphrase Max Weber, people's problems are defined in terms of how the bureaucratic organization is set up rather than having the organization set up to respond to the people's problems. When this occurs, questions of structure dominate questions of substance; means dominate ends.

In other words, change is inevitable. Yet, there is often resistance to change. Thomas Huxley puts it another way: "Perhaps the most valuable result of all education is the ability to make yourself do the thing you have to do when it ought to be done, whether you like it or not. It is the first lesson which ought to be learned, and however early a person's training begins, it is probably the last lesson learned thoroughly."

During the first part of the twentieth century, the public schools had a captive audience and little competition. It has only been within the last 10–15 years that the public schools have had to face serious competition. This was due largely to the public schools trying to be all things to all people. They serve all kinds of students with all kinds of social, emo-

---

1. Kotler, Philip, *Marketing For Non Profit Organizations* (Englewood Cliffs, NJ: Prentice-Hall), p. 38.

2. Ibid., pp. 38–39.

tional and physical problems, and with dwindling support from home and the community.

In addition, competition has increased for the shrinking dollar, the number of private schools have increased and this generation of students was raised while being entertained by television and the mass media. Most recently major corporations have been buying up school textbook publishing companies. Perhaps their plans are to add to the competition by pumping education into the home after normal school hours via satellite, or "the eye in the sky." If the public schools are perceived as continuing to be unresponsive, plans for this type of education might begin in five years. Initially, such an effort might start with after-school instruction but could be expanded to go much further.

To respond to competition, the public schools cannot merely sell the public on its programs and services, especially not just during millage elections when all that the schools need is more money. Instead, the public schools must continuously market its programs and services in response to the changing needs of its clients and the competition from without.

The private sector has become increasingly aware that to maintain its competitiveness in an international economy, a prerequisite is a highly skilled work force, albeit a work force that the private sector has to train. However, if that same work force has to be educated, the private sector realizes that it cannot pay the bill. Even if the private sector could, it couldn't do it fast enough to remain competitive. It is essential that the basic education of all students be improved, in the area of employability and literary skills, good health practices, and the ability to live, work and play in a pluralistic world. Finally, we see perhaps the principal reason why many people are paying attention to the public schools. It is not necessarily for humanistic reasons but for economic reasons. It goes without saying that the private sector has had to face the same problems. The techno-economic revolution affecting the entire world affects the private sector just as it does the public sector. The private sector has come to that realization more quickly because profits determine their ability to stay in business. Public schools must forge a new strategy through partnerships with all sectors of the community in order to help the country become more competitive with the rest of the world.

MISINFORMATION ABOUT PUBLIC EDUCATION

Although the public schools can do much to improve their delivery of services, any suggestion that public education is failing the nation is simply not true. We're getting record levels of education, reports *USA TODAY* in its September 22, 1988 issue. The article goes on to say we're staying in school longer, and a record number of us are getting high school diplomas and college degrees. A census report says today:

1. 76% of adults over 24 were at least high school graduates, up 51% from two decades ago.
2. One in five have a college degree, which is double the 1967 rate.
3. In 1940, 24.5% of people 25 and older had finished high school: 4.6% were college graduates.[3]

USA Today goes on to say, "Boosting college rates, growing opportunities for minorities and women, emphasis on career advancement refresher courses, and tuition aide, are helps in answers to what has to happen in this major revolution." "Other 1987 findings reported for adults over age 24: college degrees were held by 24% of men and 17% of women; 81% in the west had completed high school; 77% in the mid-west; 76% in the northeast and 71% in the south. The metro area had a 78% high school completion rate, and rural areas had a 69% rate. One-third of the US 12.4 million college students are now at least 25 years of age."[4]

Despite record levels of educational attainment, concern about education has grown. In the last ten years, there have been numerous studies on public education such as: *A Nation At Risk; Action for Excellence; Academic Preparation for College; Making the Grade; Education and Economic Progress Toward a National Education Policy; The Celebration of Teaching; High Schools in the 1980's;* and *High School: A report on American Secondary Education.* In general, they suggest that a poor job has been done. Instead, the position laid out by *USA Today* makes it clear that public education is doing better than ever, but it is simply not enough. In fact, the United States, as a nation, is doing better than ever but is simply not keeping pace with the emerging economic leaders in the world. Finger pointing will not bring a solution to the problem. The institutions of this nation must respond together and respond quickly.

Nationally known economist David Pearce Synder, in a 1988 speech

3. *USA Today* newspaper, Thursday, September 22, 1988, front page.
4. Ibid.

in Colorado Springs, said, "The average techno-economic revolution runs about 30–35 years. No nation which was preeminent prior to a techno-economic revolution was preeminent at the conclusion of that revolution."[5] As an example, the British Empire was a preeminent nation prior to the Industrial Revolution. However, because it did not adjust to change, Great Britain was not preeminent after the Industrial Revolution.

Regarding preeminence, the United States has decided, on a national policy level, that we want to remain preeminent after the current techno-economic revolution. Therefore, our mission is established. The questions are: (1) Do enough voices exist in the country to help us understand what the mission entails? (2) What must be done to achieve the mission? and (3) Are we hungry enough?

Wrong Approach

Other bits of information which the public does not understand: (1) by the year 2000 the total of all minorities in this country will outnumber the current white majority for the first time in the history of the United States; (2) minorities are dropping out of school much faster and in much higher numbers than the current majority population; and (3) minority grade point averages, test score results, attendance rates and graduation rates are lower. Yet, minorities and women will make up approximately 80% of the work force in the year 2000.

At a time when the country needed to support public education to benefit the nation's future work force, just the opposite occurred. The U.S. Constitution leaves the control of public education to the states. Yet, states have been shifting the financial burden to taxpayers at the local level. Percentage shares of the total educational budgets have been decreasing at state levels and increasing at local levels. Some states are now taking steps to reverse that trend. Of course, he who has the gold makes the rules. So, along with an increased share of education costs, states are establishing more requirements of local school boards, which means less control at the local level.

The federal financial support to education illustrates an even more graphic picture. Nick Penning, legislative specialist for The American Association of School Administrators and a member of The Committee

---

5. Snyder, David Pearce, "Speech" in Colorado Springs, Colorado, Cheyenne Mountain Inn, November 20, 1988.

for Education Funding (which represents about 100 of this nation's education associations), said,

> During the last eight years, the average percentage of local school district education budgets derived from the federal government dropped from about nine percent (9%) to six percent (6%). Within the same period of time, the percentage of the total federal budget devoted to education went from 2½% to 1.7%. Translated into fiscal 1989 dollars, that represents 21.9 billion dollars for education nationally. If the percentage of the federal budget devoted to education had remained at 2½%, the 1989 fiscal year federal budget would contain 31.2 billion dollars instead of 21.9 billion dollars.

We also increased graduation requirements without helping students, who were already having difficulty in school, achieve mastery and/or receive necessary remediation. We increased student tracking. We pushed more students out of school than were dropping out prior to the studies. In general, we took the wrong approach! The way to really get results is to collaborate at the school level.

In short, public education has done a better job than ever before, but it is not enough in a techno-economic revolution. However, the output of business, industry and government has not been much better. The bottom line is that the nation as a whole must forge a new strategy. In order to increase its competitiveness and meet the techno-economic revolution challenge, the strategy must be forged together. Finger pointing serves no purpose. Partnerships which emphasize service and sacrifice are part of the solution and do have purpose. Add to this human resource contribution reasonable increases in funding at all levels and the needed changes can be achieved.

Role of the Media

Communications is at the heart of all relationships and fosters understanding. The media has a leadership role to fill. The print and electronics media, as professional communicators, are key in what kind of message goes out about public education. In working with the media, public education representatives need to understand the distinctions of news reporting, features and editorials:

1. The news is who, what, when, where, why and how. The media has no responsibility to print/broadcast "good" news. The job is to report the news (a neutral word). The reason people often perceive the news as "bad" is because, thank goodness, the norm is still

usually what we perceive as good. In other words, most people arrive to work safely, so the news is about John Smith who had an accident, not about John Smith arriving at work safely and on time.

2. Features are subjective and are a good way for more in-depth focus on programs in public schools. Considered "soft news," features will always lose in the very competitive battle for space and time. However, features are often very popular with subscribers and listeners, so it is always worth the time to enter this battle by providing information and opportunities for features.

3. Editorials are opinions of the media leaders. Time spent with media leaders is usually very influential, in that it provides them with a perspective they need for judging significance of news.

The media's main goal is to get the facts and be objective in reporting them to the public. When the media has balanced coverage, covers the school board meetings, creative programs within schools, etc., along with the stories about irate parents, the public has a broad framework in which they can place the "negative" stories.

It is vital that public educators give the media the information they need, both formally and informally, so that stories are not as likely to be reported out of context. When members of the media have the information they need to understand all sides of critical issues, they can relate those issues to the public. When media management understands the importance of public education to the preservation of our democratic society and economic health, they can help establish priorities beneficial to the nation's well-being, thus assuming and asserting their leadership roles.

THE CHANGING STRUCTURE OF SOCIETY DICTATES CHANGES IN ITS INSTITUTIONS

As discussed earlier, we are in a worldwide, techno-economic revolution, and, as such, the need for change is rather astounding. Even more startling, however, are the subtle societal changes which have already occurred and of which many people are still unaware. As an example, in 1955 the four-member nuclear family, which consisted of an employed father, a non-working mother, and two school-age children existed in 62 percent of this nation's households. In 1986, such a nuclear family existed in only 6 percent of the households nationally. Many students who leave home for school in the morning leave an empty house and arrive back home in the evening to the same empty house. If you took attendance in the average classroom today, you would find, more often than not, that students have a different last name than their parent or guardian. A further illustration of changes in our society is the fact that 62 percent of teenagers believe that their lives will be harder than those of their parents. In the history of the United States no future generation has ever thought that its life would be more difficult than the generation of its parents.

Instructor Magazine, Secondary Edition, fall of 1988 has compiled the following list of statistics on today's teenagers:

> 42% of teenagers believe there will be a nuclear war in their lifetime, and that one in 16 seniors drink alcohol daily; one in five high school seniors smoke cigarettes each day; each day 3,000 teenage girls become pregnant; one in 5 girls and one in 10 boys have actually attempted suicide; 5,000 teens under 19 commit suicide yearly, 50,000 attempt it; and that auto wrecks account for 70% of accidental deaths, the leading cause of deaths of 15- to 25-year-olds; 56% of teens do not use seat belts, and 1.1 million teens from the ages of 11 to 17 leave home each year; 15% of girls have been sexually abused by age 16, and half of all rape victims are under 18 years of age; 2.5 million teens are infected with sexually transmitted diseases every year; and 85% of the teens who appear in court are functionally illiterate; one-third of the students between 16 and 19 years old work 15 to 20 hours per week; and 25% of all students who enter high school nationwide do not finish; in some areas 60% of all students drop out of school; 40% of teenage girls who drop out of school do so because they are pregnant or already a parent.[6]

The above list represents a staggering set of concerns for our next generation of adults. Our country has simply not responded. These problems are not insurmountable, but they are major problems which are systemic throughout the country. It will take change in the structure of our society to correct them and to put us in the position to maximize our resources and return to preeminence.

We often harken back to the values and benefits of the nuclear family. While it is foolish to think we can recreate the roles played by the members of the 1955 nuclear family, we can recreate the benefits derived. As an example: (1) After-school study centers can replace mom helping

---

6. *Instructor Magazine,* Secondary Edition, Fall, 1988, pp. 4–39.

with homework; (2) latchkey programs in schools and businesses before and after school can replace mom being home; (3) mentors, big brothers and big sisters can help give the love, attention and guidance that mom provided; (4) fostering the relationship between senior citizens and students, both during and after school, can further provide the love, attention and guidance missed when both parents work; and (5) pre-school centers for students and parents can close the kindergarten/first grade achievement gap.

In order to (1) meet the challenges brought on by the techno-economic revolution; (2) address the negative changes which have occurred in the structure of our society; and (3) recapture the values of the nuclear family, we as a nation must view the times of crisis as times of opportunity and mobilize the country to action. We must return to the values of service and sacrifice to community, state and country. We must become hungry again! These values coupled with specific solutions will return our nation to a position of preeminence in a challenging new international marketplace.

Morris Massey, in his two video tapes, sets a very interesting stage for us. In his first tape, titled, "What We Are Now, Is What We Were When" he says, We basically developed our value systems by the time we were 10 years old and in large part based on the environment in which we were living, and what was going on at the time." In his second video tape which is entitled, "What We Are Now, Is Not Necessarily What We Have To Be," Massey suggests, "We can change as individuals and groups. In order for that change to occur, we have to reach people at their level of personal significance."[7]

David Pearce Snyder in, *Strategic Knowledge For Leadership And Learning,* published in 1987, talks about change and under what circumstances people change. He says, "That indeed there are circumstances under which people change, they change when:

1. they perceive that the change is inevitable;
2. the benefits of the change will be quickly realized;
3. tools for adaptation are readily at hand;
4. the risk of change is diminished by some form of insurance or backup with surplus resources; and

---

7. Massey, Morris, Video Tape, "What We Are Now Is What We Were When."

5. the change can be comfortably integrated with other basic aspects of life."[8]

Snyder placed change within the context of the techno-economic revolution. He talks about how inevitable the forces of change are. He illustrated his point by discussing: (1) baby boomers and beyond, under which he details the baby bust; (2) women in the work force; (3) the baby boom; echo; zero growth; working moms; (4) latchkey kids; and (5) everyone going back to school for retraining, etc., etc.

The History of Pre-Eminence

In "Learning for Life in Revolutionary Times," printed in the *Journal of Studies in Technical Careers,* Snyder talks about the techno-economic revolution in more specific terms. He says,

> Throughout history there's never been a major techno-economic transition, during which the dominate nation prior to that transition has remained pre-eminent following the transition. Circumstances generally mitigate against large successful enterprises undertaking significant innovations. He says smaller newer enterprises, on the other hand, are generally forced by their circumstances to innovate simply to offset the competitive advantages processed by large-scale dominate producers. The characteristic result of this dynamic is that smaller less profitable enterprises and less prosperous nations have historically captured marketplace dominance during periods of economic transitions. Today a growing number of economists are referring to the Pacific Rim countries as a second growth engine of the world economy that is capable of playing such a takeover roll in the current economic situation. He says these are clearly revolutionary times.[9]

Snyder believes that this techno-economic revolution will take virtually a generation or more to be completed, or about 30 to 35 years. During this 35-year period, many new jobs will be created, most of which will require a trained work force. During the transition many people with high degrees of education and training will work in more menial positions than their training prepares them for. Yet, there will be few self-supporting jobs for people without a skill or college degree. It will be a difficult time for some who will be caught up in this transition. Education will be the cornerstone to help us through the revolution.

---

8. Snyder, David Pearce, "Strategic Knowledge for Leadership and Learning (Washington D.C., E.S. Press, 1987), p. 4.

9. Snyder, David Pearce, "Learning For Life In Revolutionary Times": Imperatives for American Educators in A Decade of Techno-Economic Change, JSTC Volume IX, Number 2, Spring, 1987, pp. 99–100.

Many people will feel the need to be engaged in some form of education to retrain themselves, understand what is going on, keep current, or fill leisure time. All this will occur at a time when resources will be tight and competition for the dollar fierce. Instead of the refrain, "Only the strong will survive," we will hear, "Only the well trained and educated will prosper."

The Challenge for the Schools

The challenge for the public schools is to restructure itself. Harold Hodgkinson, in a speech on November 10, 1988 in Colorado Springs, said, "Eighty percent of the work force of the year 2000 will be made up of women and minorities."[10]

The key, therefore, is a highly trained, educated and motivated work force in which all people regardless of circumstance have basic skills and equal opportunity. If this occurs, productivity will be at an all-time high and place the United States back on the top of the international productivity list. This is essential because our economic lives depend on it. When only three workers (one of the three will be a minority) will provide for every one retiree in the future, compared to seventeen workers providing for every retiree two to three decades ago, those three must be productive. If they are not, business and government will falter and world preeminence will be a faded dream. In order for all human resources to be maximized, discrimination on the basis of race, creed, color, national origin, sex and handicapping condition *must* become passé.

The philosophy of the schools will need major change. The revolution will require the elimination of the "bell-shaped curve" where the majority get A's, B's, or C's and a certain number fail with D's or F's. In its place will be the term "mastery." In this approach every student eventually will "get it" or "learn it." "Remediation occurs until prescribed "mastery" occurs. In remediation a student might complete their work in "after-school study centers" or in "extended summer learning." In addition, this remediation may take place after graduation, when, like Iaccoca, superintendents guarantee services by returning unprepared students back to school for retraining. In any event, there will be no stigma attached to this approach—only the realization that people develop at their own pace.

---

10. Hodgkinson, Harold, Speech on National and State Demographics, Cheyenne Mountain Inn, Colorado Springs, Colorado, November 9, 1988.

So the specific questions are: What do we do in public education to gain greater public support and thereby increase the resources necessary to do a more effective job? How do we convince the public that they will get value for value, that the quest for dollars is deserved?

Marketing Versus Selling

As indicated earlier in this chapter, until the last decade or so public schools of this nation had basically a captive audience and very little competition. As a result, public schools have had very rudimentary public relations operations. This is really obvious when we compare the size and expertise of public relations departments in public schools with those of the private sector.

In the business world you receive degrees in marketing and have highly trained people who run large marketing departments. Marketing represents all aspects of what a company or organization does. Yet, in the public schools, not only is there no such degree within the field, there are few highly trained people and virtually no large marketing departments. The public sees no need to have a public relations staff or marketing department, because such amenities are seen as fluff.

Philip Kotler, in *Marketing Management,* does an excellent job defining the difference between marketing and selling and even makes a distinction between these two concepts and the concept of product. Kotler defines marketing as "Human activity directed at satisfying needs and wants through exchange processes."[11] The selling concept is identified as "a management orientation that assumes that consumers will normally not buy enough of the company's products unless they are approached with a substantial selling and promotion effort."[12] The product concept is defined by Kotler as "a management orientation that assumes that consumers will respond favorably to good products that are reasonably priced and that little company marketing effort is required to achieve satisfactory sales and profits."[13] It is Kotler's opinion that marketing is based on customer satisfaction and strategies designed to create that satisfaction. In fact, the goals of the organization are satisfied only when the customer is satisfied.

---

11. Kotler, Philip, Prentice-Hall, Englewood Cliffs, N.J., p. 5.

12. Ibid., p. 13.

13. Ibid., p. 12.

If we look at Kotler's definition of the product concept, we note that it can be based on a lack of competition. Therefore, no need exists to work on customer satisfaction because the services needed are essentially provided only by the organization. Does this look like the public schools of the past? As for the selling concept, public schools have engaged heavily in this type of activity during millage campaigns—and primarily millage campaigns only.

The client approach of the public schools has been one of selling, and the sales pitch has primarily been used when money has been needed. This process has gone on and on for years and has worn thin. The solution is for the public schools to adopt en masse the more sophisticated "marketing" approach to its business. That means concentrating on customer satisfaction through the exchange process—value for value.

Marketing Tools

Public opinion surveys, community surveys, and market penetration are but a few components of marketing. These tools are used to find out what the client thinks of the organization, what kind of job they feel is being done, and what they expect the organization to do. This information is matched with the resources that the organization has to determine what its marketing strategy ought to be and what additional resources may be needed to deliver what the client expects. These are techniques, procedures and theories, which for the most part are foreign to public schools. Its only been recently, within the last decade or two, that public schools have begun building their public relations departments.

In the business world, marketing is a process which touches virtually everything that a company does from the time it conceives something it wants to sell to the time it is actually sold. In public education we need to look at marketing in exactly the same way. We need to understand that over 90 percent of our school image is who we are and what we do. Public education must understand the simple axioms that, "Your greatest ambassadors are your employees and that nothing sells products like word of mouth."[14] Marketing is a consumer-oriented process. Its foundation is one of exchange, a value in exchange for value. When the people see something of value in their schools, they buy it, exchanging their support and tax dollars for what they desire. Therefore, "Public Schools, Good and Getting Better," "Public Schools, No Better Place to Learn,"

---

14. Macomb, Marketing Plan, Macomb Intermediate School District, Mt. Clemens, MI, p. 2.

are some examples of a marketing approach to the business of public education.

Surveying Clients

One of the cornerstones of a quality marketing plan is a survey of clients. A good community public opinion survey on public education consists of research done to accomplish the following objectives:

1. to determine community perceptions towards public education;
2. to assess community expectations of the schools;
3. to determine community attitude toward current education issues, which are relevant to district planning efforts;
4. to measure public support for various ways to cope with changing fiscal needs;
5. to provide a basis for comparing attitudes in a given school district with national and state attitudinal assessments; and
6. to satisfy state accountability and accreditation requirements of surveying public opinion regularly and to assess needs and desires for information about the district and its programs every five years.

An effective survey requires: (1) a professionally developed survey instrument or questionnaire; (2) a scientific random sampling of residents to be used for the study, broken down in such a way as to allow the district to make comparisons from one aspect of its community to another; (3) professional interviewing techniques in administering the questionnaire; (4) professional analysis and reporting; and (5) implementation of the findings.

The survey ought to focus on mission statements, goals and objectives, as well as program importance, future goals, and equity issues. It should also address communications and community involvement, comparison of parents to non-parents, questions pertaining to teachers and the teaching act itself, and questions of facilities and funding levels.

Once the survey is completed, part of the implementation process is to develop a concept for the marketing plan. There are several strategies: defensive marketing, offensive marketing, flanking marketing, or all-out guerilla marketing.[15] Perhaps the best rule for a good marketing strategy is analogous to the football axiom that "the best defense is a good offense, or the best offense is a good defense." Either way, both an

---

15. Ibid., p. 4.

offensive and defensive marketing approach would probably make the most sense, be the most direct and be the least insulting to the community. There are a series of questions one should ask when developing a marketing plan: (1) "What is the perception of the district within the community? (2) What image or perception do we want the community to have of us? (3) Who is our competition? (4) Is the position that we would like to have in the community a reasonable one and one that we can actually finance? and (5) What are we doing and/or saying that represents what we really are?"[16]

Once that process is completed, a good marketing plan may be developed. Some good cornerstones in terms of objectives might be:

1. to demonstrate to the community that the public schools are doing a good job of teaching basic skills;
2. to alert the staff about what the public perceives about the schools;
3. to help the schools be more responsive to the public;
4. to help school staff improve their communications with the public;
5. to provide a communication plan which can be duplicated in schools throughout the district;
6. to get the board to adopt a marketing strategy;
7. to educate and help the public understand why public relations and marketing is important in todays techno-economic revolution; and
8. to produce the materials that help communicate the image and perception that we want the district to have.[17]

In short, public education needs to become more sophisticated by understanding the difference between marketing and selling and, therefore, embrace a marketing concept. From there, a marketing plan must be developed that will properly position the school district within the minds of the clients. And finally, schools must become more responsive through marketing penetration and marketing strategies to help the public understand why education is a big business, and must be treated with sophisticated big business principles, thus maximizing efficiency and effectiveness.

---

16. Ibid., pp. 8–9.

17. Ibid., pp. 8–9.

Role of the Leader

One aspect of gaining public support that should not be overlooked is the importance of a strong leader at the head of an organization. Only one name is needed to show how important a strong leader is in marketing—Lee Iaccoca!

For years chief executive officers in the private sector have cultivated each other to make sure they know about one anothers' businesses and to support common causes. C.E.O.'s in public education have not seen this networking as a top priority for many because supporting public education was a given. Also, the professional preparation and background of most educational leaders is educational administration, not marketing.

When a school district has a strong leader who manages his/her district professionally, one who is an articulate advocate of public education and is viewed as a visionary in the community, public education gains stature along with the leader.

Personal contact is the key. Education leaders need to:

1. Join the same networking organizations other C.E.O.'s do
2. Talk to them in business terms instead of "educationeese"
3. Make sure they understand the schools are big business
4. Show them the bottom line—public education's "product" is vital to the economic health of their businesses.

The involvement of the public education C.E.O. cannot be one-sided. It is important that the education leader join private sector C.E.O.'s in their organizations and helping support their priorities. When business people and other citizens perceive the education leader as an effective, efficient leader they are more willing to give their support to public education because they trust that their additional resources—time, commitment and financial support—will be used judiciously. An effective, articulate public education leader will have a major impact on how public education is viewed, thus becoming a key to the marketing plan.

FORGING A NEW STRATEGY

The meta-message is that when enough people think and act together they form the "critical mass" necessary to forge a new public education strategy. The foundations needed for successful implementation of the strategy are:

1. understanding what is at stake;
2. dedicating ourselves to service to country, state and community;
3. dedicating ourselves to more self-sacrifice;
4. electing and appointing leaders who can:
   a. trumpet the cause
   b. motivate people to act
   c. conceptualize and frame the issues
   d. articulate the issues and
   e. eloquently issue the challenges
5. building partnerships between and within all segments of each community that requires personal time energy and commitment.

Imagine if the major advertising companies in this nation, each state and each community were to join forces with the secretary of education, state superintendents and local superintendents to put the kind of sophisticated ads we see on television selling the traditional goods and services we see to sell and market education. The ads could be put on television, radio, as well as on the sides of busses, cabs, billboards, benches, pens, pencils, literature, etc. Just imagine the power of this one approach.

Forging a new public education strategy through partnerships is the answer to our problems. Suggestions for such an approach can be taken from Colorado Springs School District Eleven in Colorado Springs, Colorado where we have begun to develop such an approach. The following is a reprint of the Student Performance and Achievement Initiative (SPA) in Colorado Springs, which identifies this school district's partnership strategy.

COLORADO SPRINGS SCHOOL DISTRICT ELEVEN

Student Performance and Achievement Project[18]

I. Philosophy

Public education in the United States has entered a new era requiring a highly literate, employable, and productive work force. This new era will literally demand that every person achieve mastery of certain basic skills in order to move from school to work, school to college, or college to the work place. The bell-shaped curve which dictates that a certain number of people will fail is no longer acceptable. Instead, mastery and remediation will become the passwords of the day. Each person will be required to have basic skills, even if they take a longer period of time to achieve.

The continued forging and emergence of new partnerships between all segments of the community will be a prerequisite to the success of the United States in this new public education philosophy.

II. Goals

A. Literacy skills for all students which will enable them to move from school to work, school to college, or college to the work place. Mastery and any necessary remediation must occur in all the basic areas which should include technology, health issues, communications, reading, writing, math, science, and the arts.

B. Employability skills for all students. Employability skills are those skills necessary to be successful in the work place. As an example, punctuality, reliability, dependability, understanding the rules, getting along with other people, dressing properly, communicating well, meeting expectations, doing more than expected, etc.

C. Preparation for all students to live in a pluralistic society. It is important that we learn to live, work, and play with people both alike and different from ourselves, especially in view of the nation's changing demographics.

18. Student Performance and Achievement Project (SPA), Philosophy, Goals and Strategies, Colorado Springs, School District Eleven, Colorado Springs, Colorado, November, 1988.

D. Good health practices for all students. In order to maximize individual potential to learn, students must eat, sleep and exercise properly and be free of debilitating drugs, alcohol and chemicals.

III. Strategies for the Educational Partnership

A. **Preschool Education Programs** — These programs help young people coming into school to get a good start and not begin school far behind other students.

B. **After-School Study Centers** — Students do not have to go home to an empty house. They can receive from trained educators and volunteers after-school help on their studies, as well as study skills assistance.

C. **Latchkey Centers** — These services can be provided by the private sector. The schools can coordinate the use of the buildings and bid contracts out to the private sector so that students have some place to go before and after school.

D. **Remediation to Obtain Mastery** — Students are permitted to go to summer school, free of cost; to spend time after the school day getting help. This approach will insure that all students achieve mastery in prescribed areas.

E. **Technology Training** — All students are provided training in the use of computers and other related technology for the future.

F. **Mentorships** — All students who can benefit from a mentor should be assigned one. A mentor is a person who adopts a student and works with them on their studies, their goals, aspirations and provides general guidance.

G. **Homework Hotlines** — Phone lines set up and run by school districts Monday through Thursday each night of the week and staffed by professional teachers. Students can call in for help on their homework—cable television can augment the process.

H. **Vocational/Technical Education** — Enhance vocational technical education. Set up more area skill centers which serve as capstones to school programs (11th and 12th grade). Change graduation requirements to meet needs of students. Retrain staff if necessary. Train counselors to steer many college-bound students to get some vocational/technical education. College is not necessary for many, especially when they have a skill which permits them to lead highly productive lives.

I. **Career Counseling** — Enhance career counseling services for all students. Increase use of computer software and counselor time for this type of work.

J. **Health Counseling** — Open health counseling centers in schools, and staff them with trained professionals. Move ahead on issues like drug and alcohol abuse, pregnancy, etc.. Coordinate these efforts with local government and non-profit agencies.

K. **Guaranteed Services** — Establish mastery levels in all subject areas for each grade level. All students graduating should have reached mastery levels in all basic areas. To the extent a graduate cannot perform at the mastery levels indicated and it can be proven, return the student to the public school system until mastery is obtained (night school can be used for convenience to all).

L. **Affective Domain** — More attention, by all partners, to tender loving care, respect, time for play, and development of the total student in the mental, physical, emotional and spiritual areas.

M. **Teacher, Principal, and Staff Support** — All partners must give greater support to teachers, principals and the staff who work directly with the students.

IV. THE EDUCATIONAL PARTNERSHIP—SCHOOLS, PARENTS, BUSINESS, COMMUNITY, GOVERNMENT, AND LEGISLATURE

Students grow and flourish when nurtured in an educational environment. The home, school, and community environment play major and vital roles in a student's success or failure. Only through a working partnership of the home, community and school can success be attained. Coordination of these three major factors provides each student the opportunity, motivation and skills to be productive members of society and lifelong learners. The following commitments made by each segment of the school/community are examples of shared responsibility through partnership. The key to successful partnerships is human resource contribution. In other words, individual service to community.

A. Colorado Springs District #11 Commitment

1. Improve student attendance and eliminate student discontinuance or dropouts.
2. Improve graduation rates.
3. Improve student transition from school to college, college to work, and school to work.

4. Improve student competency in all areas, especially reading, writing, mathematics and technology.
5. Improve student performance and achievement as citizens and workers.

B. Parent Commitment

1. Provide a regular time and place for study and homework.
2. Provide a consistent bedtime and proper night's rest.
3. Know where their children are and who they are with.
4. Teach the child to respect his/her property and that of others.
5. Promote the child's self-confidence.
6. Provide the child a good diet and medical care.

C. Student Commitment

1. Commit to proper rest and nutrition for a healthy body and mind.
2. Promote cooperation between parents, teachers and others to enable them to reach their full potential.
3. Dedicate to regular homework completion (nightly and weekends).
4. Recognize the impact of and refrain from alcohol, drugs and suicidal behavior.
5. Seek assistance when needed and share support systems through peer counseling and positive interaction with fellow students.
6. Improve graduation rate, dropout rate, test scores, etc..

D. Business Commitment

1. Provide employees who have schoolage children 2 days per year to visit schools.
2. Allow personnel one day per year to visit and become acquainted with the schools.
3. Provide visitation and in-service for school personnel at the business work site.
4. Join with educators, legislators and other community leaders to support public education.
5. Sponsor support of education through business industry advertising.
6. Encourage student visitation, internships and jobs at the business site.

E. Government Commitment

1. Engage in greater inter-agency cooperation with public education.
2. Form partnerships with public education.
3. Foster positive image and perception of public education.
4. Visit two schools per year.
5. Invite public education personnel and students to view and participate in government.

F. Legislative Commitment

1. Provide legislation that brings focus and credibility to the need for education and literacy for all people regardless of circumstance.
2. Provide local level legislation that fosters improved student performance, achievement, attendance and graduation rates.
3. Provide funding to support statutory and regulatory obligations.
4. Observe at least two classrooms each school year.
5. Become personally involved in the schools.

G. Senior Citizen Commitment

1. Work in foster grandparent relationship with local schools.
2. Encourage other senior citizens to become involved with investment in public education.
3. Commit to the re-establishment of the extended family relationships of the past; to include children of their neighborhood.
4. Consider being a mentor for a student.
5. Re-commit to the value and importance of public education.
6. Join the community and its accountability school movement.

H. Community Members and Organizations

1. Make a commitment to visit a local school one day per year.
2. Foster coordination between the school and churches.
3. Coordinate services of schools and community agencies.
4. Make a personal effort to serve on a school committee, board, or advising group.
5. Learn more about what help the schools need and pitch in.

"Public support and the quest for dollars" is directly tied to the perception of getting what you pay for. In today's world of rapid change, we are not always sure we get what we pay for.

Public education is producing record levels of education and yet is losing "public support and the quest for dollars." Why? Because a great deal more is needed from public education and all of this country's institutions to remain or regain preeminence in a worldwide, techno-economic revolution. Moreover, more students than ever before are bringing their problems to school and staying through graduation. At the same time, the nuclear family is disappearing and today's teens, for the first time in U.S. history, feel that their lives will be more difficult than those of their parents. In short, the schools are faced with more students, with more problems and less support than ever before. Add to this scenario the fact that 80 percent of tomorrow's work force will be made up of women and minorities; yet many minorities have the lowest achievement levels. This points to the potential for an even less produc-tive work force in the future, at a time when our nation's levels of productivity are already too low. Further complicating matters is the "graying of America." As a result of this phenomenon, only an average of 22 percent of the adults in this country have children in our schools. The other 78 percent of the population often feels no personal connection to the schools and, therefore, see no reason to support them with tax dollars. So "tax revolts" toward public education increase when just the reverse is needed. Instead of responding with a marketing approach, which is designed to help the taxpayer see the value of the exchange process (tax dollars for quality education), the schools continue using the worn-out selling approach and usually only when money is needed.

Obviously change is needed. However, the needed change is difficult for public schools. They are bureaucracies which, by their nature, are slow to change. People do not like their institutions to change rapidly. Since virtually everyone went through the public schools, they have an opinion on how they ought to be run, which is essentially the way they were when they went through them. Change is even more difficult for public schools, because much of the change is in response to clients' changing needs and competition from without. While bureaucracies resist change, the bureaucracies of the public schools were also never designed to address competition.

Much information and misinformation abounds about public school performance. However, research clearly indicates that the public schools are producing record levels of education. Compared to the forties and fifties, today's public schools are outstripping them in many areas of performance like graduation rates, attendance rates, etc.

Financial support to public education from state and federal sources has been gradually falling off in the last decade or so. Federal support has dropped from 2.1 percent to 1.7 percent of the federal budget—about $10 billion per year in today's dollars. Until recently, states have been shifting a greater percentage of budget cost to the local levels, further exacerbating local taxpayer revolts.

While all of this has been going on, society has been changing too, especially the family. The nuclear family of the fifties, a father, non-worker mother and two children, which made up 62 percent of all families, is gone and replaced by families where both parents work or single-parent families. Often, young people are left to fend for themselves during large parts of the day. As a result of these and other pressures at home and in society, today's teenagers feel, for the first time in this country's history, that their life will be more difficult than their parents (and are described by statistics which provide gruesome indicators of teenage problems like suicide, drug abuse, pregnancy, etc., at all-time highs).

Well, it becomes obvious that change has and is rapidly occurring all around education, and much of it is not good. As a result, schools must change to meet the needs of students, especially the change which has been negative. As an illustration, where in the past we *needed* large numbers of unskilled labor, today and tomorrow we need large numbers of highly skilled labor. In other words, no longer is it acceptable for students to fail or "not get it."

Education around the country often uses the "bell-shaped curve" where so many students get A's, B's, C's, D's and F's. Now and in the future D's and F's are unacceptable. They are unacceptable because where only 3 people will be working for everyone retired, compared to 17 in the past, the 3 must be highly productive. Education must replace the bell-shaped curve with the concept of mastery and utilize remediation to achieve mastery or simply allow more time for those who need it. Thinking, communicating and writing skills will need major improvement. And the ability to live, work and play with people like as well as different from themselves is now a prerequisite for today's students. These changes are only a few of those needed.

A major assist in the change needed by the public schools is a totally different approach to its clients. The public schools should adopt a "marketing versus selling" approach to its clients. The marketing approach should be ongoing and be represented in everything the schools do. In short, public education will regain full "public support and win the quest for dollars" when the public perceives that an even exchange is occurring. Marketing by definition requires an organization to give its clients value for value or an even exchange of services for dollars provided. In order for this to occur, many more school districts will need to develop marketing departments. They will need to hire trained and educated marketing staff and set aside the resources necessary for success. Comprehensive short- and long-range marketing plans need to be developed and implemented. The leaders of public education must themselves become masters of marketing because their efforts can make or break the image of their respective districts.

The solution is forging new strategies together. A cornerstone of this effort is adopting a new philosophy that requires mastery of basic skills for all students and includes remediation until mastery becomes a reality. Major goals, which underpin this philosophy, include basic skills, technology training, and personal health acquisition for all.

Achievement of the above goals can be reached by strategies which include, but may not be limited to: preschool education, after-school study centers, latchkey centers, remediation to obtain mastery, technology training, mentorships, homework hotlines, vocational/technical education, career counseling, health counseling, and guaranteed educational service attainment.

However, partnerships of the entire community should be the driving force to accomplish the philosophy, goals and strategies just outlined. These partnerships should include: the schools, parents, students, community, government, legislatures, business, and senior citizens.

The components of the educational change plan are the same components which keep any corporation or organization vital and current. They are: (1) leadership with vision and courage; (2) well-developed goals, objectives and strategies; (3) implementable action plans; (4) marketing and client-centered approaches; (5) partnerships emphasizing service; and (6) collaboration at the school level where the mission is centered.

REFERENCES

Downs, Anthony. *Inside Bureaucracy.* Boston: Little, Brown and Co., 1967.
Hodgkinson, Harold. Speech on National and State Demographics, November 10, 1988, Cheyenne Mountain Inn, Colorado Springs, Colorado.
Instructor Magazine, Secondary Edition, Fall, 1988.

Kotler, Philip. *Marketing Management* (Analysis, Planning and Control). Englewood Cliffs, NJ, Prentice-Hall, 1976.

Kotler, Philip. *Marketing for Non Profit Organizations.* Englewood Cliffs, NJ, Prentice-Hall, 1975.

Macomb Marketing Plan, Macomb Intermediate School District, 44001 Garfield, Mt. Clemens, MI.

Massey, Morris. Video Tape #2, "What We Are Now Is Not Necessarily What We Have To Be."

Massey, Morris. Video Tape #1, "What We Are Now Is What We Were When."

Snyder, David Pearce. "Learning for Life in Revolutionary Times": Imperatives for American Educators in a Decade of Techno-Economic Change, JSTC Volume IX Number 2, Spring, 1987.

Snyder, David Pearce. *Strategic Knowledge for Leadership and Learning.* Washington D.C., E.S. Press, 1987.

Student Performance and Achievement Project (SPA). (SPA philosophy, goals strategies and partnerships). Colorado Springs School District Eleven, 1115 North El Paso Street, Colorado Springs, Colorado 80903.

USA Today, Thursday, September 23, 1988, Pg 1.

Weber, Max. "Essays on Sociology." H. H. Gerth and C. Wright Mills (ed and transl.). NY: Oxford University Press, 1946.

Chapter 12

SCHOOLS, CENTER STAGE—AT LAST

Robert Wood

> *Urban renewal has breathed fresh life into vast stretches of the nation's cities. Ramshackle structures have been razed, glass towers have risen, and city blocks have been beautified with plants, parks, and walking spaces. Cities have spacious convention centers, new hotels, and banks that look like great cathedrals. But what about the schools?*[*]

What about urban schools, indeed—the great city school systems with enrollments in the tens and hundreds of thousands; teachers by the thousands; massive service operations in transportation; custodian and security activities; food preparation and delivery. The canvas covers sprawling New York City with its $3 billion plus annual budget; Los Angeles attempting to teach in eighty-plus languages and dialects; Chicago battered year after year by bitter teacher strikes; Jersey City officially declared "bankrupt" by the state commissioner of education; Baltimore buffeted by continual breaches of security in repeated acts of student violence. And, then there is the long, sad list of city school systems struggling to provide teaching and learning under court-ordered desegregation rules and regulations: Denver, Boston, Cleveland, St. Louis, Louisville, Dallas—across the nation. Each caught up, in Joseph Viteritti's phrase, "in a very complex and turbulent environment that envelopes the system . . . a political setting . . . with an array of intergovernmental institutions . . . accountable to a wide variety of constituents . . . [for] the problems of inner-city communities."[**] After two decades of trying to absorb desegregation crises, bilingual and special needs education, rampant drugs, and urban fiscal crises, big city systems lurch toward the nineties. What are their prospects?

---

[*]From The Carnegie Foundation for the Advancement of Teaching, *An Imperiled Generation: Saving Urban Schools,* 1988.

[**]From Joseph P. Viteritti, *Across the River: Politics and Education in the City* (New York: Holmes & Meier, 1983).

This question is raised—and responses formulated—in the context of five years of a national public spotlight on education in general. The first year for a flurry of education reports was 1983—*A Nation at Risk, Making the Grade, Action for Excellence*—which awoke the nation to an educational crisis. And these were followed—and the reform impulse buttressed— by an avalanche of more than thirty books, research studies, articles, and pamphlets prescribing a smorgasbord of specific recommendations.

For school systems in general—but not city schools—the exposure proved constructive. The public and political responses, especially at the state level, were pervasive and, on the whole, impressive. Governors and legislators, who in the seventies avoided public educational programs as if they were the plague, rushed to embrace the new cause of "saving our children." Their reform packages were varied—some emphasizing regulation (that is, competency testing for students and teachers, as in Texas); some subsidies (minimum teachers' salaries, as in Connecticut); some radical choice theories (as with parental school selection in Minnesota) —but all of the 50 states did *something.* Master-teacher plans, school-based management reforms, extended school days, computer-assisted instruction, language labs, and "real" social studies popped up across the country like wild flowers in random bloom.

For all the profusion, three principal characteristics of the reform program have shaped results to date. First, the programs are size-neutral and wealth-neutral. That is, until this year, few reform laws gave particular attention to the particular plight of large cities, specifically the special characteristics of their school populations and the special demands on their resources. Second, the programs are teacher oriented—the skills, morale, and commitment of the teacher in the classroom are deemed to be the critical factor in reclaiming an educational enterprise from mediocrity or worse. Third, except for the Twentieth Century Fund report, *Making the Grade,* in 1983 and The Carnegie Foundation's *An Imperiled Generation* in 1988, the reports and reforms have not engaged the federal government; neither, in any real sense, did the 1988 presidential election. Given the overall hostility of the Reagan government to domestic programs, this lack of emphasis on the federal role may simply signal prudence or pessimism on the part of the authors and commissions. Nonetheless, the prospects of reform *without* federal aid are increasingly slight.

These characteristics have both limited the agenda of school reform and, by slighting big urban systems, seriously impaired the general renewal of our cities. We need to be clear as to the limitations that the reform framework has imposed before we shape a broader agenda for educational policy. We need to understand as well that without school reform, other prospects of big-city regeneration—job creation, strong neighborhoods, and a vibrant downtown service economy—are not likely to be sustained. Schools *are* the linchpins for economic and social urban recovery, and economic policy and urban policy must place schools at center stage. They need to do so, not just for humanitarian concern for the lives of the next generation, but for bread-and-butter basic reasons of providing skills and attitudes appropriate to the new economy in the new world-competitive arena that the United States faces today.

Limitations: (1) A School is a School is a School

The 1983 "Big Three" reports were national in outlook, analysis, and recommendations and so were most of the thirty-four studies and investigations that followed within the year. In their effort to take into account the 16,000-odd local school districts in the United States, the diagnosis of educational shortcomings and prescriptions for eliminating them understandably focused on the "typical" district. Perforce, in the eighties, that average district was suburban, middle-class, mostly white, college oriented, and reasonably well off. So, few if any of the initial reports emphasized the quite distinct and much more disparate central-city issues.

Not until 1988 did the Carnegie Foundation—the principal private institution working on educational policy—focus on urban schools. Not until June 1988 did *Education Week*, the national news organ for K–12 professionals, turn its attention directly to the glaring mismatch between the availability of instructional talent and the magnitude of at-risk students' needs. In *Reform at 5: The Unfinished Agenda,* a special report the paper editorialized, "Nowhere are the changing contours of American society more visible than in its cities. And nowhere are the demographic indicators for school failure so concentrated. Though rural poverty is extensive and though large proportions of minority students live outside the central cities, it is primarily in these urban areas that the debilitating combination of intense poverty, racial and cultural isolation, low parental achievement levels, and inadequate community supports can be found.

"To these bleak indicators will be added, in most inner cities, the additional burdens of ill-maintained school facilities and scant resources. But the crucial blow to an urban child's chances for academic success could well be administered inadvertently in the classroom—by a stream of teachers whose training is inadequate and whose professional morale has been crushed by a system that offers them few rewards for creativity and little incentive to remain."

Noting the lure of non-urban schools in attracting the 96,000 new teachers turned out each year (only 9% of the graduates wanted to teach in city schools), *Education Week* summarized the comparative attractions in these tables drawn from a 1987 national survey:

Table I
Teachers' Role in Decision Making: Percent of Teachers Reporting "No Control"

Decisions Made	Urban Schools	Other Schools
Setting goals	17	6
Selecting course contents	29	14
Selecting textbooks and materials	36	12

Table II
Teachers' Reports on Students' Health: Percent of Teachers Agreeing
Child Health and Neglect Are A Problem

Conditions Reported	Urban Teachers	Other Teachers
Abused/neglected children	49	36
Undernourished children	37	13
Poor health among children	34	16

Understandably, teachers respond to market attractions. The best teachers go to the best-paying schools with the best working conditions and avoid conditions which range from unattractive to unsafe where beginning teachers get the worst assignments. Not only does the urban teacher shortage grow increasingly severe, the preparation of new teachers is rarely oriented toward the special characteristics of the urban student. Dean Patricia Graham of Harvard describes the void:

Nobody has ever tried to educate to really make at-risk kids achieve academically. Individually, yes, but not as a group. Nobody has ever

Table III
Teacher Ratings of Discipline Problems at Their Schools: Percent of Teachers
Reporting Behavior "A Problem"

	Urban Schools	Other Schools
Student apathy toward school	81	67
Absenteeism	78	51
Student turnover	58	25
Disruptive behavior in class	53	30
Drugs	53	48
Vandalism	52	26
Alcohol	51	56
Theft	48	23
Violence against students	32	9
Racial discord	19	5
Violence against teachers	13	3

really had that as a primary goal. We have cared about keeping these students in school, keeping them on the attendance roles, but we have not cared deeply about making sure these youngsters were able to read difficult and complex pieces of literature and write sensibly about them. Never have we cared about that.

But there is more than "trying" and "caring" about urban kids in the mission of the big city schools. There is a dose of hard-bitten realism about the students not awakened to the joys of academic achievement, not destined to go on to college but nevertheless requiring instruction and support. So the final report of the Commission on Work, Family, and Citizenship, *The Forgotten Half,* emphasizes the concerns and at present limited future of these young Americans:

Who are the Forgotten Half? In nonstatistical terms, they are the young people who build our homes, drive our buses, repair our automobiles, fix our televisions, maintain and serve our offices, schools, and hospitals, and keep the production lines of our mills and factories moving. To a great extent, they determine how well the American family, economy, and democracy function. They are also the thousands of young men and women who aspire to work productively but never quite "make it" to that kind of employment. For these members of the Forgotten Half, their lives as adults start in the economic limbo of unemployment, part-time jobs, and poverty wages. Many of them never break free.

Opportunities for today's young workers who begin their careers with only a high school diploma or less are far more constrained than were those of their peers of 15 years ago. Typically, they cope with bleak job prospects by delaying marriage and the formation of their families. Many stop looking for work altogether. Disappointed in their ambitions and frustrated in their efforts to find a satisfying place in their communities, an unacceptably high number of young Americans give little in return to their families, their schools, and their work— institutions that have often shortchanged them. A kindlier society would support the Forgotten Half; a more gentle people would encourage them. A pragmatic nation would acknowledge that its very future depends on them.

In a very real sense, then, the track record of urban schools does not turn on SAT scores and college placement. It depends rather on the excellence of vocational education and more specifically on its match with the emerging service-informational economy. The critical skills now are communications and personal relations, and the major danger a failure to acknowledge how critical the role of vocational education is. Long thought to be the "sick man of the Balkans" in education, it needs to be brought front and center again.

Moreover, there is a third clientele in urban centers that the schools presently address only in the most tangential and amateurish way: adult education, especially adult literacy. In Jonathan Kozol's sometimes sensational but essentially well-grounded analysis of the illiteracy problem in America, the author estimates one-third of the nation—60 million people— cannot read at a level "equal to the full survival needs of our society." By Kozol's calculations almost 25 million cannot read the poison warning on a can of pesticide.* In most affluent Connecticut, topping the nation in 1988 in income per capita, 340,000 people are functionally illiterate. Yet, adult education is usually "overtime" and "plus" assignments in many urban schools, a low-grade patronage system in which neither curriculum nor the adult students are taken seriously. Absent either city or state priority, the schools and their voluntary agency and community college counterparts typically reach about 12 percent of those adults in real need of help.

All these very special tasks—extra support for the academically able, effective preparation for those not going on to college, catch-up educa-

---

*In Jonathan Kozol, *Illiterate America* (New York: Anchor, 1985).

tion for adults—suggest that "urban-specific" school remedies need to be high on the education agenda in the 1990s. Otherwise, the next metropolitan generation in America will divide even more sharply into suburban haves and urban have-nots in disturbingly dangerous ways.

Limitations: (2) The Teacher as Hero/Villain

To the failure to develop an adequate typology of school systems, and prepare different remedies for different diagnoses, must be added a tunnel vision as to the key problem in any school. What is striking about the 1983 reports and their successors is not so much the emphasis of quality over access and the litany of failures, but the almost single-minded focus on teaching. The "teacher factor" appears as almost the only variable in the equation.

Collectively, the call goes forth for master teachers, for science and math teachers, for teacher competency, for testing and for curriculum reform. The critical auxiliary roles like counseling, the critical role of management in large systems—New York, Boston, Chicago, Cleveland—all tend to disappear. Little if any word is said about policy responsibilities of school committees, about state distribution formulae, and the need to distinguish between lay policymaking and professional management.

This fixation on the classroom teacher grossly oversimplifies the analysis of how we achieve quality urban education. Al Shanker, former president of the American Federation of Teachers, recently recognized other qualities of schools and the need for teacher involvement. Rejecting the outmoded "time and motion" approach, Shanker wrote about the necessity of involvement and the participation of teachers in school management. He did not advocate autonomy for the classroom teacher but rather their active role in shaping programs and goals.

My observation in Boston's hundred-plus schools is similar to Shankers: there is considerable autonomy and power in the Boston classrooms—the power of the closed door. During a conference on how to improve middle schools, a teacher said, "Well, I guess I have to come and listen to all this stuff from experts because it's in the staff development part of the Boston teacher's contract. But I tell you I don't have to pay any attention because when I go into that classroom and close that door, that classroom is mine." That is a fact of school life and *should* be a fact of school life.

But the corollary to autonomy is accountability and some sense of community. The teacher autonomous, but not responsible, is a teacher under stress and in need of support training. He or she is "overloaded." A reliance solely on the autonomous teacher is likely to produce an educational bazaar: rows of shops and stalls selling miscellaneous goods like an Oriental market. In short, the role of the teacher may be the centerpiece of a successful strategy for the urban educational community to reclaim its rightful share of resources, public respect and esteem, but it is only one component in the educational system.

Nationally, that system is an extraordinarily complex one, intermingling public and private institutions with such prolific abandon as to astonish most foreign observers. Sixteen thousand separate school districts in fifty states; state departments of education which are often barely in charge; local systems of extraordinary diversity. Across the country the educational enterprise is a very weak, complicated organization faced with a mission that is extraordinarily complex. It is a "soft" system of some 3 million teachers undertaking a very "hard" function of transforming 46 million ignorant, undisciplined children into competent, effective, and civil adults.

Moreover, at the local level, where large urban school systems are involved, we combine two kinds of organizations in our schools. One is the *headquarters pattern* in which superintendents, together with state agencies, oversee activities going on in the field, literally hundreds of schools in scores of districts. The second kind are *site-specific organizations,* the individual schools themselves where education is finally delivered. These two organizational complexes are quite different.

The site-specific schools, where the faculty is enclosed and where they deal with themselves and with their children, are comparable to prisons and hospitals. That is, teachers and principals are trained professionals dealing with helpless people. Training a professional to manage as a principal in a site-specific organization requires a different curriculum than typically found in the schools of management, whether at Yale, Harvard, M.I.T., or Rutgers. Headquarters-field school organizations are in some ways comparable to other large public and private enterprises, but the appropriate behavior at the isolated sites requires a quite different mind-set and bundle of skills.

Finally, not only is our educational system enormously complex, it is also not autonomous—although our American ideology would have it so. Our folklore has it that education is free from politics, that it has a unique function in American society. That ideology—like all ideologies—

conceals rather than reveals social reality. And nowhere is the disjunction of myth and reality more apparent than in urban schools.

The urban players especially — the students, the parents, the teachers, the administrators — do not function under a protective dome, as in a sports arena, sealed off from the environment. We are in a larger political and social system. We have competing subsystems — welfare, transportation, health, economic development. And Milton Friedman and Bill Bennett, the tax credit and voucher advocates to the contrary notwithstanding, education is not a market. This system does not work by the rational calculations of Adam Smith, informed judgments of its clients and its consumers, students and parents cannily calculating costs and benefits. Quite often, school board members have favorite contractors; custodial staffs operate with carefree independence; leaders in parents' associations conceal larger political ambitions.

In short, for urban schools we have a complicated system with two kinds of organizations within the system. We are also a subsystem which is dependent on a political system. Unless performance standards of each of our components — principals, superintendents, counsellors, state agencies, school committees, and advocate groups — are clearly understood, we cannot effectively specify the function of the classroom and the role of the teacher or the substance of effective teacher preparation. We run the risk of making the teacher the culprit for failures by the rest of us. Singling out the teacher and the teacher alone is a one-factor fallacy — attractive for its simplicity but guaranteed to fail.

Indeed, it is the performance of other components — actors other than the teachers — that has consistently impaired the performance of urban public schools. Recalcitrant school committees defy federal court orders, dabble in personnel appointments, intervene in contract awards, and abdicate policy responsibilities. Central office staffs resist decentralization efforts and hover around headquarters as moths drawn to the candle flame of power. Superintendents come and go. Staff development programs for principals languish. When one contemplates the most important shortfalls in the system, the components where the slippage is greatest, the focus of reform on the classroom and the individual school seems all the more misplaced. *Site-specific* reform is only part of the problem. The large part is in headquarters-field performance, and urban political systems seem singularly disinclined to address the management issues of the larger system. So, New York has toyed with reforming the Board of Education for almost a generation without any real change.

Boston goes from city-wide to district representation with no noticeable results. Mayors come and go and schools continue to decline.

Limitations: (3) The Timid Federal Government

When President Carter honored his campaign obligations to the National Education Association and the American Federation of Teachers by proposing the creation of a Federal Department of Education, he faced a suspicious and reluctant Congress. Part of the price he paid for congressional acceptance of his reorganization plan was a legislative history that made crystal clear that education was *not* a prime federal responsibility. This month the Supreme Court, in ruling on the right of students for free transportation, in clear and specific language rejected a claim that access to education is a national constitutional right. At best, then, the federal government plays a marginal role in school reform, and states are perforce the principal actors.

But that role *at the margin* can be a critical one. For a generation the federal effort has been aimed at assisting *compensatory* education, aid to the poor, bilingual education, special education for the handicapped, and special assistance to systems undergoing school desegregation. Ever since the Elementary and Secondary Education Act of 1965, the federal government has been the prime force for legitimizing and advancing equal opportunity, greater access to education. Although the national share of school revenue has never exceeded 10 percent, that share has been critical in historically neglected areas such as vocational education and "impact aid" to local districts where the federal presence is deemed to place special burdens. Increasingly, since the Great Society, it has been the principal vehicle for maintaining the balance between attention to the principle of access or equality, as well as to the principle of quality.

The Reconciliation Act of 1981—probably the Reagan administration's most decisive step in shaping the domestic agenda—set in motion the policies that would result in the present deficit. But also, by its transformation of a series of categorical grants into a few block grants, it gave the states a much greater part to play in equal opportunity activities. In effect, that act, and the subsequent budgetary restraints placed on education, restricted more explicitly than ever the limited federal role that Carter had acknowledged. Moreover, by his actions and his words, the present Secretary of Education, William Bennett, has sought to go further than the Congress would accept in his steadfast efforts to minimize federal responsibilities and to de-emphasize the importance of compensatory education. It remains to be seen what President Bush's real agenda will be, although his campaign commitments to the schools are surprisingly comprehensive and specific. But certainly an "education president" is required if the marginal but critical federal role is to have impact.

Extra Tasks

The three broad limitations of school reform made clear there still remains to be acknowledged the extra duties, civic and otherwise, assigned to schools today. The typical middle-aged teacher today was not trained— and did not sign on to be—a peacekeeper, a specialist in linguistics, race relations, and psychological adolescent disturbances. She or he was expected and found professional satisfaction in teaching "regular kids" regular subjects. The Twentieth Century Fund puts it this way:

> ... We have always demanded a great deal of our schools, but never before have we demanded of them as much as we have over the past thirty years. On one hand we have charged them with being the melting pot, the crucible for dissolving racial divisiveness, and on the other for sustaining, and even exalting, ethnic distinctiveness.
> The schools, moreover, have had to provide a wide array of social services, acting as surrogate parent, nurse, nutritionist, sex counselor, and policeman. . . .
> ... The schools have had to cope with more children, and especially more problem children, than ever before—those who are without the rudiments of English and those who are unmotivated or prone to violence, quite apart from those who are physically handicapped. Problems have also come about as a result of the ready availability of drugs, the growing number of family breakups and the increased permissiveness in those remaining intact, the distractions of television and of easily affordable video games, the growth of underworld culture.

These special tasks add to the overload that the reform penchant to blame the teacher has already created. They are most prevalent in big city school districts, where the largest number of hard-to-educate students are found. If ever there was a catch-22 in professional life in domestic America it is with the conflicting demands on educators: ensure an effectively trained labor force capable of world-class competition and keep the peace. The truth is education for too long has been the battlefield for other people's wars—which other public figures in other arenas have not been willing to fight. Draft dodgers in income maintenance, health, social support services—they have passed the buck to the schools.

New Times, New Policies

If we understand that it is the *whole* urban school system that we must reform and not just one component, and that education is the primary task and not the resolution of broader issues of language, societal access and equity which the larger political system must resolve, then what strategies are appropriate for the nineties and beyond? What can we expect from each level of government and the private sector?

Constitutionally and in terms of resources, the federal role will remain a limited one, except where constitutional rights are concerned and courts continue to hold sway. But that role, even if constrained, can be a far more effective one. Beyond the scope of this chapter are the lessons learned painfully as to appropriate and constructive ways in which remedial law can be practiced.* In the federal assistance program area, however, besides achieving funding levels consistent with needs in poverty, bilingual, and special needs programs, the greatest opportunity lies in the revision of the "impacted areas" grants originally designed to deal with the school burdens of military installation. Today's conditions suggest, as *Making the Grade* recommends

> that federal impact aid should be used when large numbers of aliens and immigrants, many of whom are poor, place a special burden on local school districts. Given the Supreme Court decision reaffirming the right of children of illegal aliens to equal educational opportunities, the federal government has an obligation to temporarily assist states and localities facing added costs for educating these children, who usually need special help.
>
> A related problem is the plight of localities in economic distress— mainly in the nation's central cities but also in impoverished rural areas where there is an undue concentration of low-income groups, where high unemployment persists, and where there is a clear and urgent need for better education of the young. The Task Force thus urges that federal attention and assistance go to depressed localities that have concentrations of immigrant and/or impoverished groups as well as those that are already making strong efforts to improve their education performance. . . .

These programs need not be gross budgetary additions—they can replace impact aid in areas where defense activities create economic booms and which, since Eisenhower, every president has protested as pork barrel.

---

*For a more extended treatment of this issue, cf. Robert Wood, "Professionals at Bay: Managing Boston's Public Schools" (*Journal of Policy Analysis and Management*, Vol. 1, No. 4, 1982), pp. 454–468.

The Carnegie Foundation's recommendations are also timely for urban systems. They include Head Start funding to cover all eligible children by the year 2000; increased appropriations for child nuitrition programs and Chapter One of the Education Consolidation and Improvement Act; support for summer and afternoon enrichment programs and for teacher-renewal activities. Especially important are the proposal for an urban school facilities low-interest loan program, and incentive aid for curriculum innovation and links with community colleges and other urban institutions of higher education. The target here is explicitly the 100 largest cities.

For the students not going on to college, the Grant Commission has four specific strategies in its report, *The Forgotten Half,* including expanding family support funds, new youth service programs, and better employment reference services. Its centerpiece is *Fair Chance: Youth Opportunities Demonstration Act,* which proposes federal legislation to orchestrate a combination of education, training, and service programs for specified target areas. In an up-to-date version of Lyndon Johnson's Model Cities program, the commission calls for $250 million annually "to provide for financial access and support services to guarantee education and training to every youth in demonstration grant target areas who can profit from further study and job preparation." Every type of educational and employment service is to be offered and the target area would be "saturated" by a "case management system."

Even with these additions in federal programs, however, the states still must continue to carry the prime constitutional and financial responsibilities for effective aid to urban districts. Here, the need is both the correction of aid distribution formulae presently too often skewed in favor of suburban districts to give special emphasis and help to the large cities. States have struggled for years to develop genuinely equalizing minimum foundation programs, spurred on by federal and state courts as in Texas, Massachusetts, and Connecticut, but with limited and usually unsatisfactory results. Suburban legislators have usually exercised the decisive influence in constructing educational grant programs, and although the equations "tend" toward helping densely populated areas with high needs, the save-harmless clauses still provide major assistance to the wealthiest communities with the least-needy students. To date, only court intervention has provided substantial relief to large cities, and it is not certain that that relief is either sufficient or will endure.

So it is at the local level that more fundamental—if probably more elusive—issues remain to be grasped. System-wide reform—in the policy-making process, in top-level management practices, in all the aspects of communications, decentralization, and personnel development that characterize the reshaping of large ponderous, bureaucratic organizations—is the principal requirement. New York City's 110 Livingston Street, 26 Court Street in Boston—the headquarters of the largest local public bureaucracies in their cities—are symbols of administrative incorrigibility, what David Rogers has called "a model of bureaucratic pathology"—overcentralized, fragmented, compulsive in rule making, insulated from parents and students alike. Genuine reform of these systems call for the kind of radical surgery that Lee Iacocca applied to the Chrysler Motor Corporation when it teetered on bankruptcy. Certainly, the drastic shake-ups are required—on school committee structures, in superintendent offices, at headquarters' and districts' staffs—and they are awesome in political impact.

The actors whose behavior are most in need of substantial modification are not teachers but are outside the classroom—sometimes far outside. Union leaders and union lawyers, not only for the teachers but custodial, administrative, transportation, and other staffs, are prime movers and shakers, and union contracts powerfully affect managerial authority and discretion in staff assignments, transfers, layoffs, and disciplines. In this heyday of participatory democracy, urban parents, often paid to be agitators, are strenuous critics and advocates, especially in matters of class size, discipline, and curricula content. State department administrators wield power in the regulations they write and the subsidies they grant. Media, electronic and print, can make or break superintendents, school boards, and the system itself as they establish "sensational" images of violence, corruption, or illiteracy. If the system is involved in judicial proceedings, with desegregation, special needs, student rights, bilingual issues before the court, the orders of judges and the ideology of experts are prime influences on school performance.

Most important of all, of course, are the character, temperament, and style of the lay boards which govern most big city systems. Frequently, they are components of the large urban political organizations, their members aspiring to higher office and vying for opportunities for public recognition. Sometimes the committees and boards focus on internal patronage and contracts, solicit campaign contributions from teachers, and insist on management prerogatives in the award of contracts. Even when committees are not "political" in the derogatory sense of the word, they are often cumbersome in size, confused and ill-prepared to deal with matters of public policy, hobbled by anachronistic procedures and strictures in statutes. If the question is which component in an urban school system is most urgently in need of reform, the answer is not the teacher but the lay policy board or committee. In this context, support for the classroom and advocacy of school-based management are at best necessary but not sufficient reforms. At worst, they simply may evade the central issues of leadership and professionalization.

So students of urban schools, their problems and potentials are likely to come to quite different conclusions than the authors of the "national" reform reports. They do not quarrel with the thesis that what goes on in the classroom is the ultimate purpose of school management. But determining what goes on — and making it accountable — requires strategies far more complex than enhancing "teacher power."

So, in Boston, Raymond Flynn, the current mayor, has determined that the schools are too vital to the economic and social well-being of the city to be left to the school committee. He has established his own advisory council. In New York, calls for reform of the Board of Education have come from the president of the board itself. And in New Jersey, since 1975, the state legislature has mandated annual evaluation of local districts, authorized remedial plans for those found wanting, and mandated corrective state action if the plans are not implemented. Indeed, in 1978, New Jersey found the city of Trenton to have failed to implement a remedial plan. The state "took over" and a "monitor general" assumed command of the city schools. In 1980, the State Supreme Court sustained the state.

Now, seven years later, this month precisely, New Jersey has done it again. It has declared the Jersey City school system out of control, with rampant patronage, waste, fraud, and abuse. And it has assumed command through trusteeship once again.

Educational history does not reveal many instances when one American state or city enthusiastically followed the lead of another state or city in preempting local government — let alone New Jersey and Jersey City. Most cities and states prefer to do things, public or private, their own way. But single city solutions do not seem to work so far as the critical linchpin of urban regeneration is concerned, the resurrection of the once proud urban schools. Strange as it may seem to the other 49 states and 140 largest cities, Jersey City may be a prototype. At least, an entire urban system stands indicted and a comprehensive reform is underway.

At least in New Jersey, state educational leaders understand that tinkering with the classroom, placing sole reliance on teacher behavior is not sufficient. It is headquarters reform, as well as site-specific school base management, that is critical if our urban school systems are to climb back to even adequate performance.

Chapter 13

OF STATE CAPITALS AND CATALYSTS: THE POWER OF EXTERNAL PRODDING

Marsha V. Krotseng

A Responsive Climate for Reform

The emergence of education reform as front-page news and a hot political topic ranks among the "man bites dog" issues of the 1980s. Playing dual roles as both constituents and critics, governors, state legislators, corporate executives, blue-ribbon commissioners, noted journalists, and private citizens brought education to the fore early in this decade and subsequently have kept schools and colleges in the spotlight. Specifically, April 1983 headlines in *The Washington Post, The New York Times,* and *The Wall Street Journal* proclaimed, "Panel Urges Measures to Halt Decline of Education in America"; "Commission on Education Warns 'Tide of Mediocrity' Imperils U.S."; and "U.S. Panel Decries American Education." By August 1986 the action had intensified on another front, and the press reported: "New School Reforms Are Pushed: Governors Propose National Standards for Education" and "Governors Seek Greater Authority Over Operation of Public Schools."

As former U.S. Secretary of Education Terrel Bell reflects, these widely publicized proposals "hit a responsive chord"; suddenly, "education was on everyone's front burner" (Bell, 1988, p. 131). "Quality" and "excellence" became the catchwords of the times as reform-minded officials like New Jersey Governor Thomas Kean called for a "renaissance" in American education. What makes these developments especially noteworthy is their origin outside the usual academic circles. External forces rushed in where many educators initially feared to tread. Given the disconcerting decline in educational quality, elected state officials simultaneously grew less hesitant to intervene in this once-sacred realm and more independent of educational leaders (Casteen, 1985). Only belatedly did the classroom teacher and university professor participate in proposing reforms. Indeed, they expressed "gratitude" for the vigorous leadership of influential state officials (Futrell, 1986, p. D3). For the most part, education reform in the eighties is a complex and intriguing story of just such external involvement.

As Bell's reference to the "responsive chord" implies, America's social and political climate not only permitted but actually encouraged intensified activity by individuals from outside the ivy-covered walls of academe. The broad societal context of the 1980s thus fixed the course for subsequent education reform efforts. In 1983—the year the nation learned it was "at risk"—unemployment exceeded 9 percent, although inflation had fallen from the double-digit figures of 1980. North Carolina Governor Jim Hunt, along with his Arkansas compatriot Bill Clinton and a host of other political leaders, linked education with jobs and economic development. A quarter century earlier, immediately after *Sputnik* had fueled concern over America's educational fitness, the unemployment rate had been 6.8 percent with inflation below 3 percent. Passage of the National Defense Education Act attested that in 1958 defense and national preparedness—not economics—were the key issues connected to education.

The Great Society's campaign against poverty in the mid-1960s became a national effort to enhance educational opportunities for those at the lower end of the socioeconomic spectrum. After more than a decade, however, federal training and jobs programs had lost their former momentum, and states were left to solve the problem of high unemployment in 1980. Indeed, recent "concern with economic development has been more pronounced at the state and regional levels than it has been at the federal level." For one thing, governors probably are "more sensitive to high unemployment levels than are federal political leaders since the falloff in revenues and increased demand for social services invariably wreak havoc with state budgets" (Useem, 1986, p. 21). Their responses displayed regional variations as unemployment figures differed from the frost belt to the sun belt and, in most cases, effectively addressed this close-to-home issue.

In fact, since the early 1980s "states have emerged as new engines of innovation in job creation, economic development," and, concurrently, education (Doyle and Hartle, 1985b, p. C1). Analysts Denis Doyle and Terry Hartle attribute this phenomenal change to "a dramatic transformation in the quality and competence of state government." "Remarkably sophisticated and professional," the reinvigorated states have demonstrated competence "to address problems that only a decade ago seemed beyond their grasp" (Doyle and Hartle, 1985b, p. C1). For example, the energetic pursuits of Governor Lamar Alexander and his administration brought the Saturn plant—and the accompanying possibility of thousands of new jobs—to Spring Hill, Tennessee.

Thus, in contrast with earlier eras, the specifics of reform in this new age of education have been initiated at the state level rather than by the federal government. The Great Society has been transformed into the "bully pulpit." This latter role suggests Xerox chairman David Kearns is "one of the most important things" Uncle Sam can provide. While individuals "may disagree with the Reagan administration's positions on education issues, . . . no one can ignore the fact that his administration has changed the terms of the agenda and raised the public's consciousness about education" (Kearns and Doyle, 1988, p. 104).

Cabinet-Level Catalysts

Scattered stirrings of public consciousness surfaced prior to the 1983 publication of *A Nation at Risk.* By the time the report appeared, California and Florida already had enacted measures to improve education. Yet in the words of California Superintendent of Public Instruction Bill Honig, this was the "moment of maximum popular shock." The National Commission on Excellence in Education crystallized public consciousness overnight, and Terrel Bell, Reagan's first secretary of education, became an instant celebrity. As the country's top education official and organizer of the National Commission, Bell was invited both to "Meet the Press" and to "Face the Nation" in addition to appearing on all the morning television network news shows. Consequently, Bell not only secured but, in fact, rejuvenated a presidential cabinet position which was itself at risk. With education on everyone's agenda, the stage was set for the appearance of a new Secretary of Education, William J. Bennett, in 1985.

Bennett ensured that education would remain a dominant issue for popular discussion and spirited debate. When he spoke, educators listened . . . and, at least at first, refuted. Often, the rebuttal was directed as much at him as at the proposals or allegations he set forth. Consequently, the secretary himself appeared as newsworthy as his charge. However, whether or not his audience shared Bennett's philosophy, the secretary succeeded in generating lively arguments—and education benefited by holding the public's attention. Whatever the personal biases of Bennett's constituents, they felt compelled to react; his comments could not be dismissed. Through generating this conversation with the American public, Bennett succeeded in his perceived role. The U.S. Secretary of Education, he emphasizes, deals in wholesale rather than retail. Like his predecessor, Bennett has remained a significant spokesman on educational issues even after leaving his cabinet post by authoring several books and addressing a variety of audiences.

Yet, until 1988, the Reagan administration "asked Congress either to reduce sharply or to eliminate money for almost all higher education programs" (Wilson, 1988, p. A23). Other education programs fared similarly. While President Reagan declared that chances for improving education in 1988 were the best in twenty years, Senate Majority Leader Robert Byrd countered that the administration's "Three R's" of education were rhetoric, reduction, and retrenchment. State governments thus "starved into self-reliance" by federal budget policy seized control by implementing educational initiatives that Washington could—or would—not. By acting as a catalyst that prompted state action, the Reagan administration's education policy was a "triumph, although one that was hardly planned" (Doyle and Hartle, 1985a, p. 63). "The attitude used to be . . . if you got in trouble the federal government would be available as a last resort. . . . [However,] the states no longer believe that the cavalry is coming over the hill. They realize that the responsibility will continue to be theirs, and they have decided to carry it out" (Timpane quoted in Doyle and Hartle, 1985b, p. C5). Indeed, in promoting educational excellence, the states and their dynamic elected officials undeniably have taken charge.

State Capitals Seize the Initiative

Governors, in particular, adopted the education challenge as their own. Two years after the report of the National Commission on Excellence in Education, the education policy arena clearly had shifted to the states. A national survey found governors enthusiastically leading educational reform by "proposing spending increases in every state, forming task forces and commissions and responding to the national dissatisfaction with public schools with programs and proposals" (Richburg, 1985b, p. A9). "No self-respecting governor [was] without his or her commission on economic growth, technology, and education" (O'Keefe, 1984, p. 13). As portrayed by at least one national publication, the governors were "no longer simply patrons" but rather education's new policy chiefs (Caldwell,

1985, p.   , it was the rare governor who did not devote a large
portio?   ?er time, energy, and political capital . . . to nuts-and-
bolts ?   educational policy" (Caldwell, 1985, p. 1). This so-called
"Ed?   ernor" became a familiar symbol of the times, effectively
dis?   "Education President" of a former era.

i?   did the nation's governors identify with the education
             1985 the National Governors' Association (NGA) undertook
          study which culminated in a 171-page document titled, *Time*
          The Governors' 1991 Report on Education. Released on August
        this report differed from the products of numerous other
      sions and task forces because for the first time: (1) the governors
    ?lves had been actively involved in the research; (2) the governors
    ?d seven tough issues usually skirted by professional educators; and
    ?e governors planned to monitor and publicize through follow-up
  orts the results achieved during the next five years (NGA, 1986).
Among the seven "tough issues" examined by the governors were:
teaching, leadership and management, parent involvement and choice,
readiness, technology, school facilities, and college quality. Their recommendations included calls for strengthening teacher preparation, for a
national board to define teacher standards, for rewarding principals and
schools for performance, and for systematically assessing student outcomes in colleges and universities:

> As the primary source of funds for public higher education, the
> states have a major stake in the quality of postsecondary institutions
> that goes beyond measures of input and processes. State attention must
> be directed to the outcomes of the higher education system—namely,
> measuring how much students learn in college. (NGA, 1986, p. 156.)

Such intense gubernatorial scrutiny and action are unprecedented in
the history of American education. As observed in the preceding pages,
modern governors readily acknowledge a correlation between first-class
universities and a sound state economy. "The networks of research activity around Boston, the Research Triangle in North Carolina, and
California's Silicon Valley are cited by envious state officials all over the
country as examples of the benefits of close ties between industry, state
government, and higher education" (Davis, 1988, p. A52). Specifically, a
skilled work force and a good educational system are now considered
crucial—particularly if a state's economic future is tied to its attractiveness
to high-technology industry (Richburg, 1985a).
With this inherent bi-partisan appeal (What astute politician would

ever publicly oppose measures creating additional jobs?), Republican
and Democratic governors alike have placed education as a top political
priority, a theme which resounds across the nation in their inaugural
and state of the state messages. State chief executives of both parties are
equally able to claim tangible education reforms. While crediting such
Democratic governors as James Hunt of North Carolina, Bill Clinton of
Arkansas, Robert Graham of Florida, Richard Riley of South Carolina,
and William Winter of Mississippi for their successful education initiatives,
columnist David Broder (1987) expressed greater surprise that the Republicans had matched them "step for step." For instance, Iowa's Republican
Governor Terry Branstad, backed by the teachers' union, superintendents,
and school boards, convinced his legislature to increase the education
budget by $92 million and raise starting salaries by 24 percent. John
Ashcroft challenged the presidents of Missouri's state-supported colleges
and universities to define their goals and then evaluate the extent to
which students were meeting them. Yet another Republican, Rhode
Island's Edward DiPrete, advanced a dropout-prevention program for
students of kindergarten age and above which gained approval during
the 1987 legislative season.

Comparable reforms have spread from Trenton to Tallahassee and
across the country to Sacramento. New Jersey's alternative certification
program has opened the teaching profession to talented and skilled
individuals who lack formal teacher education courses. Connecticut and
California have established an interstate teacher assessment consortium.
Following its earlier no-pass, no-play regulations for public school students,
Texas has adopted a basic skills assessment program for higher education.
Alabama, Oklahoma, Tennessee, and Wisconsin are among the states
studying the mission statements of their colleges and universities, while
in 1987–88 Michigan incorporated institutional mission statements in its
appropriations process. Even Mississippi has shed its traditional image
under the enthusiastic leadership of progressive Governor Ray Mabus,
whose program of educational investment yielded one of the highest
teacher salary increases in the United States during 1988.

In his introduction to the 1986 National Governors' Association report,
then-NGA chairman Lamar Alexander of Tennessee stressed that governors would remain involved in education "for the long haul." The
illustrative state actions outlined above combine with the realization of
the proposed National Board for Professional Teaching Standards to
bear witness to the depth and longevity of the governors' educational

commitments. To help grasp the full extent of this gubernatorial influence, four recognized "education governors" of the 1980s—Bill Clinton, Robert Graham, James B. Hunt, Jr., and Thomas H. Kean—are profiled below and their primary accomplishments summarized.

"Education Governors" of the Eighties

These four governors represent three geographic regions of the United States and both major political parties. Clinton and Graham, both Democrats, reside in the Deep South, while the Democratic Hunt hails from the Border South. Kean, a Republican, comes from the Mid-Atlantic states. All are united in having been judged outstanding governors of recent times by University of Virginia political analyst Larry Sabato. In addition, each has chaired the Education Commission of the States, a national alliance organized in 1965 to enhance communication and cooperation among governors, state legislators, professional educators, and lay leaders dedicated to educational improvement.

Bill Clinton. A former Rhodes Scholar, lawyer, and faculty member at the University of Arkansas Law School, Bill Clinton became Arkansas's—and the nation's—youngest governor in 1979 at age 32. Holding out the promise of substantive educational reform in his first Inaugural Address, Clinton declared,

> In education, we have lingered too long on or near the bottom of the heap in spending per student and in teacher salaries. We must try to reverse that. However, we must be mindful that higher quality education will not come from money alone. The money must be but part of a plan which includes better accountability and assessment for students and teachers, a fairer distribution of aid, more efficient organization of school districts, and recognition of work still to be done in programs for kindergarten, special education, and gifted and talented children.

From that moment until the close of his two-year term in 1981, the Democratic governor took steps toward achieving these expressed priorities. Yet Arkansas's true educational reawakening awaited Clinton's reelection in 1982. His 1983 inaugural and state of the state addresses iterated the demands for better basic education, higher teacher salaries, and diversified vocational and high-technology programs. In the fall of that year, the governor convened a special session of the legislature which enacted new standards for the public schools and increased the sales tax to foster improvements in higher and vocational education. In persuading his constituents to raise the tax, Clinton capitalized on the interdependence of education and economic development. Among the new standards, the one which brought Clinton the greatest note — as well as "the most notoriety" — was his insistence that all teachers pass a basic competency test to retain their certification (Jaschik, 1986, p. 25). The legislature also approved an Educational Excellence Fund cultivating Clinton's reputation as the governor who "pour[ed] millions into education" (Jaschik, 1986, p. 25).

Higher education profited from $32 million invested in new science and engineering facilities, a $2.2 million increase in the student loan fund, $3.4 million for selected college improvement programs, and $800,000 for creation of a merit scholarship program designed to reverse the outward flow of Arkansas's best and brightest. "Ultimately," Clinton insisted, "every governor should be able to say that high school seniors need not leave their state or attend an expensive private institution to receive an 'absolutely first-rate education' " (Jaschik, 1986, p. 25).

Clinton also successfully advocated basic skill improvement programs for teachers unable to pass the competency test, testing programs for administrators, improved job training opportunities for unemployed adults and vocational students, and heightened involvement in education by the business community — all in the name of excellence with accountability. As the governor remarked in a 1985 address, these educational triumphs brought "general praise and approval, [not only] within our borders but far beyond this state." This acclamation included Clinton's selection as chairman of both the Education Commission of the States and the National Governors' Association in 1986 — the first state chief executive to simultaneously hold both offices. Clinton has been a frequent speaker for such educational organizations as the American Association for Higher Education (AAHE) and the American Association of Colleges for Teacher Education (AACTE). In addition, he contributed to the *Time for Results* report by leading the NGA Task Force on School Leadership and Management, subsequently authoring an article asking "Who Will Manage the Schools?" for the November 1986 *Phi Delta Kappan.*

Robert Graham: A Phi Beta Kappa graduate of the University of Florida, Robert Graham took Florida's gubernatorial oath in 1979 and quickly established his priorities in his first inaugural address:

> Whatever the issues, whatever the demands of the moment, whatever our other concerns, we must never hesitate to fulfill our greatest obligation — that of teaching our children.

That year Graham's state of the state message encouraged state government to assume a greater share of the tax burden for public schools; at the same time he maintained that the proper state role in education should be that of concentrating on student performance, setting statewide standards, and monitoring those standards closely. In addition to increased per pupil funding for public schools and community colleges, the governor earmarked a special appropriation for "improving the excellence of the programs in our state universities" (State of the State, 1979). As a tangible goal and standard by which to judge progress, Graham resolved to place Florida among the top twelve states in the nation in educational quality by 1986. In terms of raising teacher and college and university faculty salaries, the state did make tremendous strides, although not quite as rapidly as the governor had anticipated. By 1982, Graham informed the legislature and citizens that "Florida's public school system is progressing toward the excellence we seek, with students scoring higher on basic skills and scholastic aptitude tests. We are proud of our children and teachers."

However, Graham's second term beginning in 1983 ushered in the real impetus for excellence. As his state of the state address affirmed, "By improving our schools, community colleges and state universities, you can help Florida attract the new high-technology businesses that will dominate the economy of the United States into the twenty-first century." The governor devoted over half of that speech to education, demanding greater accountability of students, teachers, and administrators; more rigorous academic standards; enhanced instruction in mathematics, science, and foreign languages; and scholarships for mathematics and science teachers. Moreover, he stated, "We must pay what it costs to reduce the class sizes so more learning can take place" and recommended tax increases to fund the desired excellence.

Graham's strategy succeeded; that legislative session enacted the nation's highest graduation standards, provided for a Master Teacher Program, expanded the school day, and supported local district implementation of merit-pay plans. Graham also noted the greater number of citizens volunteering their time to schools as well as the productive partnership of education, government, and business exemplified by a program linking American Transtech Company, Florida Junior College, and the Florida Department of Education. Urging the 1984 legislature to continue to back these reforms with ample resources, he observed,

Excellence is not a bill we can pass and sign into law in a single session. Excellence requires years of continuous concerted effort. . . . Within the past two days, our state's largest newspaper published a survey showing that two of every three Floridians think the public schools are getting better—and two of every three Floridians want them to keep on getting better. And two of every three say they are willing to pay higher taxes if it means better schools.

In demonstrating their confidence in our work, and by volunteering to work in hundreds of our schools, Floridians are showing they take education seriously.

Throughout his gubernatorial term, Graham sought to broaden his perspectives by stepping into an unfamiliar role—such as that of a teacher—one day each month. He participated in the Southern Regional Education Board, the National Commission on Reforming Secondary Education, and the National Foundation for the Improvement of Education. He also contributed to the *Time for Results* effort by serving as vice chairman of the NGA's College Quality Task Force.

James B. Hunt, Jr.: James B. Hunt, Jr., was inaugurated governor of North Carolina in January 1977. His state of the state message referred to education as a top priority: "We [in North Carolina] believe deeply in education; we know it is the door to a better future. . . . The money we spend on education is the best money we spend." This message effectively established Hunt's agenda and foreshadowed the attainments with which his eight-year administration would be credited. In working toward his ideal of a state educational system which taught every child to read and which thus inspired the citizens' confidence, Hunt championed a Primary Reading Program; a rigorous standardized testing program; the minimum competency test required for graduation; and a Community Schools Act which opened facilities to the general public.

In addition, Hunt convinced his legislature to support basic skills instruction; programs for exceptional children; remedial instruction; the nation's first residential school for the gifted in science and mathematics; a governor's school for students gifted in the arts; and more stringent high school graduation standards. By 1981, the governor could report that these programs were yielding tangible results. According to his state of the state address,

For years, North Carolina has been way down in the national education scores. But now, for the first time ever, our students in grades one through six have scored at or above the national average in reading, language, spelling and math. Our students' SAT scores are up, while they are dropping in other parts of the nation.

Not only did the School of Science and Mathematics lead the nation in the percentage of national merit scholarship semi-finalists, it also stimulated better instruction in those subjects throughout the state's public schools. And, across North Carolina, the dropout rate decreased.

Hunt began his second term by calling for more than tax dollars. "My goal during the next four years," he explained, "will be to get more people helping to make their schools excellent." "Will you help teach a child to read?" he asked the public. The governor himself set the example by finding time in his hectic gubernatorial schedule to tutor students. Further, Hunt spent many hours visiting schools and classrooms. In 1983, he applauded the successful "adopt-a-school" program as well as the establishment of the North Carolina Business Council on Science and Mathematics Education. Hunt designated that year as "The Year of the Public School" and encouraged citizens to "rally around the public schools . . . to get more personally involved in them . . . and to mobilize the forces for education across our state. The key to economic growth is education—the public schools, the community colleges and the universities." Hunt's administration accomplished the most extensive changes in the public schools (including increased teacher salaries) since the days of Governor Terry Sanford, the archetype "Education Governor" of the early 1960s and Hunt's mentor (Pearce, 1982).

Hunt proved a thoughtful and energetic participant in regional and national education organizations. He chaired the Southern Regional Education Board, served on the Business Advisory Council of the Education Commission of the States following his term as ECS chairman, took part in the Carnegie Forum Task Force on Teaching as a Profession, and, in 1987, was selected to chair the newly organized National Board for Professional Teaching Standards.

Thomas H. Kean. A former American history and English teacher and political science professor, Kean became New Jersey's chief executive in 1982. His inaugural address that year reflected this education background and firmly established Kean's gubernatorial goals:

> We must strengthen our commitment to the basics of education: Reading, writing, and arithmetic. At the same time, children and teachers must never be inhibited from striving for excellence, or searching out new horizons of intellectual growth.

Kean quickly moved to shift the emphasis in his state's educational system from "the maintenance of mediocrity to the attainment of excellence" (State of the State, 1983). He reorganized the New Jersey Department of Education; involved top state higher education business, labor, and government leaders on a Commission of Science and Technology; and donated the proceeds from his inaugural ball to initiate the Governor's School at Monmouth College. Like his North Carolina contemporary Jim Hunt, Kean officially declared 1983 the "Year of the School" to "bring into focus the compelling need to develop ideas and techniques to improve our system of education, public as well as private" (State of the State, 1983).

The following year, the Governor's State of the State Address called for raising the minimum teacher salary to $18,500 (at that time the nation's highest) coupled with a Master Teacher Plan of Incentives, grants to teachers for developing program proposals to improve student learning, a controversial alternative certification program for liberal arts graduates wishing to teach, increased professional standards, scholarships for top students agreeing to teach in New Jersey upon graduation, enhancement of education in the humanities and foreign languages, alternative education for disruptive students, improvements in technical and high-technology programs, and an increase in the Educational Opportunity Fund to encourage continued minority enrollments at state colleges and universities. Increased taxes subsidized these—and other—education reforms.

Convinced that "the quality of teachers depends on the quality of colleges," Kean also aimed initiatives at higher education. "The state that ignores its public colleges," he acknowledged, "is going to suffer in the long run. It's going to suffer economically, and its image is going to suffer. The best and brightest students may go elsewhere, and stay" ("Rising expectations," 1985). Thus, he challenged Rutgers University and the state colleges to fulfill their potential—to push for excellence and attract world-class scholars to New Jersey; millions of state dollars backed this challenge. Within a year, Kean was able to introduce five renowned scholars to the legislature, observing, "These people have two things in common: They are the best in their field and now they teach in New Jersey" (State of the State, 1986).

Kean gained endorsement by the New Jersey Education Association during his 1985 reelection campaign—the first time that organization had ever sponsored a Republican gubernatorial candidate. His second term has been characterized by a move to more effectively assess college outcomes. The New Jersey legislature committed $1.7 million to assessment between 1986 and 1988 and approved Kean's request for an additional $1 million in grants for specific programs on campuses across the state and $850,000 for state officials to use in developing assessment programs (Blumenstyk, 1988b).

A much sought-after speaker, Kean has addressed audiences from Atlantic City to San Francisco, including the American Association of Colleges for Teacher Education and the Council for Financial Aid to Education. He chaired the NGA Task Force on Teaching, served as a member of the Carnegie Forum Task Force on Teaching as a Profession, was invited to membership on the National Board for Professional Teaching Standards, and remained actively involved in initiatives of the Education Commission of the States after concluding his term as chairman in 1986. Using a public forum to highlight the importance of gubernatorial action, Kean wrote in the November 1986 *Phi Delta Kappan* that state chief executives

> should develop incentives to encourage more professional school environments. They should challenge the higher education community to rebuild teacher education and support those who take up that challenge. They should listen to teachers, principals, and board members and focus the energy of those people on what must be done. Above all, governors must emphasize that it isn't the teacher recruitment program they are interested in, but the people—the people who teach children.
> ... Without the support of governors, there will be no progress on the emerging agenda for the reform of teaching. (Kean, 1986, p. 205.)

Building Political Reputations on Education

Indeed, the news of the 1980s has been—and continues to be—that of governors putting themselves and their political reputation on the line for educational improvement. The four discussed in this chapter represent a mere handful of state chief executives who have worked vigorously to strengthen the educational systems of their states. Former Republican Governor Lamar Alexander of Tennessee led his state's "Better Schools Program," together with the career ladder and school choice movements and funding for excellence. Virginia Democrats Charles Robb and Gerald Baliles respectively raised high school graduation requirements and won $4.5 million from the General Assembly for colleges and universities to use in devising their own assessment programs during the 1988–1990 biennium. And, former South Carolina Governor Richard Riley, a Democrat, focused national attention on his state with his far-reaching 1984 Education Improvement Act. Featured in both *The Washington Post* and *The Wall Street Journal,* this act mandated a penny sales tax increase for education programs, yielding $240 million in 1986–87. Since this law took effect, average SAT scores of South Carolina students indicate one of the largest gains in the country and increases have been reported in both attendance and the rate at which high school graduates go on to state colleges (Putka, 1988). One Arkansas superintendent has labeled his state "the epicenter of education reform" (Vobejda, 1988, p. A12).

Astute Advisors: In the Governor's Shadow

Behind the scenes, however, these governors have benefited from the support and guidance of some extraordinarily knowledgable and capable education advisors. Prior to his appointment as Assistant Secretary for Educational Research and Improvement with the United States Department of Education, Chester E. Finn, Jr., held a professorship at Vanderbilt University where he could offer advice to Lamar Alexander. As Virginia's thoughtful and distinguished Secretary of Education, John T. Casteen, III, served with Governor Charles Robb before accepting the presidency of the University of Connecticut. Another university president, Robert C. Dickeson of the University of Northern Colorado, employed his superb managerial and analytical skills as Colorado Governor Roy Romer's chief of staff. Lowell J. Paige, higher education advisor to California's George Deukmejian, lends his job experience gained as a dean at U.C.L.A. and as an assistant director of the National Science Foundation. And, former professor Tom Duncan and Richard Mills are recognized as highly respected advisors to Missouri's Governor John Ashcroft and New Jersey's Governor Thomas Kean, respectively.* A study conducted by J. Wade Gilley and Kenneth A. Fulmer of George Mason University confirms that governors are indeed relying more heavily on the guidance of such individuals rather than on the college officials in their states (Gilley and Fulmer, 1986). Ultimately, then, these chief education advisors are in a position to effect more specific policy changes than generally realized.

---

*Mills left New Jersey to become Vermont's Commissioner of Education.

Blue Ribbon Commissions

Governors and state legislatures also have made extensive use of the blue ribbon commission as a strategy for planning and policy development. Blue ribbon commission and special task force recommendations are expected to make news and, consequently, "to make things happen" (Johnson and Marcus, 1986, p. 3). Such external panels have the advantage of viewing situations with a different lens, and they can present bold—even controversial—proposals, particularly if their citizens represent a wide range of backgrounds. For instance, one Texas committee initially recommended the merger of several state higher education institutions in 1987. New Jersey has charged a number of panels which have dealt solely with higher education issues; these include a Blue Ribbon Panel on Teacher Education, the Commission on the Future of the State Colleges, and the Governor's Commission on Science and Technology. Connecticut, Florida, Georgia, North Carolina, North Dakota, Tennessee, and Washington are among the many other states which have turned to such outside bodies in the 1980s. The University of Maryland employed this general approach as a means of examining its mission and clarifying institutional goals. Headed by former University of Minnesota president Malcolm Moos the effort resulted in *The Post-Land Grant University*, a remarkably comprehensive and, in some respects, "adventurous" document as it urged the University to concentrate on its strengths and to institute differential pay policies for high-demand fields (Johnson and Marcus, 1986). Of course, the noteworthy reports by the National Commission on Excellence in Education (1983), the Twentieth Century Fund Task Force on Elementary and Secondary Education Policy (1983), and the Education Commission of the States Task Force on Education for Economic Growth (1983) all paved the way for the states to move forward in education.

The Business Connection

Former Governor Richard Riley garnered grass-roots support for his 1984 reform bill by turning to local businessmen. In fact, key South Carolina businessmen joined legislators on the education commission charged to create a "strong but politically acceptable package of reforms" (Richburg, 1985a, p. A3). The business community responded to the governor's efforts by raising $100,000 which financed a media blitz aimed more at pressuring state lawmakers than the public. In Texas, at the request of then-Governor Mark White, the highly visible business leader H. Ross Perot chaired his state's school reform commission. IBM Chairman John F. Akers has emphasized in his speeches that the key to America's future competitive ability is allowing children far less time to watch television and far more time in school. Indeed, businessmen like Perot and Akers displayed genuine concern for education as America's business community assumed a major role in the development of educational policy for the first time in over a quarter century. "Business and industrial associations, both nationally and at the state level, supported reform proposals, even on occasions when omnibus bills raised state taxes to assist schools. . . . [For instance] the nationally prestigious Committee for Economic Development (CED) issued reports specifying reform agendas" (Guthrie and Koppich, 1988, p. 30).

Xerox Corporation Chairman David T. Kearns has set forth his own marketplace-based plan for restructuring the country's entire educational system in the book, *Winning the Brain Race: A Bold Plan to Make Our Schools Competitive*, co-authored with Denis P. Doyle. Kearns and Doyle's agenda comprises: (1) choice for parents, students, and teachers; (2) restructuring schools from the bottom up; (3) professionalism in teaching; (4) high standards of academic achievement; (5) values of democracy and citizenship in a core curriculum; and (6) an increased federal role in research.

Education as a Bookstore Best-Seller

Several other authors of the 1980s transformed the state of American education (and proposals explaining how it might be remedied) into a best-selling theme at the bookstore. In 1987 Allan Bloom and E.D. Hirsch, Jr., succeeded in sparking heated debate around a normally predictable issue with their respective books, *The Closing of the American Mind* and *Cultural Literacy*. The timing was excellent; as Boston University President John Silber noted, the public proved ready for a readable indictment of education. Bloom's rhetoric aside, he basically prescribed a return to the liberal arts disciplines to cure the "cultural relativism" which he insisted has riddled America's universities since the 1960s. Hirsch, on the other hand, would treat students with substantial doses of Western cultural tradition, conveniently packaged in a 5,000-entry appendix presumably representing "What Literate Americans Know."

These two works, like the policies of the Reagan administration and the proclamations of William Bennett, are just as (if not more) significant for the controversy and reactions they precipitated as for their specific content. Some critics, for instance, applied such adjectives as "elitist" and "racist" to Bloom's book. National newspapers printed excerpts from the two commentaries; the publishers have sold hundreds of thousands of copies; by mid-1988 over fifty-five reviews of *The Closing of the American Mind* had appeared in publications ranging from *Fortune* to the *National Review;* some twenty-six reviews reflected on *Cultural Literacy;* professional journal articles examined the authors' striking statements; and symposia and papers presented at professional conferences raised relevant questions. (In fact, participants in a 1987 "English Coalition Conference" showed such skepticism toward Hirsch's notion of cultural lists that the author himself was unexpectedly summoned to address the audience.) Ultimately, however, Bloom and Hirsch enlivened education; they kept—and are keeping—dialogue among educators and the public alive.

No less important but perhaps more heralded in the academic community than among the general public was Ernest Boyer's major study, *College: The Undergraduate Experience in America.* This thoughtful 1986 work by the president of the Carnegie Foundation for the Advancement of Teaching ambitiously considered the whole undergraduate collegiate experience from classes to the extracurriculum. Its main intent was to encourage college and university faculty and administrators to think more carefully about the importance of the undergraduate college and to strengthen this essential facet of higher education. "Our goal," said Boyer, "is not to impose answers but to help shape the debate about education in the nation" (quoted in Marchese, 1986, p. 17).

The Debate Thickens

As Boyer affirmed when his book was first published, we have, indeed, come a long way from the initial shock induced by *A Nation at Risk.*

> School standards have been tightened, teacher salaries have been raised at twice the inflation rate and we now are having a vigorous debate about how teachers should be educated and credentialed. Governors, for the first time in years, are deeply involved in school reform. (quoted in Marchese, 1986, p. 12.)

Yet, at the same time, the Carnegie Foundation president expressed deep concern over the apparent domination of testing in the reform movement. Despite the results achieved by South Carolina's 1984 Education Improvement Act, critics have charged that tests are driving the schools, with teachers devoting too much class time to test content alone. Some university faculty and administrators in other states have been wary of the "rising junior examinations" mandated in Florida, Georgia, and Texas as the gateway to college junior status or to an associate's degree. In short, a number of educators fear a tendency to measure everything that moves.

Others question the degree of influence which governors can legitimately exert over state educational systems. Strong controversy surrounded the implementation of both Lamar Alexander's Master Teacher Plan in Tennessee and Bill Clinton's teacher competency tests in Arkansas. In Oregon, Governor Neil Goldschmidt's desire to find a higher education leader able to integrate the state's educational resources with its growing international business relationships has led to accusations that he forced the chancellor of the higher-education system to resign and subsequently contributed to the delay in hiring a replacement (Blumenstyk, 1988a). Commentators suggest this situation illustrates "what can happen when a well-meaning, action-oriented Governor stumbles into the tradition-bound world of academe using conventional political tactics to make changes" (Blumenstyk, 1988a, p. A21).

Political involvement **can** become inappropriate intrusion as Education Commission of the States president Frank Newman has documented in his study, *Choosing Quality*. Still, former North Carolina Governor Terry Sanford insists that more schools "have suffered from political indifference than have ever been upset by political interference." And, according to one former state finance official, "often state government is the only force that can bring change [to the campus] . . . a governor may be the only way of achieving [the needed educational changes] through external forces" (quoted in Newman, 1987, p. 43).

Awaiting the Education Community's Response

In truth, day-to-day pressures of educating students and running a school or college often mitigate against change from within, instead perpetuating the status quo. Even American Federation of Teachers president Al Shanker has warned his educator-colleagues, "If there's an enemy, it's likely to be us" (quoted in Mitgang, 1988, p. A15). Outside questions and criticisms may be necessary to break the business-as-usual syndrome and to stimulate action. The U.S. Secretary of Education, governors, gubernatorial advisors, blue ribbon commissions, prominent businessmen, and controversial authors all can arouse the public interest, build momentum, and clear the route for reforms to progress. Such individuals are powerful and effective catalysts. However, the final realization of any educational reform lies in the hands of educators themselves. Ernest Boyer, one of those educators who is, himself, a catalyst, wholeheartedly concurs, "If educators rather than politicians take charge . . . the impact will be constructive" (quoted in Marchese, 1986, p. 14).

The ball now has rebounded to the educational community, and educators must choose whether to respond to the external prodding by keeping reform in motion. Obviously, the governors and other outside players anxiously await this next—and most critical—move. Should the educational community be caught holding the ball for an extended period of time, influential and energetic leaders from other sectors stand ready to regain control.

REFERENCES

Bell, T.H. (1988). *The thirteenth man: A Reagan cabinet memoir.* New York: The Free Press.

Blumenstyk, G. (1988a, September 7). Action-oriented governor at odds with college leaders over charge he's politicizing Oregon higher education. *Chronicle of Higher Education*, pp. A1;A21–A23.

Blumenstyk, G. (1988b, July 20). Diversity is keynote of states' efforts to assess students' learning. *Chronicle of Higher Education*, pp. A17;A25–A26.

Broder, D.S. (1987, July 29). Education is bipartisan again. *The Washington Post*, p. A23.

Caldwell, P. (1985, February 6). Governors: No longer simply patrons, they are policy chiefs. *Education Week*, pp. 1;34.

Casteen, J.T., III (1985). Educational policy at mid-decade: The state of the states. University of Connecticut, Storrs, Connecticut. (Mimeographed).

Davis, W.E. (1988, March 9). The growing politicization of state higher education makes jobs of top college officials shakier than ever. *Chronicle of Higher Education*, p. A52.

Doyle, D.P. and Hartle, T.W. (1985a). *Excellence in education: The states take charge.* Washington, D.C.: American Enterprise Institute for Public Policy Research.

Doyle, D.P. and Hartle, T.W. (1985b, September 8). The states are leading as Washington wallows. *The Washington Post*, pp. C1;C5.

Futrell, M.H. (1986, August 31). To the governors, with gratitude. *The Washington Post*, p. D3.

Gilley, J.W. and Fulmer, K.A. (1986). *A question of leadership: Or, to whom are the governors listening?* Fairfax, Virginia: George Mason University Center for Policy Studies in Education.

Guthrie, J.W. and Koppich, J. (1988). Exploring the political economy of national education reform. In W.L. Boyd and C.T. Kerchner (Eds.), *The politics of excellence and choice in education* (pp. 25–47). New York: The Falmer Press.

Jaschik, S. (1986, September 3). A governor pours millions into education. *Chronicle of Higher Education*, p. 25.

Johnson, J.R. and Marcus, L.R. (1986). *Blue ribbon commissions and higher education: Changing academe from the outside.* ASHE–ERIC Higher Education Report No. 2. Washington, D.C.: Association for the Study of Higher Education.

Kean, T.H. (1986). Who will teach? *Phi Delta Kappan, 68* (4), 205–207.

Kearns, D.T. and Doyle, D.P. (1988). *Winning the brain race: A bold plan to make our schools competitive.* San Francisco: ICS Press.

Marchese, T.J. (1986). College: Raising a new vision. *Change, 18* (6), 10–17.

Mitgang, L. (1988, September 4). Teachers take lead in trend of reform. *The (Memphis, Tennessee) Commercial Appeal,* pp. A1;A15.

National Governors' Association. (1986). *Time for results: The governors' 1991 report on education.* Washington, D.C.: National Governors' Association Center for Policy Research and Analysis.

Newman, F. (1987). *Choosing quality: Reducing conflict between the state and the university.* Denver: Education Commission of the States.

O'Keefe, M. (1984). What will the 1984 election mean for higher education? *Change, 16* (7), 12–25.

Pearce, G. (1982). Governor James Baxter Hunt, Jr. In M.F. Mitchell (Ed.), *Addresses and public papers of James Baxter Hunt, Jr.* (pp. xxi–xxxiii). Raleigh, North Carolina: Division of Archives and History.

Putka, G. (1988, July 12). South Carolina's broad school reform includes incentives or punishment based on performance. *The Wall Street Journal,* p. 54.

Richburg, K.R. (1985a, September 4). Education-reform effort sweeps southern states. *The Washington Post,* p. A3.

Richburg, K.R. (1985b, February 11). Survey sees advances in education. *The Washington Post,* p. A9.

Rising expectations: Can states help renew quality? (1985). *Change, 17* (6), 13–15.

Useem, E.L. (1986). *Low tech education in a high tech world: Corporations and classrooms in the new information society.* New York: The Free Press.

Vobejda, B. (1988, April 25). Gains fall short of goals as education reform takes its course in S. Carolina. *The Washington Post,* pp. A1;A12.

Wilson, R. (1988, February 24). Reagan seeks a record $8.8 billion for aid to students; $9.2 billion would go to university R&D, up 13 pct. *Chronicle of Higher Education,* pp. A23:A26.

Chapter 14

RESEARCH ON TEACHING
AND EDUCATIONAL POLICY

David C. Berliner

Research, unfortunately, either does not influence educational policy or influences it very slowly. There are two major reasons for this. First, policy in the educational arena influences large numbers of people who think that by virtue of having gone to school that they have informed opinions. Unlike, say, space policy, timber clearing policy, or rate setting policies for interstate commerce, educational policy is intertwined with the daily lives of people at the local level. More than in other areas of policymaking, educational policies often appear tied to the emotions, politics, social relationships, and fiscal interests of a local, vocal and broad-based constituency. When policy is made under such conditions, research ordinarily has a minor role to play. A second reason that research often fails to inform policy is that in many areas of intense public debate educational research has, until recently, been lacking or uninformative.

There appears to be no easy solution, nor perhaps would we want one, for the myriad problems engendered by the fact that educational policy is so intricately intertwined with the daily lives of the people for whom the policies are intended. But educational research has expanded in recent years, and one branch of it, research on classrooms and teachers, has yielded a useful knowledge base about which policymakers must be informed. It is time to highlight these changes in the knowledge base so that those in positions to affect educational policy learn that contemporary research on teaching and classroom processes offers them information to guide their thinking about the issues with which they wrestle.

To make this point, in one of the following sections, a case is made for the power of educational research when compared to research in physics, chemistry, or medicine. Unless policymakers believe in the power of the research undertaken in education they should not be expected to take that work seriously. To the surprise of many, educational research compares quite favorably, on a number of dimensions, to these other well-respected fields of research. Following the comparison of educational research to other fields of research is a description of some of the rich findings, concepts, theories and technologies that contemporary educational research yields. The policy implications of these illustrative cases of contemporary research on teaching and classroom processes are noted.

The Power of Educational Research

High-energy particle physics, not education, is the kind of field that usually comes to mind when someone mentions "scientific" research. Billions of dollars are spent by thousands of physicists searching for understanding that often is beyond the grasp of the common person. But we should question that field of research in the same ways that we question the research in education. We need, therefore, to ask: How good is the data that is generated in that field of research? That is, how cumulative is it? Is it cohesive, such that agreed upon understandings are emerging from the research? Hedges (1987) asked this question about research in high-energy physics and about social science research, including educational research. There are some straightforward ways to answer these questions. For example, the 10 published studies of the mass of the charged pion, or the 27 known studies of the lifetime of the lambda particle, can be analyzed by means of the chi-square statistic. This statistic can be applied to the results of every study of the same phenomena, say the mass or the lifetime of a particular particle, to check whether homogeneity or heterogeneity characterizes that set of data. A non-significant chi-square indicates that the pool of studies under examination has yielded comparable findings. If this result obtains, then the data from the different studies, conducted in different places, with different equipment, and by different investigators, is believed to hang together. That is, we may conclude that the different studies arrive at similar estimates of the phenomenon under investigation. A significant chi-square, on the other hand, indicates a non-homogenous set of estimates. If that is the case, the analysis suggests that the data does not hang together. Some of the studies that comprise the set of studies of the same phenomenon do not yield data that is comparable to what is found in some of the other studies in the set. Under these conditions we must conclude that there is an element of untrustworthiness in the data. When 13 different collections of data in high-energy physics were analyzed in this way, many of them were found *not* to be homogenous sets of data. Different investigators were obtaining different results when determining the lifetime or the mass of the particles under investigation.

Hedges conducted the same kind of analysis in different areas of social science research. He looked at the 62 studies of gender differences in spatial perception, the 18 studies of self-concept in studies of traditional and open education, and 11 other areas where a large number of studies of the same phenomenon exist. The chi-square test revealed essentially the same pattern as was found in physics — many of the data sets were not homogenous, though some were. In fact, of particular interest was one of the research areas that might have been considered among the "softest," a comparison of the data obtained from 18 different studies of the self-concept of students in traditional and open education classes. This set of data proved to be more stable, homogenous, or cumulative in nature than one would have predicted. The chi-square statistic for these data was non-significant. A rather strong case can be made, therefore, that open education has positive effects on student self-concept, because the set of data from different studies of this phenomenon are relatively homogenous. As interesting as that finding is, the general case is the more important to consider, namely, that there are some social science and educational data sets that are more dependable, or homogenous, or consistent, or cumulative, for policymaking, than data sets from the field of physics. Sets of social science research data of the same phenomenon turned out to be no less trustworthy, cumulative or valid than the data obtained in high-energy physics. Hedges began his research by asking whether the so-called "soft" sciences are really any softer than the so-called "hard" sciences. He surprised people by concluding that the soft sciences are not all that soft, and the hard sciences are not all that hard. Educational research need not be identified as one of the soft sciences. All sciences have difficulties pinning down the facts they are interested in acquiring, and physicists are no better at that than educational researchers. If physics is to be considered a "genuine" scientific enterprise, then the research in education must also be considered as a genuine scientific enterprise.

Hedges went on to address another problem that distinguishes the so-called "hard" from the so-called "soft" sciences. That is the problem of measurement. In chemistry and physics, for example, there is an absolute zero when we measure cold and heat, there is also the decibel scale for measuring sound pressure, and there are horsepower and footcandles and ohms and light-years. These scales have desirable properties that are not often found in education. In education we find such peculiar scales as grade equivalence, or we have the arbitrary scales of intelligence, or creativity, or locus of control. None of these measures is anything but ordinal in nature, with unequal intervals, no absolute zero point, and thus, from a measurement standpoint, rather crude devices. So those in the physical sciences seem to be able to measure better than those of us in the social sciences. The precision in measurement that the physical sciences achieve seem capable of is an attribute we associate with genuine and strong scientific fields. Hedges, however, looked at the estimates of thermal conductivity of certain chemical elements, crucial information in an era exploring superconductivity and other new materials for the information age. It turns out, for example, that from approximately 1960 to 1970 the accepted value for thermal conductivity in that most common of elements, carbon, changed by 8000 percent! Thermal conductivity estimates for indium changed over the decade by 242 percent; the values for the element silicon changed by 82 percent; and so forth. The lack of precision in measurement seemed not to hamper scientific progress at all in the decade that was scrutinized. Precise measurement instruments and interval or ratio measurement scales do not automatically make for a precise science. The problems of measurement plague every scientific field—education, chemistry, and physics alike. All scientists learn to live with these problems and to compensate for them, and it is for this reason that most reputable researchers are cautious about using their data to influence policy until replication has occurred.

What we have seen thus far in this comparison of educational research to research in physics and chemistry, for example, is that research in education is not intrinsically of lower value, of lesser validity, or inherently a more difficult field from which to build a reliable data base. Nor does it suffer badly, in comparison, when it comes to measurement of the phenomena about which it has interest. Science of all kind is fraught with problems of measurement, and scientists simply find ways to make do until better measures are available. The production of useful knowledge does not stop because of imprecision in systems of measurement. Rather, one needs simply to be more cautious in interpretation of that research.

The Utility of Educational Research. An issue about the research endeavor that has not yet been discussed is whether the educational research that is generated has utility—the power to affect change for the better in the ways we live and work. When we are asked to think of powerful, policy-relevant research, we may think of medical research and the impact it has had on our lives. We usually do not think about educational research. But the findings from research in education are often of greater magnitude and may lead to greater effects than in medicine. Let us look at an example presented first by Gage (1985).

A few years ago the news was released of a longitudinal study, costing $150 million, concerned about the lowering of cholesterol through use of diet and a drug. After 1906 men took the experimental treatment for 9 years it was found that 8.1 percent of them had suffered a major heart attack or died of a heart attack. In the control group of 1906 men, 9.8 percent were affected in this way. Over 9 years there appeared a 1.7 percent difference in the heart attack rates of the men in the two groups. How was news of this tiny difference, appearing after 9 years of study, greeted by the public? *The New York Times* and *The Boston Globe* featured this story on the front page. *Time* magazine used this study as its cover story. *Science* magazine held that the results of the study would "affect profoundly" the practice of medicine. The correlation obtained from the data presented, between treatment (yes/no) and effect (heart attack/no heart attack), was about .03. The variance in the measure of health used to assess the outcomes of this study (heart attack), that was attributable to the treatment (the drug and diet), was 0.1. Would we consider an educational research study that found only a 1.7 percent difference after 9 years to be useful? Would our journals accept a study that could only find a correlation of .03 between the variables that were studied? Would anyone in education think that a variable is of use if it accounts for one-tenth of one percent of the variance in the outcome measure? Let us suppose someone in education worked on a program to prevent dropouts and after nine years and a cost of $100,000 it was found that 1.7 percent more children graduated from high school. When presented with such findings would a school board call it a miracle and praise the researchers, thank the researchers for a valiant but barely successful attempt, or declare that the money was wasted in another losing effort to increase graduation rates? Would the press feature the story on the front page because the results were so encouraging? Would anyone have extrapolated from the study to determine the benefits, as physicians do? (To address medical policy issues physicians often announce from their studies that, say, 21,400 lives can be saved each year if their recommendations are followed. A 1.7 percent increase in high school graduation rates might save a community, say, $15,000,000 over 20 years through increased taxes earned, and decreased costs of welfare, incarceration, unemployment, and the like. These are known effects of high school completion. The small effect that was found, amounting to only a 1.7 percent difference between the treated and untreated groups, seems more useful when extrapolated and put into terms that are both dramatic and clearly policy relevant, as is usually done by medical researchers.) Educational data is often of greater magnitude, in terms of its effects, than medical data, but it is not treated that way. When we have time-on-task variables correlating between .20 and .50 with measures of achievement, and which are found to explain between 10 and 40 percent of the variance in academic achievement, we are providing much more powerful data than that produced in many medical studies. Yet the medical studies are used to influence policy and practice throughout the nation. They appear to be more useful, but they really are not. It is just that life and death are such powerful motivators that we regard any data about those processes as important. When announcing the educational benefits of time on task, or cooperative learning, or reciprocal teaching, educational researchers can only speak metaphorically about the life-and-death consequences to our society or to an individual. Nevertheless, we should remember that educational research has the same potential for utility as medical research, it just is not perceived that way by teachers or policymakers. We must work on changing that.

These comparisons of educational research with other fields were to make a set of related points before presenting some of the findings, concepts, theories, and technology that have been generated by the educational research community. The points are (1) that some of the disciplined inquiry in education is as cumulative and coherent as is research in the physical sciences, (2) that the inherent problems of measurement in education are not dissimilar to the problems of measurement faced by every discipline, and (3) that our research often is of potentially greater power and utility than that of medical research. An understanding of these points by teachers, administrators, teacher educators, and the policy-making community is a prerequisite for attempting to use educational research to guide policy and practice in education.

Findings, Concepts, Theories and Technology From Educational Research and Their Relations to Contemporary Policy Issues.

An argument will be made that the data from the relatively new body of knowledge about teaching and learning could guide policy if thoughtfully integrated into policy discussions. As in most fields, however, research that directly answers policy questions is hard to find. It usually takes an intermediate inventive mind to translate research into either policy or practice. We will apply that inventiveness to some of the findings, concepts, theories, and technology that have emerged in recent years. We will examine whether policy at some level of the educational system might be affected by the knowledge that has been provided.

Findings. Some of the research on teaching stands alone. These are often findings that are quite likely to have some effects that we value but may not be of great intellectual and theoretical import. They are simply scientific findings. For example, teachers who provide more academic feedback, teachers who structure lessons more frequently, teachers who monitor classes more frequently when seatwork is being completed, are teachers whose students achieve higher on standardized achievement tests (Berliner, 1987). These are well-known findings, though not always well integrated into teaching practice. But what are the policy implications of these findings? One implication is that ways need to be found to release principals from some of their fiscal and administrative duties, to allow them time to visit classes to observe whether or not these kinds of research findings are applied in the classroom. The research on effective principals is supportive of this recommendation. Principals that spend more time involved in instructional issues (i.e. principals who spend a great deal of their time in classrooms) were usually principals of effective schools and rarely principals of ineffective schools. Another policy implication, for the higher education community, requires rethinking teacher education programs to find ways to insure that colleges of education can assure school districts that the teachers they turn out have had experience actually doing (not just reading about) these effective teaching behaviors.

Another example of a replicable finding from research on teaching is related to the variable or concept of "wait-time." This is the time that a teacher waits after asking a well-formed, meaty, higher-order question of students. Researchers have at least 16 replications of the general finding that when teachers wait approximately 3 full seconds after asking their questions, instead of the more usual .8 of a second, wondrous things happen (Tobin, 1987). The research reveals that some likely outcomes of adopting this strategy are:

1. The length of student response increases.
2. The number of unsolicited but appropriate responses increases.
3. The failures to respond decrease.
4. The complexity and cognitive level of student responses increases.
5. The number of alternative explanations increases.
6. The incidence of student-to-student responses increases.
7. Student achievement in science and mathematics increases.

Wait-time, by allowing students an authentic opportunity to think, seems to be a highly commendable teacher behavior. No negative side effects are known and the positive effects seem to be plentiful. If this were the report of a new drug to increase classroom attentiveness, thoughtfulness and achievement it would be heralded as a miracle drug. But it is not used much by teachers despite its replicated positive effects. It is not used, in part, because it is not well taught in colleges of teacher education, nor monitored well by those who supervise instruction at the classroom level. Thus, the policy implications are the same as noted above for the variables of academic feedback, structuring, and monitoring. But in the case of wait-time more is involved. Despite its many positive effects, wait-time slows down a class. Thus, teachers who learned about the research and agreed to try this teaching technique quickly abandoned it because it conflicted with the preexisting choices about appropriate classroom behavior that the teachers had already made. The teachers were behaving in accordance with their interpretation of district and state policies, which they believe pressure them to cover large amounts of the curriculum. They believe they are to emphasize breadth of understanding rather than depth of understanding. Teachers in New York, for example, saw value in the concept and believed that the research they read made a great case for using this variable. They would not use this teaching practice, however, "because they felt a tremendous pressure to get kids through the curriculum at a fast pace to prepare them for the New York State Regents Examinations" (Beyerbach, 1988a, 1988b). The teachers believed they had to get through all that they could of the extensive mandated curriculum, or their students would be penalized. They adopted this policy even though they believed that it was the wrong professional decision to make. These teachers were "driven by the regents." Pace became one of the dominant forces regulating their behavior and thus wait-time was simply abandoned as an instructional strategy. What we see here is the case of research that is useful, that informs us how children can be led to think deeper, clearer and in a more sophisticated way, and in ways that help them achieve better. But the implementation of these findings is hampered by conflicting state and local policy about how school achievement is to be measured and how school districts and teachers will be rewarded. If breadth of knowledge, as measured on a wide-range multiple-choice test, is the criterion by which teachers and schools are to be judged effective, then teachers' actions are quite understandable. Different conceptions of achievement and the role of the teacher need to be promulgated if the empirical findings about wait-time are ever to become a part of a teachers' routinely used behavioral repertoire. Unless state policies were to change, classroom practices are not likely to change. The interaction of conflicting values is what we uncover when we reflect on why wait-time is not used in the classroom. This is an interesting case for policy analysts to consider.

Some educational research findings are quite straightforward. They might easily have an impact on state and local finances and the ways we think about the process of schooling. The findings with regard to retention in grade have those qualities, though, as we shall see, research does not usually influence policy quickly and easily. For example, it is estimated that the state of Arizona retained in grade over 15,000 school children last year, mostly in the early elementary grades. Nationwide estimates of the numbers of school children retained in grade vary but are probably well over 1,250,000. The costs of public school education in Arizona are relatively inexpensive by nationwide standards, approximately $3,000 per student per year. Thus, Arizona's decision to retain students in grade one year will cost the state $45,000,000 (R. Doyle, 1989). And that same decision might cost the nation $5,000,000,000. This five billion dollars might be a wise investment if research supported the decision to retain a student in grade. Such a costly decision should have positive consequences for the students involved or for society in general. But research informs us that the decision to retain students in grade is absolutely the wrong decision for the majority of the students for whom retention in grade is considered. A student who is allowed to go ahead with their age-mates is estimated to achieve 15 percentile points higher on standardized achievement tests than a student that is retained in grade (Holmes and Mathews, 1984). Moreover, the students retained in grade are likely to have lower self-concept and poorer overall adjustment than the students of equal ability who were allowed to remain with the cohort with which they started school. And the evidence on dropouts in America reveals that one of the strongest predictors of dropping out of school before high school graduation is retention in grade. Thus, the real costs to society of school policies that try to maximize the numbers of students retained in grade are much higher than the five billion dollars noted above, since the economic costs of failing to complete high school are substantial and must be included in determining the total costs to society of this kind of school policy. These straightforward findings beg to be considered by policymakers who are increasingly calling for tougher standards and leaving back students who do not keep up with their age-mates. These same policymakers, however, also want to reduce dropouts and save money. These are competing policy agendas. They cannot exist side by side. The research findings about the effects of leaving students back a year call for a reconceptualization of school retention policy by state and local school boards, and by the teachers and administrators within a district. Unfortunately, such policy reappraisals are not readily discernable.

Other research findings illuminate the philosophical debates about the nature of schools in a multi-cultural and multi-lingual country and could impact the policy decisions that flow from those debates. For example, many states are currently debating "English Only" propositions, and in some states constitutional amendments to this effect have passed. The putative goal of such propositions is to have minority and immigrant children speak English as rapidly as possible, perhaps through immersion programs of instruction, and to phase out bilingual education or shorten it dramatically. (Other motives for this kind of legislation are not not nearly as pleasant to consider. They include racism, ethnocentrism, xenophobia, and the like.) Issues about language, which always touch upon cultural identity, are emotional issues, not issues where facts can easily influence policy. Nevertheless, it is clear that the "facts" from research in bilingualism support a different policy than most of America desires or now has in place. The research demonstrates that balanced bilingual children have cognitive (as well as economic) advantages over those that do not have such bilingual ability. For example, Kessler and Quinn (1987) studied sophisticated language use, such as the use of irony or metaphor. Two groups were compared. One group was from a barrio public school in a Southwestern city. These were bilingual students in the fifth grade with a measured reading level on standardized tests at about the third grade level. The comparison group was from an elite private school in the northeast, also fifth graders, with a tested reading level at about the seventh grade. The results of such a comparison are usually easy to predict. But in this case, on the sophisticated language measures, the poor, barrio, bilingual children outperformed the richer children of the elite school. Similar effects are demonstrated in other studies (e.g. Hakuta, 1989). This set of studies is the basis for concluding that balanced bilingualism provides a child with cognitive advantages. This is as true of Turkish-German bilingualism as it is of Spanish-English bilingualism. Yet, our current national policy seems to be designed to squelch a child's heritage language in elementary school, and then, when the child reaches high school, teach the child a foreign language! Research suggests that we should set out from the beginning of schooling to build the child's heritage language as teachers search for ways to help the child make a transition into English. Research also informs us that it is the late exit bilingual programs (slow transition) which are more effective than the early exit (fast transition) programs. This finding also goes against current public beliefs and many school policies. But the research convincingly suggests that it is better to build a child's heritage language and slowly promote the transition of the child into regular English instruction than to suppress the child's heritage language and try to make the transition as rapid as possible. Moreover, since balanced bilingualism yields cognitive advantages, policies should be developed so that *every* child should be receiving genuine and extensive amounts of foreign language instruction from the earliest school grades. From a developmental perspective it appears better to teach foreign language skills as early as possible rather than wait until the child is older. So, nationally, with a few noteworthy exceptions, we see school language policies that are unequivocally incompatible with research evidence. This is another reason for stressing the power of our contemporary research and for attempting to convince those in policy settings that educational research has relevance to the decisions about teaching, learning and schooling that must be made. But it is reasonable to also remain skeptical about the role that research can play in policy formulation, particularly in areas of intense public debate such as surrounds the language issues confronted by our schools. Research does not easily influence public policy when the research suggests that the policies derived from deep-seated beliefs about the educational system are inappropriate. Educational policy, historically, is more often determined by social and philosophical arguments than by empirical findings.

Concepts. Educational research in general, and research on teaching in particular, does not just yield variables to study, it yields concepts with which to think about education, as well. Concepts may also be variables (e.g. wait-time is both), but as concepts they play an important and different role. Concepts are the names of things, and by naming and defining things we thereby organize our world and render it more manageable. When we begin using precise concepts like "allocated time," or "reinforcement," descriptive concepts like "gifted" or "learning disabled," or even such abstract concepts as "at risk" and "instructional leadership," we are developing our technical vocabulary, our language to communicate with each other. Education has been viewed from within and without as a field of practice and not primarily as a technical/scientific field. Thus, a rich set of concepts, derived from research, and used to describe practice in something other than lay terms, was not developed until recently. Concepts, like variables, have policy implications by helping us think differently about the phenomena that is of interest to us.

For example, time on task has, in recent years, become a key concept in thinking about schooling. Virtually everyone understands that a student will not learn much if he or she does not pay attention. Attention, engagement, or time on task is a prerequisite for learning to take place. The importance of this concept was made clear in a series of studies in which it was found that students in different classrooms spent vastly different amounts of time on task (Berliner, 1979, 1987; Fisher, Berliner, Filby, Marliave, Cahen and Dishaw, 1980). In one classroom a teacher may allocate 50 minutes to mathematics instruction each day and in another classroom a teacher may allocate 16 minutes to mathematics instruction each day. (Note: Allocated time is another useful concept for thinking about actual time spent in the area of the curricula that is of interest.) In the former classroom the teacher might have been skilled enough to keep students on task about 90 percent of the time, while in the latter classroom the teacher might have been able to keep the students on task about 50 percent of the time. The result of the teaching practices in these two classes is actual time on mathematics tasks of 45 minutes versus eight minutes per day. This leads to a difference in terms of time on task of almost 3 hours per week in the two classes. On-task instructional time is 400 percent more in one class than another. As might be expected, achievement will be different in the two classes. So the concept of time on task can be used as a variable to describe differences among classrooms in the time actually spent interacting with the designated curriculum materials. And the concept can be used as a variable in predicting achievement, which it does quite well, correlating with achievement usually at between .20 and .50, and usually accounting for between 10 to 40 percent of the variance in student achievement. But most of all, the concept can be used to think about how schools and teachers organize themselves. Are they using time wisely? Are students provided with enough time on science tasks in the elementary school curriculum to actually learn anything useful over the academic year? If someone believes that students are not writing well, the first question to ask might be whether students are spending any time doing writing? If someone is concerned about Japanese students' mathematics achievement, in comparison to American students' mathematics achievement, they could examine the American teachers, the students' interests and abilities, the cultural emphasis and value that the nation places on mathematics, or the curriculum materials for studying mathematics. But armed with the concept of time on task one might first ask whether the time students spend on mathematics in the two countries is the same? In fact, the most parsimonious explanation for why Japanese children excel at mathematics in comparison to American students is because Japanese students spend vastly greater amounts of time doing mathematics tasks. Policy implications flow easily from such a conclusion. Mathematics could be given more time in the existing curriculum. School days, weeks, and years could be lengthened. New motivational systems could be tried out to increase the amount of time students are willing to spend on mathematics. Mathematics in the elementary school could be taught by specialists who would insure that the mathematics that is learned is the best for increasing mathematical understanding and mathematical achievement. Time is a scarce resource. Schools that do not spend it well have students that do not achieve well (Teddlie, Kirby, and Stringfield, 1989). Thus, time on task is a concept to be prized when thinking about schools, since it well connected to empirical evidence and so laden with conceptual utility.

Another concept that has been useful for thinking about schooling and student achievement is that of "curriculum alignment." This concept refers to the fact that the curriculum that is taught should be aligned with the outcome measure that is used to assess the effectiveness of instruction. If it is desirable to teach two-column addition without regrouping, then ability to perform two-column addition without regrouping should be what is assessed. A test of two-column addition that demands under-standing of regrouping is not aligned with the curriculum being taught. When there is little overlap between a test and the curriculum that is offered, it is likely that the test is *under*estimating achievement by a considerable amount. This happens frequently in the United States of America when nationally standardized tests are used to assess instruction in a local school district that has created a curriculum to serve their local purposes. Teachers, in the interest of fairness to their students, and schools, in the interest of fairness to their teachers, must take care to match the curriculum and the test used to assess learning and teaching. Policy implications abound from this rich concept and the accompany-ing empirical work (e.g. Freeman, Kuhs, Porter, Knappen, Floden, Schmidt, and Schwille, 1980). For example, if a school has its own innovative or local curriculum and it is considered a valued product of the staff, then standardized test results cannot be used to evaluate school effectiveness. Thus, policies that help foster local school-based manage-ment and local curriculum development may have to include resources to develop special tests that are aligned with the curriculum developed or chosen at a particular site. This is rarely done. Norm-referenced nationally standardized tests, so often used to monitor the effects of certain school policies, are likely to be inappropriate measures of achieve-ment for evaluating those policies. Criterion-referenced tests may be the instrument of choice in many situations and these may have to be developed locally. Policymakers, however, may be disappointed in such tests because they do not provide comparative information, though the information they do provide may be far more appropriate from an educational viewpoint. On the other hand, as so often happens, the outcome measure can become more valued than the curriculum. It can become the standard by which the quality of instruction is judged. When that happens a different set of policy decisions are instituted. Curricu-lum is modified to meet the items and objectives which constitute the test. In this case the tail wags the dog! This is only a sensible curriculum and instructional policy decision when the test is considered a valid indicator of desirable achievement. To compound the problem, many pressures to have students do well on the tests are brought to bear on administrators and teachers, and sometimes teachers do teach precisely what is on the test, without regard for the educational merit of the test and without taking the time to create the context that must be developed for instruction to be meaningful. Sometimes the pressure on principals and teachers to have their students score well on the tests is quite heavy and thus cheating by teachers and administrators becomes a major problem. It is apparently a widespread problem in contemporary America (Stringfield and Teddlie, in press). It appears that policies that emanate from decision makers who reify test scores have some major negative effects on educational systems.

Other concepts and ideas about the educational system are related to policies that affect the educational system in both small and large ways. For example, the concept of "grade surety" (W. Doyle, 1983) helps us to understand some educational phenomena. The concept is derived from an economic conception of classes as places where an exchange of performance for grades takes place. Students in some schools, under pressure by society in general and their parents in particular, believe they must obtain certain kinds of grades and therefore they strike certain kinds of (often unwritten) deals with their teachers. In exchange for certain kinds of performances they expect certain kinds of grades to be assigned to them. They need to engage in activities that provide them with surety that the implicit or explicit "contract" is upheld; that they will, in fact, receive the grades they need. When such a system is operating, as it is, say, in an upwardly mobile suburban community, with youngsters under pressure to eventually be accepted by "good" colleges, the creativity of their teachers can be severely reduced. For example, if a teacher wanted to teach a unit of science as a creative problem-seeking and creative problem-solving activity, that is, as a process, without clear objectives, without fixed assignments and without some multiple-choice test of molecular bits of knowledge in mind, then that teacher is likely to be condemned by the students and their families as not providing the content that the community wants. Under these conditions of teaching, the students lose their sense of surety about their grades, and students can become very anxious in such a setting. They begin to demand a more pedestrian and predictable curriculum. Thus, if the legislature and some segment of the public wants more creative classroom teachers, they may have to find ways to change grading policies, university entrance requirements, parents' understanding of what schools are to accomplish, and so forth. That is, a simple concept like "grade surety," which turns out to be useful for understanding the ways some classes in some communities operate, also has implications for thinking about a large number of interrelated school and societal problems.

Other concepts, such as "learning disabled" or "hyperactive," have been given new meanings in recent years and led to an assortment of costly educational policies. This has occurred despite the fact that many educators see the concept of learning disability as socially constructed by middle-class parents on the one hand, who did not want to have their children identified as retarded, and, on the other hand, constructed by school psychologists in order to have a cliental to justify their own activities. Hyperactivity, now often treated inappropriately by drugs, is another case in which a descriptive concept takes on peculiar meanings. Somehow, a behavioral problem was transformed into a medical problem, perhaps in this way easing the teachers' and the parents' responsibility for management of a child with excess energy and difficulty paying attention. Our concepts for thinking about teaching, learning, and the individual differences we see among students help us to organize the way we think. The concepts influence what we perceive, and thus they influence what we will ultimately do. If we had no concept like "learning disabled," as seems true of some other Western-developed countries, then there would be no need for special policies and special funding, since no problem of that kind would be evident. The concepts we use, therefore, can help or hinder us as we try to understand education and as we attempt to develop policies that will improve education throughout the nation.

Theories. Theories about teaching and learning also have policy implications. For example, metaphors are a form of theorizing, a way to describe a phenomena in such a way that we think we understand it. If elementary school teachers are described, metaphorically, as being like "mother" or "father" earth, we think we understand something about teachers and teaching. The metaphor brings to mind nurturance, love, and caring, which are, of course, important characteristics for those holding the position of elementary teacher. But that metaphor usually precludes us from thinking about the notions of competence, managerial skill and professionalism. Our metaphors, our theories about teaching and teachers, predisposes us to act in certain ways and not act in other ways. Do policies to promote career ladders and site-based management follow if our metaphor, our theory, emphasized the nurturant skills of teachers? Or, if the mother earth metaphor is used, would policies having to do with cooperative teacher study groups and in-service programs concerned with the health and safety of young students be more likely to be emphasized? At the high school level a different metaphor is often used to describe teachers. This is the metaphor of the "information giver," which also implies certain characteristics and not others. Information givers do not use television and computers to teach students, since *they* are the information givers. Media and technology cannot do that job effectively. Thus, contemporary policies concerned about computer usage in schools are likely to run afoul of the theory of instruction that permeates the high school: that of the teacher as the source of knowledge, as the information giver. If, for example, we chose a more modern metaphor to help us think about the nature of teachers and teaching, such as the metaphor of the teacher as "executive," then decision making, management, and supervision are the concepts that are quickly brought to mind. With this metaphor or theory of classroom teaching, career ladders and policies to promote site-based management make more sense (Berliner, in press). One does not formulate policy and programs related to career ladders if teaching is primarily nurturance; rather, one debates career ladder policies when notions of subject-matter competence, measurable outcomes, effectiveness, and so forth, are associated with our thinking about the work of teachers. Thus, the metaphors we use to think about teachers and teaching are directly, though subtly, influencing the educational policies that we create.

Formal theories of schooling and classroom learning have also been created (Carroll, 1963, 1985; Harnishfeger and Wiley, 1976; Berliner, 1987). The key concept in many of these theories is derived from J. B. Carroll's concept of the "opportunity to learn." It is arguably the most powerful concept in education. The theories all stress that students need sufficient time to learn the things they are supposed to learn, that is, students must have the opportunity to learn the things for which they will be held responsible. This theory, in various forms, has been subject to empirical tests hundreds of times and proved very useful. The concepts that are joined in this theory, and given mathematical notation, include opportunity to learn, perseverance of students, allocated time, engaged time, quality of the instruction, and aptitude for instruction in the particular curriculum area. Each of these concepts alone, but especially when woven into a theory, have implications for instruction and school organization. For example, to find ways to increase students' perseverance, raise the quality of instruction, and insure the maximum opportunity to learn, a form of instruction called mastery learning was invented (Bloom, 1968). Policy debates about the usefulness of this form of instruction abound, with some districts mandating mastery programs, others using it selectively, and still others declaring that it is fine for training but not education. The related set of theories are also all concerned with student time and enter the debates about the time spent by American students on their core subjects. Should the school day be longer? Should the school year be longer? Should we have after-school and Saturday schools for all children? How can we insure that time spent in schools provides students with the opportunity to learn that they need? These issues spring forth from the theories of Carroll and his disciples. Then these issues become mixed with the fiscal, social, and philosophical concerns of policymakers; and in different states and communities, different decisions are made about the time needed for schooling. The Carroll theory contains one element that is of singular importance. It is the element that describes student aptitude, such as intelligence, in terms of the time a student needs to learn a particular subject-matter area. In this formulation it is unnecessary to believe in intelligence as a fixed entity and unnecessary to regard it has having a strong genetic component. Such concerns are irrelevant in Carroll's model of school learning. Intelligence in a particular area of the curriculum—art, mathematics, athletics, reading and language arts—is demonstrated by the time needed to achieve certain tasks in the subject area. In this brilliant insight, transforming intelligence into a time-based variable, Carroll makes it possible for us to drop out of the educational vocabulary the terms smart and dumb and substitute, instead, the terms quick and slow. Important policy implications flow from this theoretical position. Schools, for example, would never be age graded if the Carroll model were followed. Students would finish twelve years of schooling whenever they could. Some would finish the standard curriculum in eight years and some in fifteen. Schools would accommodate to a student's rate of progress instead of organizing themselves around the untenable assumption that all students can (and should) proceed at precisely the same rate. Contemporary school policies, reflecting the kind of social Darwinism that was prevalent at the end of the last century, are designed to sort out the smart from the less smart. These policies are based on the assumption that students fall along some continuum running from dumb to smart, reflecting, in some way, their genetic endowment. But from Carroll's theory we can take a position that is theoretically more sound and certainly more humane, namely, that students fall along a continuum that runs from slow to fast. Adoption of the former position allows too many teachers to fail students who cannot keep up and to abandon them as worthwhile human beings because they appear not to have the requisite intelligence to perform as expected. Adoption of the latter position calls for the accommodation to students' aptitude (rate of learning a particular subject) and a belief that almost every student can achieve the criterion set for achievement if given the amount of time that is needed by that particular student. A good many problems in contemporary education are circumvented when this theoretical position is used to design schooling. No doubt, however, a whole set of new problems would emerge, but the policies that are derived from the Carroll model are appealing ones and need to be tried out.

Technology. Practitioners generally rely upon those in basic fields of inquiry to help them in their practice. In this respect the practice of education is no different than the practice of medicine or engineering. One difference, however, is that unlike the biology-medicine linkage and the physics-engineering linkage, an extensive educational research community was virtually nonexistent until a few years ago and thus made almost no impact on the practice of teaching. Scientific findings are relatively new in education. As they are established, technology flows from them just as it does in other fields. Technology in teaching, like any other form of technology, is simply the practical use of scientific achievements. Already mentioned was that the basic model or testable theory of school learning proposed by Carroll (1963) had been developed into technology, mastery learning, by Bloom (1968). Scientific investigations of the benefits of cooperative learning, by Slavin (1983) and others (Johnson and Johnson, 1975; Cohen, 1982; Sharan, 1980), have yielded training manuals and instructional guides that help a teacher turn these scientific investigations into classroom practices that have a high probability of working. But technology requires adaptation. When cooperative learning is used, teachers, parents and school boards have to reassess their beliefs about the role of students and teachers in classrooms. If students are to be considered capable of instructing each other, then what sort of schools will we have in the future, since a rather pervasive current conception of schooling is that teaching is telling and learning is listening? What happens to that cherished American tradition of competition if there is an infusion of cooperative learning in the schools? How can teachers be prepared to teach in a cooperative fashion when our schools of education have no laboratories for them to practice for a week or more this complex form of teaching? The evidence for the usefulness of this new technology is clear. But beliefs about schooling and students, and methods for teacher education must be addressed by policymakers as they try to promote cooperative learning in the schools. It is not enough to demonstrate that a new technology is useful. Each new technology has associated with it some new ways of thinking and requires new roles to be played by the users of the technology. These social and psychological issues must be part of the policymakers' thinking if there is to be a reasonable chance that some new technology for instruction will become institutionalized in the schools.

Research on classroom teaching and learning also has provided a technological innovation called reciprocal teaching (Palincsar and Brown, 1984). In this form of instruction teachers and students take turns asking questions about prose materials. The goal is to build the students' competence in asking who, what, when, where and how questions, in order that the students could learn to answer comprehension questions. The students in the original study were performing at around the fifteenth percentile in reading comprehension. After only fifteen days of instruction, for a short period of time each day, the students were performing at about the seventieth percentile on standardized tests of comprehension. Moreover, the positive effects were still noted months later and in other areas of the school curriculum. This study would surely have been declared a "monumental breakthrough" if the field had been medicine. Headlines in the press might have declared "Miracle Cure For Comprehension Deficit Found." But in education this new technology is vastly underutilized. Teachers do not always hear about research findings, and even when they do, many do not know how to manage classrooms in ways that would allow them to break out into small groups or engage in individual instruction. Some teachers also may find it difficult to take the role of student and engage in a genuine reciprocal activity, since to do so may undermine their authority in the class. It is not a simple issue for those who make policy to confront. One cannot simply pass a motion "that henceforth, reciprocal teaching will be used." Information in education is not immediately transformable into policy. Nevertheless, the new technology—technology that works—needs to find its ways into the schools, and those in policy positions need to explore the ways this can be done in some sensible manner that is respectful of teachers and their needs.

Other technology derived from studies of teaching exists. Outcome-based instruction, for example, is one such innovation that many districts are adopting. In this form of instruction the criteria for instruction in a curriculum area are very well defined and the tests to assess instruction are well aligned with the curriculum. Teachers instruct primarily in those areas that are assessed. The outcomes determine instruction. Such systems have been very effective in some communities, but it calls for a redefinition of the role of teachers and a different sense of professionalism for teachers than is ordinarily the case in education. Policymakers considering this form of instruction, and the evidence of effectiveness that exists, have to think deeply, also, about the instructional means as well as the ends that are desired. It is too easy in outcomes-based education for education to become simply training for test taking. This may be what some communities desire, but others do not want their schools working in such ways.

In a number of areas of instruction new technology that usually works is available. But the technology cannot and should not be imposed on teachers and schools by those in positions to set policy. Rather, the new technology, whether a new curriculum, new video and computer systems, or the kinds of instructional technology described above, must be thoughtfully examined by those in positions to influence policy. The information that is available must be shared with teachers and others that might be affected by adopting the new technology. Small pilot studies of the new technology should be instituted, rather than asking everyone to adopt a new program at once. Money should be allocated for a number of years to support teachers that try the new technology. And both formative and summative evaluation should be supported. Policymakers would be deluded if they were to think that the route from "good research idea" to "well-functioning school practice" was an uncomplicated, linear, sequence. Educational policy, like policy in public health, welfare, agriculture, national park management and military defence, simply does not work that way.

Conclusion

Research on teaching and learning in the last few decades has been fruitful. Dozens of illustrations of new findings, concepts, theories and technologies could have been cited rather than the ones chosen above. One research line, related to how expectations affect another person's behavior, touch on all four areas (Cooper and Good, 1983; Good and Brophy, 1984). There are scores of *findings* related to teachers' expectations and students' classroom behavior and achievement; the *concept* of expectancy has found a place in attempts to explain the performance deficits among minority and poor students; *theories* of interpersonal communication and influence have been created to account for the findings and hypotheses associated with this construct; and *technology* has been derived from the theories and findings associated with the concept, taking the form of a program called TESA (an attempt to change *T*eacher *E*xpectations and *S*tudent *A*chievement). Or, for illustration, the research *findings* and associated policy implications about expert teachers could have been used (Berliner, 1988); a rich set of *concepts* with policy implications have also been described by Rosenshine and Stevens (1986), who argue that a set of teaching functions must be fulfilled by every effective teacher in areas where the outcomes are explicit (i.e. mathematics as opposed to social studies); and *technology* could also have been illustrated by the program known as Missouri Mathematics (Good, Grouws and Ebmeier, 1983) or the research-based classroom management programs developed by Evertson (1984) and Emmer and their colleagues. The last two decades have been fruitful, indeed, and the relationship of this burgeoning body of powerful and useful literature to educational policy must be clarified.

We have made the case above that replicable *findings* about instruction are plentiful. For illustration we have noted how academic feedback, structuring behavior by teachers, and active monitoring of their classes has had positive effects on student achievement. We have seen how research on wait-time, retention in grade, and bilingualism addresses issues that concern policymakers. We noted, also, how there is rarely any direct link between replicable, reliable, useful research, and the creation of policy. A recent notable exception to this rule is the research on the longitudinal effects and return on investment of early childhood education. But even here the policy community deals with many other issues than the ones addressed by educational researchers. This theme—the convoluted way that research affects policy—was true also for the *concepts* that research provides us with. For illustration we used the concepts of time on task, curriculum alignment, and grade surety. These are informative and rich concepts. But they do not easily give rise to educational policy. It was pointed out, above, that our educational *theories* have some special qualities. Our metaphors for discussing teaching and learning affect the way we think about problems and usually limit our thinking. Fresh metaphors need to be sought to help policy analysts think creatively about the problems they are addressing. Well-substantiated theories, such as J. B. Carroll's, provide us with important concepts and help us to understand the linkages between those concepts. By using this theory to interpret some phenomena within the larger educational system, new insights arise about the ways that schooling can be organized. Finally, illustrations of new instructional *technology* were presented. These technologies create expectations for the improvement of schooling, but they will not do so directly, quickly, or without resistance. New technology must fit into existing beliefs and patterns of schooling, or new beliefs and patterns must be promulgated in order to integrate the new technology into the school and classroom. It is not easy to change people and institutions, either by building better mousetraps, or providing irrefutable evidence, or by setting forth new policies (Cuban, 1984). Education, however, is not unique here. Witness resistance to economic change in China or Russia, failure to acknowledge changes in consumer preferences by the American auto industry, the failure of prohibition and recent anti-drug laws, the inane continuation of subsidies to tobacco farmers and the suicidal continuation of cigarette smoking among a large proportion of the population, and so forth.

The difficulty in setting and enforcing policy in education merely makes the task difficult, not impossible. As the research community in education grows and respect for the findings, concepts, theories and technology that it yields also grows, we can expect more informed debates about educational policy. But the social, political, philosophical and fiscal issues that policymakers must attend to always exert great influence on their decisions. Research must, therefore, be seen as just one of the many sources of information and beliefs from which policy is derived. We probably cannot improve much on our ranking in the set of concerns that policymakers must consider. But we can improve on the quality and usefulness of our research, attempting in this way to illuminate some of the problems faced by those charged with the task of making educational policy.

REFERENCES

Berliner, D. C. (1987). Knowledge is power. In D. C. Berliner and B. Rosenshine (Eds.), *Talks to teachers.* New York, NY: Random House.

Berliner, D. C. (1979). Tempus Educare. In P. L. Peterson and H. J. Walberg (Eds.) *Research on teaching.* Berkeley, CA: McCutchan.

Berliner, D. C. (1987). A simple theory of classroom instruction. In D. C. Berliner and B. Rosenshine (Eds.), *Talks to teachers.* New York, NY: Random House.

Berliner, D. C. (in press). If the metaphor fits, why not wear it? *Theory into Practice.*

Beyerbach, B. A. (1988a, April). *The interaction of research, policy, and practice: A case study of a research group attempting to implement wait time.* Paper presented at the meetings of the American Educational Research Association, New Orleans, LA.

Beyerbach, B. A. (1988b, April). *Comparing researchers', teachers', and students' perspectives on a line of research attempting to implement wait-time in classrooms.* Paper presented at the meetings of the American Educational Research Association, New Orleans, LA.

Bloom, B. S. (1968). Learning for mastery. *Evaluation Comment*, 1(2).

Carroll, J. B. (1985). The model of school learning: Progress of an idea. In C. W. Fisher and D. C. Berliner (Eds.), *Perspectives on instructional time.* New York, NY: Longman.

Carroll, J. B. (1963). A model of school learning. *Teachers College Record*, 64, 723–733.

Cohen, E. (1982). Expectation status and interracial interaction in school settings. *Annual Review of Sociology*, 8, 209–235.

Cooper, H. M. & Good, T. L. (1983). *Pygmalian grows up: Studies in the expectation communication process.* New York, NY: Longman.

Cuban, L. (1984). *How teachers taught: Constancy and change in American Classrooms: 1890-1980.* New York, NY: Longman.

Doyle, R. (1989, April). *Resistance of conventional wisdom to research evidence: A critical look at the grade standards approach to underachievement.* Paper presented at the meetings of the American Educational Research Association, San Francisco, CA.

Doyle, W. (1983). Academic work. *Review of Educational Research*, 53, 159–199.

Emmer, E., Evertson, C., Sanford, J., Clements, B. & Worsham, M. E. (1984). *Classroom management for secondary teachers.* Englewood Cliffs, NJ: Prentice-Hall.

Evertson, C., Emmer, E. T., Clements, B., Sanford, J. & Worsham, M. E. (1984). *Classroom management for elementary teachers.* New York, NY: Prentice-Hall.

Fisher, C. W., Berliner, D. C., Filby, N. N., Marliave, R., Cahen, L. S., & Dishaw, M. M. (1980). Teaching behaviors, academic learning time, and student achievement: An overview. In C. Denham and A. Lieberman (Eds.), *Time to learn.* Washington, D.C.: National Institute for Education, U.S. Department of Education.

Freeman, D., Kuhs, T., Porter, A., Knappen, L., Floden, R., Schmidt, W., & Schwille, J. (1980). *The fourth grade mathematics curriculum as inferred from textbooks and tests.* IRT report No. 82, East Lansing, MI: Michigan State University, Institute for Research on Teaching.

Gage, N. L. (1985). *Hard gains in the soft sciences: The case of pedagogy.* Bloomington, IN: Phi Delta Kappan.

Good, T. L. & Brophy, J. (1984). *Looking in classrooms* (3rd ed.). New York, NY: Harper and Row.

Good, T. L., Grouws, D., & Ebmeier, H. (1983). *Active mathematics teaching.* New York, NY: Longman.

Hakuta, K. (1989). Language and cognition in bilingual children. In *Advances in language education.* Los Angeles: University of California, Center for Language Education and Research.

Harnischfeger, A. & Wiley, D. E. (1976). The teaching learning process in elementary school: A synoptic view. *Curriculum Inquiry*, 6, 5–43.

Hedges, L. V. (1987). How hard is hard science, how soft is soft science? The empirical cummulativeness of research. *American Psychologist*, 42, 443–455.

Holmes, C. T. and Mathews, K. M. (1984). The effects of non-promotion on elementary and junior high school pupils: A meta-analysis. *Review of Educational Research*, 54, 225–237.

Johnson, D. W. & Johnson R. T. (1975). *Learning together and alone*. Englewood Cliffs, NJ: Prentice-Hall.

Kessler, C. & Quinn, M. E. (1987). Language minority children's linguistic and cognitive creativity. *Journal of Multilingual and Multicultural Development*, 8, 173–185.

Palincsar, A. M., & Brown, A. L. (1984). Reciprocal teaching of comprehension-fostering and comprehension-monitoring activities. *Cognition and Instruction*, 1, 117–175.

Rosenshine, B. and Stevens, R. (1986). Teaching functions. In M. C. Wittrock (Ed.), *Handbook of research on teaching*. New York: Macmillan.

Sharan, S. (1980). Cooperative learning in small groups. *Review of Educational Research*, 50, 241–271.

Slavin, R. E. (1983). *Cooperative learning*. New York, NY: Longman.

Stringfield, S. & Teddlie, C. (in press). *Among school children*. White Plains, NY: Longman.

Teddlie, C., Kirby, P. C. & Stringfield, S. (1989). Effective versus ineffective schools: Observable differences in the classroom. *American Journal of Education*, 97, 221–236.

Tobin, K. (1987). The role of wait-time in higher cognitive level learning. *Review of Educational Research*, 57, 69–95.

Chapter 15

DON'T BLAME THE SCHOOLS FOR CHANGES IN VALUES, CULTURE, AND FAMILIES

Richard D. Lamm and Richard A. Caldwell

What's wrong with America's schools? Inquiring minds in government, industry and the general public want to know.

In 1983, the United States Department of Education published *A Nation At Risk*, which alleged that "the educational foundations of our society are presently being eroded by a rising tide of mediocrity" and that our education failures are equivalent to "an act of unthinking, unilateral educational disarmament."[1]

Six years have passed, but true reform has been elusive. Countless commissions and task forces, private foundations, and corporations have studied the issues and published recommendations. But the fact remains— American education is inferior to our major competitors'. Perhaps a quarter of our eighteen-year-olds are functionally illiterate. International achievement tests show American students lagging behind in math, science, even geography.[2]

We would suggest that much of the problem with the American education system lies outside the realm of the schoolroom and is not subject to correction within the school room. This is not to say there isn't much to correct within the American education system. Clearly there is. But much lies outside the schoolroom and has not received enough discussion or attention. We must, if we are to correct the problem of educational failure, look outside the classroom to changing American values, behavior, and culture.

It is unrealistic and unfair to assign as "educational failure" the current low performance standards of many of our students. Children born to single women in poverty, who grow up in often disrupted circumstances, are not the same students which challenged previous generations of teachers. A larger and larger percentage of American children are being born to families that do not have the material or emotional wherewithal

288

to produce children capable of taking advantage of a normal classroom. We scapegoat the schools for faults that lie deeper within our society.

Schools are not separate from the supporting environment. We suggest schools are largely the products of their environments, and the fundamental determinants of educational success or failure are found in the larger social and valuational setting in which the school operates. Prescriptions for more of the "old time school religion," i.e. more homework, a tougher curriculum, more discipline, longer school days, etc., will not work, however well-intentioned, because they treat the symptoms of educational decline, not the causes.

The schools we have are the products of our society and its core values. Since the fifties, our values have changed. Society is different. It may be better; it may be worse. But value change has consequences. A complex society is built on a core of shared values; so are the schools.

Thomas P. Rohlen,[3] an expert on Japanese schools, has pointed out that Japan's schools produce a highly competent and competitive high school graduate because Japan fundamentally is a society devoted to education and to learning. On the other hand, we would argue that the progressive failure of American schools stems from a lack of clear public standards—standards that are deeply felt within society, not just promulgated by political leaders—underscored by a series of value changes that have occurred over the past thirty-five years.

Something very dramatic has happened to the way Americans act and react to the world, and we suggest that it is having a significant impact on our declining educational results. There has been a "Great American Value Shift" which must be better recognized.

Each reader is free to make up his/her own list, but we believe that most Americans will identify in our list and theirs' elements of an increasingly overindulged, permissive and hedonistic society. The Roman Juvenal observed "luxury is more ruthless than war." America has lost many of the stern virtues that made us great in the first place. If our kids and schools are falling behind, they find their twin in our trade deficit, federal deficit, falling productivity growth rates, and lack of savings. Our educational inadequacies mirror our societal inadequacies.

Schools are a symbolic mirror in which we see reflected the problems of our entire nation. They are the generational way station in which we glimpse our future.

Diane Ravitch, one of America's foremost education critics, has made a similar point that we will get the schools we deserve:

. . . Despite our dissatisfaction, we will not soon transform our educational system. It is not that it can't be done. The problem is that we lack consensus about whether there should be a common curriculum, and whether there are knowledge and skills everyone should have. If we believed that it was important to have a highly literate public, to have people capable of understanding history and politics and economics, to have citizens who are knowledgeable about science and technology, to have a society in which the powers of verbal communication are developed systematically and intentionally, then we would know what we wanted of our schools. Until we do, we get the schools we deserve, which accurately reflect our own confusion about the value of education.[4]

James Fallows in his book *More Like Us*[5] observes, "In the long run, habits, values and behavior of ordinary people determine national strength." Senator Patrick Moynihan similarly states, "The central conservative truth is that it is culture, not politics, that determines the success of society."

We thus must look at our national values and culture. Shakespeare said, "A hungry lion hunts best." American students are today competing with students from Japan, Korea, Taiwan, West Germany, who are "hungry lions." Their cultures stress education, hard work, delayed gratification, a strong will to succeed. Too many American students believe that success is their birthright and that a good job is guaranteed by the U.S. Constitution. They watch television while their international counterparts do four or five times the amount of homework. "Hungry lions" do hunt best.

A powerful book on the role of culture in the success of peoples is Larry Harrison's *Underdevelopment is a State of Mind: The Latin American Case.*[6] In it he discusses blacks from the same tribe who were placed part in Barbados and part in Haiti. In Barbados they fell under the influence of English culture and, while the road wasn't easy, they now run a successful democracy with a relatively high standard of living. The same people in Haiti fell under the influence of a different culture and did not come close to duplicating the success of their neighbors in Barbados.

Harrison observes, "My own belief is that Barbados's absorption of British culture over three hundred years is the principal explanation of its success. The liberalization of Barbadian society is closely linked to the liberalization of British society. . . . It is (however) not just 'enlightened colonialism' that is in play. It is not just the imposition by a colonial power of European institutions that results in elections, a free press, literacy and public health programs. It is also the absorption by the colonized people of the colonial power's values and attitudes over an extended period that gives vitality and durability to the imported institutions."

The point is an important one. Some nations succeed and other nations fail partly because of their culture and values. Even within a nation, certain groups have greater success rates, not because they are smarter, but because they stress ambition, education, hard work, success and a belief in social mobility. Japanese Americans, Jews, and Chinese Americans are the most economically successful people in the United States; yet all have faced special hurdles and barriers. All have been discriminated against by the majority community. Yet as a group they have succeeded brilliantly. Their attitudes, values and culture allowed them to overcome barriers seemingly insurmountable by others.

Today, we are in an historic struggle of tremendous importance over which values will dominate our national life. Either we are moving toward a new synthesis between traditional commitments and new forms of personal fulfillment, or we are approaching a fragmented, anomic society wherein the family is a shambles, the work ethic has collapsed, personal freedom is restricted, and the economy is increasingly uncompetitive.

But formulating a sense of public purpose in America and bolstering the required value system is not an easy task. The United States Constitution, in general, and the Bill of Rights, in particular, are monuments to the spirit of individualism. The founders were concerned with the limits of political action, enlarging the sphere of individual rights and diminishing the potential range of state action and abuse. They assumed that the common good and a valid sense of community would emerge from the cumulative actions of individuals.

Unfortunately, true reform of the educational system will require a new social consensus on goals and outcome. We must agree on the level of knowledge and skills that everyone should have. We must define high educational attainment as in the nation's interest, not just the individual's. We must sacrifice short-term gain for long-term results.

Values change over time. The America of the 1990s will not replicate the America of the 1950s. We still espouse a belief in achievement and success, in activity and work, in efficiency, pragmatism, and humanitarianism; but we also care about personal pleasure, material things and high profits, instant happiness, and ourselves, not our communities.

—We are paying the price of our success. America's material success is legendary and both admired and envied. The foundation of lasting wealth as we prepare to enter a new century is knowledge, not land, not labor, not military power, not even accumulated capital. In this sense, education is the ultimate intergenerational issue. Without a revitalized educational system, this generation's legacy to the next will be a poor one indeed.

THE GREAT AMERICAN 30-YEAR VALUE SHIFT

1950's	1990's	Consequences/Results
Saving	Spending	Federal Debt
		Trade Deficit
Delayed	Instant	Narcissism
Gratification	Gratification	
Ozzie and Harriet	Latchkey Kids	71% National High
		School Graduation Rate
Certainty	Ambivalence	Marriage Encounter
Orthodoxy	Skepticism	*Spy Magazine*
Investing	Leveraging	Low rate of
		Productivity Growth;
		Michael Milken
Unionization	Chapters 11 & 12	Decline of the
		Middle Class
Lifetime Employer	Outplacement	Look Out for #1;
		Alienation
Neighborhood	Lifestyle	Failure of Community
		Single-Issue Politics;
		Age Segregation;
		Ethnic Conflict;
		Gentrification
Middleclass	Underclass	Drugs; Gangs; Teenage
		Grannies; Colombia
Export	Import	Acura; Infiniti;
		Lexus; Fax; VCR's
Public Virtue	Personal Well-Being	Decline of Polity;
		Voter Alienation
Civil Rights	Affirmative Action	Lawsuits & Lawyers
Sputnik Scare	Bilingual Education	Ethnocentrism
Mom & Dad	Nanny/Day Care	Peers Replace Parents
Press Conference	Photo Opportunity	*People* Magazine
Achievement	Fame	Ratings & Polls
Knowledge	Credential	University as
		Secular Church
Fooling Around	Sexual Revolution	AIDS; Madonna
Manufacturing	Service	Computers;
		Information Systems;
		Eye strain
Industry	Technology	Bright Collars

Value-added	Mastercard	5-Year Car Loans; Repossessions
Problems	Pathologies	Analysis Paralysis
Newspaper/Radio	Media	30-Second Spot; Orwell Lives
Hope	Happiness	Preference By L'Oreal
Bomb Shelters	Crack Houses	Edward Bennett
Organization Man	Murphy Brown	Androgyny
NATO; Godless Communists	Commie Capitalists	Trading Blocks; New Alliances
Psychoanalysis/Neurosis	Support Groups/Serial Killers	Big Book Sales
Cheeseburger, fries, shake	Cheeseburger, fries, shake	American Cultural Hegemony
USA	Japan	"Japanaphobia"
New York	Tokyo	Des Moines
Harry; Ike	George Bush; Jim Wright	Nightline
Regulation	De-regulation	Re-regulation
Cash	Credit	Cash
Containment	Economic Security	Trade Sanctions
Deterrence	Terrorism	Metal Detectors
Upward Mobility	Downward Mobility	The Homeless; Heavy Metal; Shrinking Middle Class
Duty	Divorce	Despair
Elvis	Cinderella; Ratt; Poison; Metallica; Tesla	Elvis
Life	*People*	Geraldo; Oprah; Phil
"We"	"Me"	"Them"
Voyeurism	Affairs	Celibacy
Equity	Renting/Leasing	Balloon Payments
Repression	Acting-out	Repression
Organized Religion	Cults; TV Preachers	Authoritarianism
Heroes	Cover Girls	Cynicism
Internationalism	Isolationism	Personality Politics; "Psychiatrization" of Foreign Leaders (Raisa as role model)
Public Troubles	Private Issues	Greed; Fear; Insularity
Sherman Adams	Iran-Contra	Docudramas; "Infotainment"
B-52	*Challenger*	Pessimism
Money	More Money	Even More Money
"Do What You're Told"	"Do What You Want"	"You Do It"

"To Get Along, Go Along"	"To Get Ahead, Push Ahead"	Ivan Boesky; George Roberts, Henry Kravis; RJR
Punch Card	Motorola 68030 Microprocessor; Cray supercomputer	Information Overload; *Extra Strength Tylenol*
I Love Lucy	*I Love Lucy*	*I Love Lucy*
California Battery	Mandatory Drug Testing	Corporate Sovereignty; Huxley Lives; Drug Abuser "Boot Camps"
Young	Middle Age	Old

ENDNOTES

1. National Commission on Excellence in Education, U.S. Department of Education. *A Nation at Risk.* Washington, D.C.: U.S. Government Printing Office, 1983.
2. *American Agenda: Report to the Forty-First President of the United States.* Washington, D.C.: Times Mirror, 1988.
3. Rohlen, Thomas P. "Why Japanese Education Works." *Harvard Business Review.* September–October, 1987.
4. Ravitch, Diane.
5. Fallows, James. *More Like Us.* Boston: Houghton Mifflin, 1989.
6. Harrison, Lawrence. *Underdevelopment is a State of Mind.* Lanham, MD: Madison Books, 1985.

A CONCLUDING NOTE:

THE CHALLENGE AHEAD

Laurence R. Marcus and Benjamin D. Stickney

What began in the latter 1970s as a series of localized tremors of dissatisfaction with educational quality rumbled into an earthquake of national proportions as business and community leaders, parents and politicians across the country began to demand more of the schools in the early 1980s. *A Nation at Risk* (1983) emphasized the centrality of education to America's continuing technological development and to our ambition of regaining the lead position in the global economy. Since then, community after community, state after state, college after college have committed themselves to a quest for educational excellence. The reform activity has been so broadly based and so sustained that we have referred to this period as the "Age of Education."

As befits such a massive renewal effort, a stock-taking is in order. One important gauge of the impact of the reform movement is the increase in per-student spending, up 46 percent between 1982 and 1987 to $3977 (Evangelauf, 1989) and continuing to grow to $4800 by 1989, approximately twice as much in real terms as in the mid-1960s (Finn, 1989). It is fair to ask what all this money has bought. In many regards, the record is impressive: curricula have been revised; standards have been strengthened; high school graduation requirements have been expanded; teacher salaries have been improved; and the gap between whites and minorities has begun to narrow on some tests. Even critics as staunch as Vanderbilt's Chester Finn (1989) concede that significant progress is being made at the bottom end, that "rudimentary skills are nearly universal." Test scores for minority students are on the rise (Evangelauf, 1989), blacks having increased some 28 points on the SAT math test and 21 points on the SAT verbal test, for example, between 1979 and 1989 (Mitgang, 1989a).

A Job Not Finished

But, it is there, perhaps, that the consensus ends. Finn (1989) points to reports by the National Assessment of Educational Progress and others to conclude that students continue "to emerge from the typical school in possession of mediocre skills and skimpy knowledge." For example, only 5 percent of the 17-year-old high school students possess the reading skills to understand and to use information contained in technical materials, literary essays and historical documents. Only 6 percent are proficient with multi-step math problems and basic algebra. Equally discouraging is the demonstrated ability of only 7 percent of these students to infer relationships and to draw conclusions from detailed scientific knowledge. Facility with historical and social science data is also weak: only 25 percent know the years when Lincoln served as president; most cannot explain what a government budget deficit is; only about one-third can define *profit;* and familiarity with national and world geography is poor.

In addition, the knowledge and skill levels of those going on to college has not increased appreciably, and performance has been mixed on college admissions tests. After increases in recent years, the SAT dropped two points in 1988 and another point in 1989 to rest at 903 (427 verbal, 476 math). The ACT increased by .1 to 18.8 in 1988 but declined to 18.6 the following year. The gap between white and black SAT takers increased to 200 points in 1989 as a result of a two-point gain by whites to an average score of 937 in the face of an unchanged average among blacks (Evangelauf, 1989; Mitgang, 1989a). Collegiate basic skills tests (measuring reading, writing, computation and algebra skills) used in New Jersey's public colleges and universities reveal only the scantist of improvements between 1979 and 1988. Similarly, 30 percent of the higher education institutions in the 15 states that comprise the Southern Region Education Board have reported that at least half of their entering students are academically ill-prepared for college-level work (Finn, 1989).

More evidence that indicates that the problem has not been licked comes from the sixth annual "Wall Chart," issued in May 1989 by the Education Secretary Lauro F. Cavazos; it revealed that the 1987 high school graduation rate slipped to 71.1 percent, a decrease of one-half of 1 percent from the previous year. Declines in the graduation rates in 31 states outweighted the increases experienced in 19 states. Cavazos pointed out that only one state, Minnesota, graduated at least 90 percent of its high school students, a goal that he challenged the rest of the nation to achieve (Evangelauf, 1989).

Meanwhile, reports that contradict these gloomy figures are being presented by numerous school districts as they announce increases on standardized achievement tests used in elementary and secondary schools. Such proclamations have become so universal as to prompt some to point to a "Lake Wobegon effect," named after the mythical Minnesota town made famous by the radio program, "A Prairie Home Companion," where all of the children are "above average." In 1987 the Friends of Education, an educational watchdog group headed by Arizona physician, John Cannell, claimed that all 50 states were reporting above average scores on the major national standardized achievement tests. This finding was confirmed a year later by the U.S. Department of Education. A draft of a follow-up Friends of Education report, released to the press in September 1989, indicates that all but two states, Louisiana and Arizona, were reporting above average scores, as were 83 percent of the 5143 elementary school districts and 73 percent of the secondary school districts surveyed. The organization's skepticism about the reported scores is highlighted by the example of two states: 65 percent of Georgia's second grade pupils exceeded the national norms on the Iowa Test of Basic Skills and 75 percent of Kentucky's third graders scored above average on the Comprehensive Test of Basic Skills; yet, literacy levels, college entrance examination scores and results on the Armed Services Vocational Aptitude Battery Scores for Georgia and Kentucky residents are among the lowest in the nation. Cannell's research revealed a variety of improprieties by teachers and principals before, during and after the test administrations so as to yield higher scores. The group also has alleged a widespread practice of teaching to the tests (Mitgang, 1989b).

Losing Steam?

This increase in local test scores, whether or not they are, in fact, reflective of student achievement, is causing a dangerous complacency. Finn (1989) believes that reports of rising scores falsely assure parents and the public that the problem lies elsewhere, not in the local community. Secretary Cavazos, too, believes that the country has failed to recognize that we continue to have an "educational deficit." The result, claims Cavazos, is a loss of steam for the educational reform movement (Evangelauf, 1989).

Critics also contend that reform efforts have not been based on a coherent sense of expected educational outcomes and have ignored the fact that students learn in direct proportion to the time spent studying a given subject. They lament that as recently as 1987 only 30 percent of the graduating high school class had completed four years of English and three each of math, science and social studies. Further, they hold that the reform movement has become "dominated by the conviction that it is not really important to know anything in particular," that the teaching of facts has been replaced by an educational approach that seeks to improve critical thinking and higher-order cognitive skills (Finn, 1989).

Can it be that the failure to realize the goal of lifting the educational achievement levels of American youth is the product of an overoptimistic view of what has been accomplished to date, along with a misplaced concentration on process rather than product? Probably not. Surely, it is important to keep the public focused on the existence of an educational deficit. If some school officials and teachers have sought to turn our attention away by going to the extreme of manipulating test scores to make themselves look better, shame on them, but it should be recognized that the full weight of the responsibility for the problem of the schools may have been unfairly heaped upon them. As former Secretary Terrel H. Bell (1988) has stated, constructive criticism of schools and colleges is much more effective than "teacher and professor bashing." In any event, with less manipulable tests producing dismaying data, with outcomes measures such as high school and college graduation rates continuing to reveal serious problems, with achievement level comparisons revealing American school children trailing their counterparts in much of the industrialized world and with international measures of economic productivity showing us to be on the decline, there should be sufficient data to keep all eyes focused on the issue of the quality of education.

To the second criticism, it is true that in response to a world where the generation of new information and the application of new technologies are proceding at an unparalleled pace, increasing numbers of educators have posited that schools should focus on the development of critical thinking and higher-order cognitive skills. Few teachers, however, would ever attempt to argue that one can develop such skills in the absence of a full reservoir of facts. So, if Finn is correct that process has become dominant in today's schools, it should not be all that difficult for teachers to bring process and product into balance.

While the reform movement's success has yet to be demonstrated conclusively, it must be kept in mind that the downward slope of our educational system was long in the making. It was not until the spring

1983 release of *A Nation at Risk* that this reform era gained momentum; new approaches began to be implemented over the next several years. It can be said that the current wave of reform has probably arrested the decline. Realistically, the ascent to our former position will not come overnight.

While there may be many different routes to educational excellence, several themes have emerged that should be a part of the effort to regain that position: academic achievement is associated with time spent studying a subject; students involved in the learning process achieve more than students in passive learning situations; improved salaries do attract and hold teachers who have been high-achieving students themselves; effective schools have excellent principals; and well-planned parental involvement strategies can lead to a more productive usage of critical after-school hours and to the reinforcement of scholastic values.

This last point deserves special mention, given the emphasis placed on education by parents of youngsters who comprise America's most educationally successful ethnic groups. Similarly, much has been written about the widespread practice of parents in Japan insisting that their children receive after-school and weekend tutoring. It is not the case that American parents have less concern for their children than parents had a generation ago. However, the increase in the number of single-parent families, the economic necessity that requires both members of many two-parent families to work outside of the home, and the desire of increasing numbers of women for employment outside of the home have the combined results of children spending less time with their parents than occurred in the previous generation and of parents having more on their minds than how their children are doing in school. While parents have a responsibility to communicate with the schools, the schools need to do more than they have in recent years to engage parents as active partners in the educational process. This requires them to go beyond encouraging parental attendance at "back-to-school nights" and school plays. It should involve systematic programs which involve such efforts as parental signatures on completed homework assignments and graded tests, the organization of study time by parents and the cultivation of family reading hours to replace some of the time that children spend in front of the television.

Challenges to Reform

The type of reforms that have been initiated in recent years, once solidly in place on a widespread basis, will, we believe, result in achievement gains. However, without some other changes we fear that the American public will continue to be disappointed with the results of its educational system. There are several fundamental challenges to the success of the reform movement; one deals with the structure of the effort itself, another with the expectations of the reform movement, and a third with the context within which the reform movement is occurring.

Federalism Out of Balance

The first restraint on the reform movement is that the federalist balance has slipped too much toward the states. Secretary Cavazos recently commented that the role of the federal government is to bring educational issues to the national attention, to provide a spotlight for programs that are producing excellent results, to reward successful schools, teachers and students, and to reduce bureaucratic red tape (Evangelauf, 1989). Such a philosophy on the part of a national official speaking about a national crisis is an indication of how the Reagan revolution endures into the Bush administration. While it may be, as the Rand Corporation's Arthur Wise (1988) has held, that the quality of education is not as susceptible to regulation as is equal opportunity, the federal government has all but abdicated its regulatory authority regarding school improvement including the use of the budget as a policy tool.

Synchronous with its having passed the torch to state and local governments, Washington has dramatically reduced the amount of intergovernmental aid that it is making available to them. Since 1978, federal aid has declined 32 percent as a proportion of state and local revenues and has dropped by a third as a proportion of the entire federal budget. As George Mason University's Timothy Conlan (1989), a former assistant staff director of the Senate Subcommittee on Intergovernmental Relations, has pointed out, "With the elimination of General Revenue Sharing and the state-oriented restructuring of the Reagan block grants, many localities that once received direct federal funding now receive none at all."

This reduction in revenue sharing would not present a major problem if the states and municipalities were readily able to back-fill the hole created by the lack of federal dollars with new money raised closer to home. The effort of many has been monumental, but former Colorado governor Richard D. Lamm (1989) reminds us that ever since California's "Proposition 13" and the tax revolt of the late 1970s, states have been increasingly forced to turn to non-tax revenue sources such as user fees, lotteries and special assessments, all of which appear to have limited growth potential. Compounding the problem for the states, nearly every change in federal tax law during the last decade has contained provisions that inhibit state revenue generating ability. The best example of this phenomenon is the elimination of the federal income tax deductions for excise, sales and personal income taxes levied by state and local governments. If it is true that the American people are willing to pay only so much in taxes, the states and municipalities are now in direct competition with the federal government for the room at the margin for tax increases (Conlan, 1989).

With the revenues available to them, the states have put increased dollars into the ongoing operation of the schools but have not been able to focus significant sums on educational reform. Moreover, an Education Commission of the States study of spending in 47 states revealed that of the $67 billion in state funds for local school districts in the 1985–86 school year, only about 3 percent (less than $2 billion) was dedicated to school reform activities. Nearly 40 percent of that amount was directed toward teachers; only $11 million supported increased graduation requirements; testing initiatives received only $72 million. New programs and curricular revision received $552 million, an amount in excess of a quarter of the reform funds. A similar amount, $554 million, supported such structural changes as longer school days and extended academic years (Jordan and McKeown, 1988).

While these amounts may seem like significant expenditures, a closer look reveals the essence of the problem with the current condition of educational federalism. Sixty percent of the testing money was spent in only two states. Similarly, 60 percent of the money used to fund more time in school was spent in just one state. Likewise, 80 percent of the $67.3 million dedicated to programs for at-risk students was spent in one state. Even the efforts to increase teacher salaries were unevenly supported: while such measures were undertaken in 25 states between 1983 and 1987, only 16 states provided any money to fund the raises. Similarly, career ladder and merit pay initiatives were begun in 21 states, but funds were provided by only 15 (Jordan and McKeown, 1988).

While every single state has engaged in some aspect of educational reform since the publication of *A Nation at Risk* (Pipho, 1986), Astuto and Clark (1988) point out that "comprehensive improvement programs are emerging only in states that have contextual conditions to support such programs," and the others are falling behind. For example, the efforts initiated in Arkansas in 1979 to devise a new plan for educational finance remained stalled some eight years later, with little likelihood of being implemented prior to 1989 (Schoppmeyer, 1987). In West Virginia, despite legislative support for a series of reforms that accompanied Governor Arch A. Moore Jr.'s proclamation of 1987 as the "Year of Education," serious revenue shortfalls not only precluded their enactment but also led to stinging cuts to education (Meckley, Hartnett and Yeager, 1987).

The burden of funding reform, then, has fallen to a great extent to the local school districts, many of which rely on impoverished and already stretched tax bases as well as unpredictable electorates. The reallocation of money from existing to new purposes and the saving of funds through efficiency initiatives can go only so far. As has been noted by Ernest Boyer (1988), head of the Carnegie Foundation for the Advancement of Teaching, "money alone won't make better schools, [but] it's foolish to suggest that money doesn't matter." In fact, money matters so much that the unevenness in educational spending across school districts within states resulted in legal challenges to school funding formulas in 22 states between 1986 and 1988 (Camp and Thompson, 1988).

When federal funds were supporting a higher percentage of the cost of schooling, local and regional economic fluctuations did not have the same effect on educational finance that they do now. The downturn in state revenue growth experienced in the Northeast in 1988 and 1989 has meant serious across-the-board cutbacks in spending in such reform-minded states as New York, New Jersey and Massachusetts. In the latter, for example, state revenues were expected to grow by 10.9 percent in fiscal year 1989 but actually grew at a rate of only 6.5 percent, yielding a shortfall of $364 million. The result was a $31 million cut for the University of Massachusetts at Amherst. Many local school districts were forced to drop their after-school activities, while some of the more affluent districts shifted the costs for such activities to students. At Arlington High School, for example, students who wanted to play football were charged $125, while cheerleaders had to pay $80. Similarly, Lincoln-Sudbury Regional High School charged students $100 per sport (Associated Press, 1989).

Thus, at a time when an all-out effort to raise the educational standards of the nation is required in order to respond to a national problem, the current condition of federalism (popular because it has reduced federal taxes and federal regulation) has the effect of promoting different levels of educational quality in each state (and, often, school district), based on the ability of each to pay (or the current mood of the voters in localities where the electorate must approve millage increases to support higher school budgets). This has prompted some observers to call for "a national safety net to protect minimal educational quality levels in all states" (Astuto and Clark, 1988).

On September 27 and 28, 1989 President Bush took an important step in the effort to raise quality levels in all states by hosting an "education summit" attended by 49 of the nation's 50 governors as well as by every member of the cabinet except the Secretaries of State and Defense. Not since the Great Depression has such a gathering occurred. The governors unanimously pledged to set national goals for increasing high school graduation rates, for improving test scores for curbing violence and drug use in the schools, and for providing parents with the opportunity to choose the schools that their children will attend. They committed themselves to improving educational outcomes in return for reduced federal regulation, and supported the publication of an annual report card on the condition of education in their states. The president stated that the educational "status quo is a guarantee of mediocrity, social decay and national decline" and urged that "from this day forward, let us be an America of tougher standards, an America of higher goals and a land of bigger dreams." He declined, however, to commit new money to the schools, stating that [o]ur focus must no longer be on resources. It must be on results" (Warren and Roser, 1989).

While the summit, itself, represents a milestone on the road to quality education, it fell short of its potential. Rather than call for new federal initiatives that would support and complement the activities of the states, the president merely maintained the bully pulpit posture.

We believe that a higher federal profile is required, one that goes beyond rhetorical leadership, one that proposes the development of a national consensus regarding the outcomes that should be expected of our educational system and that provides a financial base that will foster the attainment of those outcomes. In suggesting that the federal role needs to be heightened, we are not unmindful of the constitutional principle that education is a state function. We are not proposing that federal dollars and regulations be used to relieve the states of their responsibilities or to diminish the level of state activity. Washington should take the lead in establishing a set of national educational goals and then should target its funds toward helping the states meet those standards. As a condition for releasing federal and state educational funds, the states can play a pivotal role in the quest for excellence by requiring school districts to present specific plans intended to meet or exceed the national goals. Such an approach would bring federalism vis-a-vis education into a more productive balance.

Education and International Competitiveness

While the reassertion of a leadership position by the federal government, combined with the infusion of a critical mass of dollars from Washington, would propel our educational system in the direction of meeting its potential, more is required if our goal of renewed international economic competitiveness is to be achieved. Joel Spring (1988) argues that the authors of *A Nation at Risk* "seem to have assumed that the economic problems of the U.S. are not being caused by problems in the economic system itself but by problems in the development of human capital." It does not appear to be the case that we lost our lead positions in the manufacturing of steel and small appliances, for example, as a result of an undereducated America. Fundamental to our slippage was our inability to be competitive at the cash register. In part this was due to lower wages in other countries (some of which became havens for American multinational corporations); in part it was the result of the economic subsidy and protectionist policies of other governments that permit their country's products to undercut the competition. Some industries that have lost market share had their American-designed products copied by foreign competitors and sold at lower cost. And, many of our corporations failed to invest in the updating and modernizing of their production divisions. Strategic changes are required in some of these areas if we are to regain our economic edge.

There are some places where we lost our position for reasons that might well be attributed to education. To be sure, the decline of our automobile industry, related both to cost and quality issues, was the result of more than worker alienation; our cars were not as well-engineered as those designed in Japan. While our educational system has produced superb engineers in the past and continues to produce some of the best, there is room for improvement in engineering education, as there is in many fields.

The problem, however, seems to be less in how well engineers are prepared than it is in how many of them are prepared. Indeed, according to the National Science Foundation (Task Force on Women, Minorities and the Handicapped in Science and Technology, 1988), among 1977's four million high school sophomores only 340,000 entered college with an interest in a major in science or engineering. Four years later, 206,000 of these students earned bachelor's degrees in those fields. By 1986, only 46,000 had gone on to earn master's degrees. It is projected that by 1992, 9700 (only .24 percent of the original 1977 cohort) will have earned doctorates in science and engineering. Certainly, the inadequate precollegiate preparation of students in mathematics and science must be overcome if the supply is to be improved.

The preceding discussion is meant neither as a nationalistic defense of our educational system nor as an argument that America does not need a better-educated population. Indeed, that we are experiencing both a knowledge explosion and a rapid technological development demand higher levels of educational attainment. However, as Henry Giroux (1989) has pointed out, schools have become the new scapegoat for our decreasing competitiveness in the international marketplace. Our educational system should be expected to contribute to the resolution of the problem, but it cannot be expected to compensate for the governmental and corporate policies that caused us to fall behind.

Education in a Troubled Time

Nor can the educational reform movement be expected, by itself, to have sufficient inertia to overcome the drag created by societal maladies that, if left unaddressed, have the potential to tear our democracy apart. Our nation appears to be polarizing economically, educationally and racially. The media is replete with reports of homelessness or its threat, of the widespread growth of "latchkey" children, of the disintegration of the traditional family, of growing numbers of unmarried teenage mothers who are having their second and third child, of young people caught in a welfare cycle three or four generations deep, of unethical and illegal activities by public officials and corporate leaders, and of an increasing pessimism about the future. Indeed, the chances of anyone being able to beat the odds in some poor urban neighborhoods (many of which are ravaged by drugs and despair) appear to be decreasing with every passing day. Yet, while we implore persons in such circumstances to "just say no" to the temptations that hold them down, our society has provided them in recent years with little of a positive nature to which they can say, "yes."

Schools cannot compensate for the totality of environmental circumstance. Accordingly, the achievement gap between American pupils and those of most other industrialized nations, in many instances, has much to do with differences in environmental condition. In Japan, for example, sociological factors such as the prestigious relationship between educational attainment and lifelong, vertical employment within a given work place, the relatively strong socioeconomic and cultural homogeneity that reduces class distinctions, and the striving for educational excellence within the ethos of the family contribute profoundly to a national consciousness that places a strong value on education. Given the horizontal mobility of the American work force, the demographic change that historically is America's social landscape, the increase in poverty, particularly among children, and the widespread changes in marital status, the schools face a herculean task in engendering national educational achievement which equals or surpasses the Japanese.

It may not be trendy in today's America to speak, as Lyndon Johnson did, of a war on poverty and a changing of the social order, but poverty represents the most serious threat to our future. Unfortunately, government activity in recent times does not appear to have been aimed at eradicating this problem. That there were federal budget reductions during the Reagan years is well known. How many people realize, though, that between 1981 and 1987 federal housing programs were reduced by 79 percent, that training and employment programs were slashed by 70 percent, that the Work Incentive Program lost 71 percent of its funding and that block grants for community development and community services fell by more than one-third? While much of America benefited from Reagan economics, many were left out of the boom; real income, adjusted for inflation, increased by $12,218 between 1979 and 1986 for the top earning quintile but fell by $663 for Americans at the bottom fifth of the economic ladder. One-fifth of all children and a majority of black children are growing up in poverty. Sadly, as a result of inadequate funding, less than one-fifth of the children eligible for Head Start programs and less than half of those eligible for compensatory education are being served by the programs (Jacob, 1988). Not only did the Reagan administration turn its back on the poor and on civil rights enforcement, but its campaign to turn back the legal clock has begun to bear fruit as the conservative-dominated Rehnquist Court has begun to limit or to strike down well-established equity measures.

Congress, too, must share some of the blame for the perpetuation of inequality. The movement toward replacing categorical programs by "block grants" was one way in which it removed funds from those who need it most in favor of those who need it less. In 1981 the Congress consolidated 29 programs from the Elementary and Secondary Education Act of 1965, many of which were targeted toward educationally disadvantaged populations. Under the umbrella of Chapter 2 of the Educational Consolidation and Improvement Act, block grants, representing a relatively unrestricted chunk of federal dollars, can be used for virtually any instructional purpose. More often than not, these funds have been used across the educational spectrum, rather than being focused on the disadvantaged.

More recently, the Hawkins-Stafford Elementary and Secondary School Improvement Amendments of 1988 (P.L. 100–297) provides another example of this phenomenon. Theretofore, schools with high concentrations of students living in poverty received a disproportionately high distribution of federal education funds. The earlier policy was based on research findings that indicate that the average level of academic achievement decreases for all students in a school as the percentage of pupils from poor families increases; that is, the rate of educational disadvantagement is higher for both poor and non-poor students in schools with high concentrations of poor children than it is in schools with low concentrations of poor children. Public Law 100-297 changed the formula for the distribution of funds from one which gave more money to per student to the counties with the highest poverty rates to one which gave grants in equal proportion to all counties that meet a poverty concentration threshold of 15 percent. The result was a shift of funds away from the counties and the states with the largest concentration of poverty. States including Alabama, Georgia and North Carolina each received increases of more than $5 million, while others such as California (down $11.1 million), Michigan (down $2.1 million), Maryland (down $1.5 million) and New York (down $14.3 million) were among the net losers. Los Angeles County and Wayne County (Detroit) lost $8.2 million and $3 million, respectively. Even for states such as Arizona, Florida and Louisiana which were net winners under this approach, their leading cities, Phoenix, Miami and New Orleans, lost significant funds (Riddle, 1988).

Former Secretary Bell (1988) reminds us that, in an era when most of the new jobs will require at least a college-level education, there are over 50 million American families in which not one member has ever earned a college degree. To make matters worse, nearly 30 percent of the nation's ninth graders (and half of those who live in our largest cities) do not finish high school. Over 40 percent of minority teenagers are out of school, and disproportionately high proportions of them are unemployed. Further, the college-going rate of minority youngsters in the late 1980s is lower than it was in 1976. Recent changes in federal spending patterns seem destined to exacerbate these problems.

If we want to reverse the trend of societal bifurcation and to restore true meaning of the promise of America (and, indeed, to insure domestic tranquility), we need to do more than to reform our educational system. Our schools can form the cornerstone of the effort, but by themselves the schools can accomplish only so much. A comprehensive program to maximize the potential of our citizency is needed; one that provides good-paying, responsible and secure jobs, adequate housing, basic health care and strong schools; one that will help our poor to establish for themselves a critical measure of security; and one that permits our children to reside in an environment of stability and direction. If we fail to recognize the interrelationship between the broader social, political and economic environment and the ability of the schools to be successful, we will never find the right set of formulae for educational effectiveness.

Again, we come back to a familiar place. Efforts such as we suggest cost money. Richard Lamm (1989), among others, contends that the United States has enough tax money to meet our critical needs, if the funds are properly focused. We concur. The transformational changes that appear to be occurring in Eastern Europe, the ethnic unrest within the Soviet Union, and the recent defense reduction offers made by the Russians might well place us at an historic point where a significant reduction in our defense spending would be possible, still permitting modest defense gains while providing a source of funds to tackle our domestic problems. Given President George Bush's desire for a "kinder, gentler nation" and his wish to become known as the "education president," the challenge is his.

Prolonging the Age of Education

We live in a time when it is said that America has a six-week memory. Indeed, it is an accomplishment (and a testimony to the faith placed in it) that education has stayed at the public fore for nearly a decade. It has taken a tremendous effort, but during this "Age of Education" substantial reforms have been initiated. Now is not the time to lay back if we are serious about fundamentally redesigning our schools. We must be careful to make honest assessments of our activity, rejecting approaches that prove unsuccessful, encouraging emulation of those that work and continuing to seek new and imaginative solutions to remaining shortcomings and emerging areas of need. We must pay concentrated attention to our urban schools, the schools that present the greatest challenge and that will be producing the greatest number of new entrants into the labor market in the years to come.

The groundwork has been laid to help our nation emerge from risk and to permit the Age of Education to have a life so long that it is fundamental to our national sense of being.

REFERENCES

Associated Press. "Pay ball: In Mass., it's first-and-$125." *Philadelphia Inquirer*, September 12, 1989, p. A-3.

Astuto, Terry A. and David L. Clark. "State Responses to the New Federalism in Education." *Educational Policy*, 2(4):361–375. 1988.

Bell, Terrel H. "How to Make Education a Top Priority." *Change*, 20(6): 20–23. 1988.

Boyer, Ernest L. "How to Give Education a Vision and Voice of Credibility." *Change*, 20(6):24–26. 1988.

Camp, William E. and David C. Thompson. "School Finance Litigation: Legal Issues and Politics of Reform." *Journal of Education Finance*, 14(2):221–238, 1988.

Conlan, Timothy J. "Federalism at the Crossroads: Conflicting Trends, Competing Futures." *Journal of State Government*, 62(1):50–55. 1989.

Evangelauf, Jean. "Education Secretary, Citing Student Statistics, Says School-Reform Movements Is Stalled." *Chronicle of Higher Education*, May 10, 1989, p. A31–32.

Finn, Chester E., Jr. "A Nation Still at Risk." *Commentary*, 87(5):17–23, 1989.

Giroux, Henry A. "Rethinking Education Reform in the Age of George Bush." *Phi Delta Kappan*, 70(9):728–730. 1989.

Jacob, John E. "Black America, 1987: An Overview," in Janet Dewart (Ed): *The State of Black America 1988*. New York: National Urban League, 1988, pp. 1–6.

Jordan, Forbis K. and Mary P. McKeown. "State Funding for Education Reform: False Hopes and Unfulfilled Expectations." *Journal of Education Finance*, 14(1):18–29. 1988.

Lamm, Richard D. "The Brave New World of Public Policy." *State Legislatures*, 15(7):31–34. 1989.

Meckley, Richard, Richard Hartnett and Jack Yaeger. "The Year of Education: That Dog Won't Hunt." *Journal of Education Finance*, 13(2):182–188. 1987.

Mitgang, Lee. "Test pattern: Some SAT scores slip." *Philadelphia Inquirer*, September 12, 1989a, p 3A.

_____. "Teachers boost test scores by cheating, report says." *Philadelphia Inquirer*, September 19, 1989b, p. 2A.

Pipho, Chris. "States Move Reform Closer to Reality." *Phi Delta Kappan: Kappan Special Report* (reprint). December, 1986.

Riddle, Wayne, "Chapter 1 Concentration Grants: An Analysis of the Concept, and Its Embodiment in Federal Elementary and Secondary Education Legislation." *Journal of Education Finance*, 14(2): 285–303. 1988.

Schoppmeyer, Martin W. "Full State Assumption in Arkansas." *Journal of Education Finance*, 13(2): 174–181. 1987.

Spring, Joel. "Education and the Sony War," Education 87–88. Guilford, CT: Dushkin Publishing Group, Inc., 1988, pp. 46–48.

Task Force on Women, Minorities and the Handicapped in Science and Technology. *Changing America: The New Face of Science and Engineering, Interim Report.* Washington, D.C.: U.S. Government Printing Office. 1988.

Warren, Ellen and Mary Ann Roser. "Education Summit Ends with a Call for Reforms." *Philadelphia Inquirer*, September 29, 1989, pp. 1A, 4A.

Wise, Arthur. "Legislated Learning Revisited." *Phi Delta Kappan*, 69 (5):328–333. 1988.

INDEX

313